Harold Cafone

Ronald L. Cramer

Janet Hamerman

Carol A. Mejia

Mary Sue Ordway

E. Brooks Smith

DeWayne Triplett

Language

Skills and Use

Special Populations Author Dale R. Jordan

Reader Consultants Rachel Hemmerly
Jeannie Tainaka

Scott, Foresman and Company
Editorial Offices: Glenview, Illinois

Regional Sales Offices: Palo Alto, California •
Tucker, Georgia • Glenview, Illinois •
Oakland, New Jersey • Dallas, Texas

Program Author

E. Brooks Smith

Book Authors

Readiness — Book Eight

Sister Gilmary Beagle, SS.C.M.

Harold Cafone

Ronald L. Cramer

Beverly Dryden

Janet Hamerman

Lida Lim

Barbara McDermitt

Carol A. Mejia

Virginia Mickish

Norman C. Najimy

Donna Ogle

Mary Sue Ordway

John Prejza, Jr.

Robert E. Quackenbush

E. Brooks Smith

Joan Smutny

DeWayne Triplett

ISBN: 0-673-12754-0

2345678910-KPK-8887868584838281807 9

Acknowledgments

Text

page 11: "Grammar" from *Beasts and Nonsense* by Marie Hall Ets. Copyright 1952 by Marie Hall Ets. All rights reserved. Reprinted by permission of Viking Penguin, Inc.

page 17: Adapted from *Holidays and Customs,* Volume 9 of *Childcraft—The How and Why Library.* © 1979 World Book-Childcraft International, Inc.

page 25: "El Train" excerpted from the book *My Daddy Is a Cool Dude* by Karama Fufuka. Text copyright © 1975 by Karama Fufuka. Reprinted by permission The Dial Press.

page 32: "Said a restless young person of Yew" from *A Lollygag of Limericks* by Myra Cohn Livingston (A Margaret K. McElderry Book). Copyright © 1978 by Myra Cohn Livingston. Used by permission of Atheneum Publishers and McIntosh & Otis, Inc.

page 59: "Do you carrot all for me? . . ." from *A Rocket in my Pocket* compiled by Carl Withers. Copyright 1948 by Carl Withers. Copyright © 1976 by Samuel H. Halperin. Reprinted by permission of Holt, Rinehart and Winston, Publishers and The Bodley Head.

page 68: Emily Neville. *It's Like This, Cat.* New York: Harper & Row, Publishers, Inc., 1963, p. 126.

page 75: Lillian Morrison, editor. Excerpts as they appeared in *Best Wishes, Amen.* New York: Thomas Y. Crowell, 1974, pp. 9, 85, 86, 124. Lillian Morrison, editor. Excerpts as they appeared in *Yours Till Niagara Falls.* New York: Thomas Y. Crowell, pp. Title Page, 81, 54, 56.

page 91: Peggy Mann. *The Street of the Flower Boxes.* New York: Coward-McCann, Inc., 1966, p. 16.

page 93: "The Acrobats" from *Where the Sidewalk Ends* by Shel Silverstein. Copyright © 1974 by Shel Silverstein. By permission of Harper & Row, Publishers, Inc.

page 96: "Clay" from *The Moon and a Star and Other Poems,* © 1965 by Myra Cohn Livingston. Reprinted by permission of Harcourt Brace Jovanovich, Inc.

page 100: E. B. White. *The Trumpet of the Swan.* New York: Harper & Row, Publishers, Inc., 1970, p. 174.

pages 102–103: Barbara M. Parramore and Dan D'Amelio. *Scott, Foresman Social Studies.* Copyright © 1979, Scott, Foresman and Company.

page 127 top: "A Dragon Fly". Copyright 1933, renewed 1960 by Eleanor Farjeon. From *Poems for Children* by Eleanor Farjeon. Copyright 1951 by Eleanor Farjeon. Reprinted by permission of J. B. Lippincott Company and Harold Ober Associates Incorporated.

page 127 bottom: "Bee Song" by Carl Sandburg. Copyright © 1960 by Carl Sandburg. Reprinted from his volume *Wind Song* by permission of Harcourt Brace Jovanovich, Inc.

pages 128, 130: Andrew Schiller and William A. Jenkins. *In Other Words, A Beginning Thesaurus.* Copyright © 1977, 1968, Scott, Foresman and Company.

Continued on page 352.

CONTENTS

UNIT THREE

UNIT FOUR

UNIT FIVE

UNIT SIX

UNIT EIGHT

UNIT NINE

UNIT TEN

Unit One

How's your grammar?

Grammar

At home it's "It's *me*."

At school it's "It is *I*."

And hippopotamuses

Are hippopot-a-m*i*.

Marie Hall Ets

In this unit you will discover how much you know about your language.

Are Your Directions in Order?

When you listen to directions, notice the order in which
things happen. When you give directions, make sure they are
in the right order.

Look at these directions. Use the map at the right to check
order.

> To get to the principal's office, enter the school and
> turn right. Walk straight to the kindergarten room and
> turn left. Walk down the hall until you come to the
> nurse's office. Turn left. The principal's office is the
> first door on your right.

It is easy to understand directions that are given in the
right order. Using landmarks, such as the nurse's office in
the paragraph above, will help.

A. Write directions for getting to the library from the
principal's office.

B. Give the following directions. Share your directions
with your class. Your classmates may have more than one
way of getting from one place to another.

  1. Go from room 104 to room 102.

  2. Go from the gym to the nurse's office.

  3. Go from the kindergarten room to the art room.

  4. Go from the entrance to room 103.

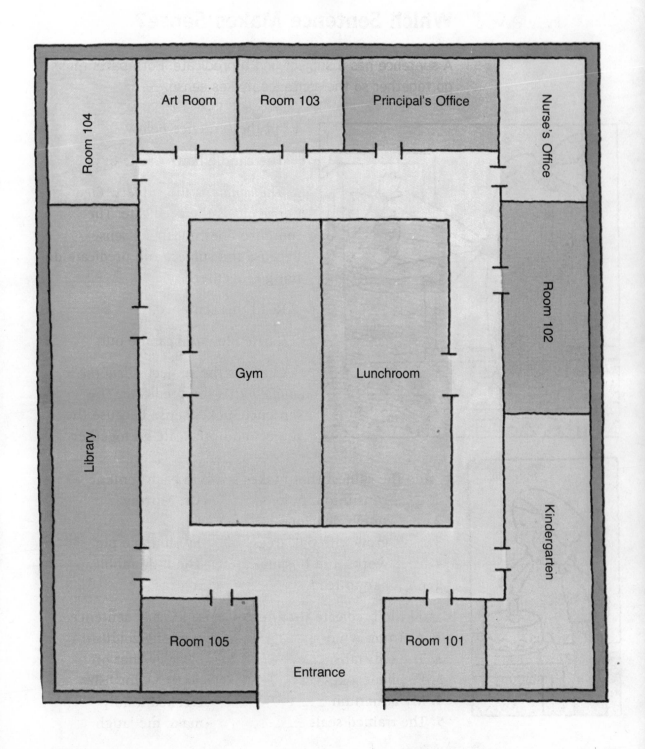

Which Sentence Makes Sense?

A sentence has a subject and a predicate. Both parts must go together so the sentence makes sense.

Read the sentence below.

The candle blew Carrie out.

The candle is the subject. *Blew Carrie out* is the predicate. The sentence does not make sense because the subject and predicate do not go together.

Read this sentence.

Carrie blew the candle out.

Carrie is the subject. *Blew the candle out* is the predicate. The sentence makes sense because the subject and predicate go together.

A. Add the subject that makes sense in each sentence.

1. _____ runs into a hole.   Dr. Murray
2. _____ smells delicious.   I
3. _____ grow into oak trees.   Fresh apple pie
4. _____ works in a hospital.   The little rabbit
5. _____ like to read.   Acorns

B. Add the predicate that makes sense in each sentence.

1. A strong wind _____.   contains goldfish
2. The old stairs _____.   blew my hat off
3. Elephant jokes _____.   do tricks for fish
4. My aquarium _____.   creaked loudly
5. The trained seals _____.   make me laugh

14

Review 3　What Are Nouns and Verbs?

Nouns are words that name persons, places, or things. Verbs are words that show action in sentences.

Read the sentences below.

> Dulcy ran fast to school.
> The teacher will read the story.

Words that name persons, places, or things are called nouns. In the sentences, the words *Dulcy*, *school*, *teacher*, and *story* are nouns.

Verbs are words that can show the action in a sentence. The words *ran* and *will read* are verbs in the sentences.

A. Complete the following sentences by choosing a noun or verb from the list.

1. The ____ punched our tickets.
2. Dad ____ some firewood.
3. ____ make milk.
4. The teapot ____ when the water is hot.
5. Our class visited a ____ .
6. I always ____ my safety belt.

Nouns	Verbs
museum	whistles
conductor	fasten
cows	chopped

B. Copy the sentences below. Find and underline 12 nouns.

1. Tanya made a boat.
2. The boat will float in the bathtub.
3. Rudy calls the dog.
4. The dog will listen for his voice.
5. Snowflakes fell to the ground.
6. The sun melts the snowflakes.

C. Look at the sentences in Exercise A. Put a circle around the action verbs. You should find 6 verbs.

Can You Build Interesting Sentences?

Some words describe the size, shape, or color of nouns. Some words tell how, where, and when an action happens.

Follow the steps to build an interesting sentence.

1. Begin with a subject and a word that tells what the subject did.

   Pumpkins rolled.

2. Add words that describe the size, shape, and color of the subject.

   Huge, round, yellow pumpkins rolled.

3. Add a word that tells how the action happened.

   Huge, round, yellow pumpkins rolled quickly.

4. Add words that tell where the action happened.

   Huge, round, yellow pumpkins rolled quickly down the road.

5. Add a word or words that tell when the action happened.

   Huge, round, yellow pumpkins rolled quickly down the road yesterday.

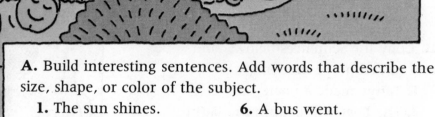

A. Build interesting sentences. Add words that describe the size, shape, or color of the subject.

1. The sun shines.
2. Horses raced.
3. Lightning flashed.
4. The balloon burst.
5. An eagle flew.
6. A bus went.
7. The waves splash.
8. Flowers grow.
9. The astronauts landed.
10. A boat floats.

B. Add to the sentences that you built in Exercise A. Tell how, where, or when the action happened.

What Is the Main Idea?

All the sentences in a paragraph tell about the main idea of the paragraph.

Read the paragraph below to find out about some unusual clothes.

Some clothes have different uses. In the United States, cowboys wear "ten-gallon" hats that can be filled with water, so horses can drink from them. In Greenland, women wear jackets that have a pouch where little children can ride. In Portugal, there are caps that men also use as purses to carry coins.

The main idea of this paragraph is that some clothes are used for more than one reason.

Write a paragraph about the picture below. Make sure all the sentences tell about the main idea.

Can You Use a Dictionary?

You can use a dictionary to find out what a word means and how to spell it.

Look at the dictionary page at the right.

Find an *entry word*. It shows how a word is spelled. Entry words are listed in alphabetical order.

Find the *guide words*. They tell what the first and last entry words on a page are.

Find a *definition*. It tells what a word means. Some words have more than one definition.

Find a *picture*. It helps show what a word means.

Use the sample dictionary page at the right to answer the questions.

1. Which entry word would come between **mammoth** and **pillow?**
   main   lemon   penny
2. Write the correct spelling of *pawper*.
3. If you got hit with a pillow, would you probably be hurt? Why or why not?
4. Which definition of *obey* means "follow the orders of"?
5. Would you grow hay in an orchard or a meadow?
6. Which meaning of *ocean* is used in the sentence *The Atlantic Ocean is off the eastern coast of the United States.*
7. Would you plant your orchard with noodles? Why or why not?
8. Use *notify* in a sentence.
9. Which definition of *mammoth* is shown in the picture?
10. Would you nibble or narrate an apple?
11. How many sides does a pentagon have?

entry word

definition

mam moth (mam′əth), **1** a large elephant with a hairy skin and long curved tusks. The last mammoth died thousands of years ago. See picture. **2** huge; gigantic: *Digging the Panama Canal was a mammoth undertaking.* **1** *noun,* **2** *adjective.*

mead ow (med′ō), piece of grassy land, especially one used for growing hay or as a pasture for grazing animals. *noun.*

nar rate (nar′āt), tell the story of. *verb,* **nar rat ed, nar rat ing.**

nib ble (nib′əl), **1** eat away with quick small bites, as a rabbit or a mouse does. **2** bite gently or lightly: *A fish nibbles at the bait.* *verb.* **nib bled, nib bling.**

noo dle (nü′dl), a mixture of flour, water, and eggs, like macaroni, but dried into hard flat strips. *noun.*

no ti fy (nō′tə fī), let know; give notice to; announce to; inform: *Our teacher notified us that there would be a test on Monday. We have a letter notifying us that she will visit us soon.* verb. **no ti fied, no ti fy ing.**

o bey (ō bā′), **1** do what one is told to do: *The dog obeyed and went home.* **2** follow the orders of: *You must obey the court's decision.* **3** yield to the control of: *A horse obeys the rein.* verb.

o cean (ō′shən), **1** the great body of salt water that covers almost three fourths of the earth's surface; the sea. **2** any of its four main divisions—the Atlantic, Pacific, Indian, and Arctic oceans. The waters around the Antarctic continent are considered by some to form a separate ocean. *noun.*

or chard (ôr′chərd), **1** piece of ground on which fruit trees are grown. **2** the trees in an orchard: *The orchard should bear a good crop this year. noun.*

pau per (pô′pər), a very poor person; person supported by charity. *noun.*

pen ta gon (pen′tə gon), a figure having five angles and five sides. See picture. *noun.*

pil low (pil′ō), bag or case filled with feathers, down, or other soft material, usually to support the head when resting or sleeping. *noun.*

a hat	i it	oi oil	ch child	a in about
ā age	ī ice	ou out	ng long	e in taken
ä far	o hot	u cup	sh she	ə = i in pencil
e let	ō open	u̇ put	th thin	o in lemon
ē equal	ô order	ü rule	ᴛH then	u in circus
ėr term			zh measure	

mammoth

pentagon

Where Do You Use Capital Letters?

Every sentence begins with a capital letter. A capital letter is also used at the beginning of certain words.

Notice the capital letters in the following words and sentences.

Sentences

We raced across the finish line.
Did we win?

Names of particular persons, places, and animals

Bill King	United States	Fluffy
Erin Murphy	Wabash River	Rover

Days and months	**Cities and states**	**Special titles**
Monday	Cheyenne	Dr.
Wednesday	Illinois	Mr.
August	Peoria	Mrs.
March	Wyoming	Ms.

Find the words in the following sentences that should begin with capital letters. Write the words.

1. i love baked apples.
2. myrna named her goldfish tom, dick, and harry.
3. Our new teacher is ms. carmen lopez.
4. my cousin, natalie, just moved here from three rivers, michigan.
5. mr. walek drives his truck to florida every week.
6. in january, dr. towns is moving to another state.
7. Last summer, we went to mackinac island.
8. The natchez county carnival is held every october.
9. my class is going to help clean the schoolyard friday after school.
10. i help make breakfast on saturday and sunday.

Review 8 Can You Use Ending Marks Correctly?

Some words can be abbreviated, or shortened. A period is used after an abbreviated word. Periods and question marks are used to end sentences.

Names of months, days, and special titles are often abbreviated. An abbreviated word ends with a period.

Feb.	Sat.	Dr.
Dec.	Tues.	Ms.
Aug.	Mon.	Mr.

A sentence that tells something or states a fact ends with a period. A sentence that asks a question ends with a question mark.

I forgot my watch.
What time is it?

A. Match each word with its abbreviated form.

1. March   5. Sunday   a. Dr.   e. Nov.
2. November   6. April   b. Feb.   f. Wed.
3. Thursday   7. February   c. Sun.   g. Mar.
4. Doctor   8. Wednesday   d. Apr.   h. Thurs.

B. Tell whether each sentence should end with a period or a question mark.

1. How can you catch a monkey
2. Hang upside down and act like a banana
3. What is a volcano
4. It's a mountain with hiccups
5. There was a fight on the train
6. The conductor punched the ticket
7. What did one eye say to the other
8. Just between you and me, there's something that smells

Evaluation

A. Write the letter of the response that tells if the sentence makes sense or doesn't make sense.

1. The dog buried the bone.
   a. makes sense
   b. doesn't make sense
2. The bone buried the dog.
   a. makes sense
   b. doesn't make sense
3. Mr. Gomez watched the boat.
   a. makes sense
   b. doesn't make sense
4. The boat watched Mr. Gomez.
   a. makes sense
   b. doesn't make sense
5. The flowers planted Sally.
   a. makes sense
   b. doesn't make sense
6. Sally planted the flowers.
   a. makes sense
   b. doesn't make sense
7. The cup broke the baby.
   a. makes sense
   b. doesn't make sense
8. The baby broke the cup.
   a. makes sense
   b. doesn't make sense
9. The beach ran to Ms. Hill.
   a. makes sense
   b. doesn't make sense
10. Ms. Hill ran to the beach.
   a. makes sense
   b. doesn't make sense

B. Write the letter of the response that tells what kind of word the underlined word in each sentence is.

1. <u>Paul</u> cooked dinner.
   a. noun   **b.** verb
2. The wind <u>blew</u> in the trees.
   a. noun   **b.** verb
3. The cat licked the <u>milk</u>.
   a. noun   **b.** verb
4. My <u>brothers</u> play tennis.
   a. noun   **b.** verb
5. I went to the <u>zoo</u>.
   a. noun   **b.** verb
6. Ed <u>will tell</u> a story.
   a. noun   **b.** verb
7. Suzie went to the <u>store</u>.
   a. noun   **b.** verb
8. Enrico <u>jumps</u> over the fence.
   a. noun   **b.** verb
9. My <u>tooth</u> fell out.
   a. noun   **b.** verb
10. Anita <u>rowed</u> the boat.
   a. noun   **b.** verb
11. I <u>will see</u> you today.
   a. noun   **b.** verb
12. <u>Mrs. Higgins</u> lives next door.
   a. noun   **b.** verb

C. Write the letter of each word that should begin with a capital letter.

1. i read about abraham lincoln.
   a b c d e

2. Ann lives in the united states.
   a b c d e f

3. Ed moved to phoenix, arizona.
   a b c d e

4. They are mr. and mrs. hill.
   a b c d e f

5. we flew over the grand canyon.
   a b c d e f

6. last june, mr. jones came here.
   a b c d e f

7. Jim got his dog fido on friday.
   a b c d e f g

8. Did you see dr. sims in may?
   a b c d e f g

9. Tim visited los angeles in june.
   a b c d e f

10. i want to see utah and wyoming.
    a b c d e f g

D. Write the letter that gives the correct abbreviation for each underlined word.

1. Today is December 14.
   a. Dec.   c. dec
   b. Dec   d. dec.

2. My uncle is Doctor Carter.
   a. dr.   c. Dr
   b. Dr.   d. dr

3. Our test is on Thursday.
   a. thur.   c. day
   b. Thur.   d. Thurs.

4. I saw Jake on Saturday.
   a. Sun.   c. sat.
   b. Sat.   d. Day

5. Can you come on Monday?
   a. monday   c. mon
   b. Mon.   d. mon.

6. Sarah's birthday is March 13.
   a. mar   c. Mar.
   b. ma.   d. Mr.

E. Write the letter of the punctuation mark that should come at the end of each sentence.

1. Did you eat yet
   a. ⊙   b. ?

2. The girl built a model
   a. ⊙   b. ?

3. Who is your teacher
   a. ⊙   b. ?

4. Where is my pencil
   a. ⊙   b. ?

5. Our jackets are warm
   a. ⊙   b. ?

6. What is your name
   a. ⊙   b. ?

7. Steve is my son
   a. ⊙   b. ?

8. Sandra went to the zoo
   a. ⊙   b. ?

Unit Two

There are many ways to get from one place to another.
Have you ever traveled this way?

El Train

Riding on the "el" train is lots of fun.
It goes up above the streets
and way down underground.
It sure does make a lot of noise.
It throws electric sparks.
People push and crowd all in;
it says "Screeeeeeeeeeeeeech"
when it stops.

Karama Fufuka

Like trains, language goes from place to place. In this
unit, you will learn some ways that English spoken in
one country is different from English spoken in another.
Like the cars in a train, the words in a sentence can be
put together or taken apart. You will learn how to make
your sentences carry your ideas just the way you want
them to.

Lesson 1   Place Names in America

The names of many places in America came from the languages of the Native Americans. Other place names came from the languages of the people who settled in America.

Thinking It Through

The map shows some American cities and tells who named them.

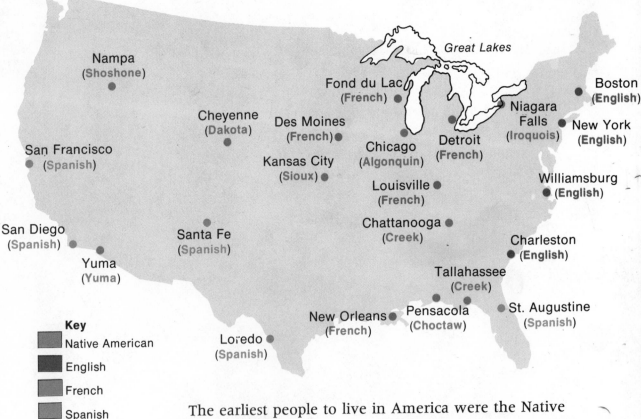

Great Lakes

Nampa (Shoshone)

Fond du Lac (French)

Boston (English)

Cheyenne (Dakota)

Des Moines (French)

Niagara Falls (Iroquois)

New York (English)

San Francisco (Spanish)

Chicago (Algonquin)

Detroit (French)

Kansas City (Sioux)

Louisville (French)

Williamsburg (English)

San Diego (Spanish)

Santa Fe (Spanish)

Chattanooga (Creek)

Charleston (English)

Yuma (Yuma)

Tallahassee (Creek)

New Orleans (French)

Pensacola (Choctaw)

St. Augustine (Spanish)

Loredo (Spanish)

Key
Native American
English
French
Spanish

The earliest people to live in America were the Native Americans. There were a million Native Americans, and they spoke 350 different languages. Some of these languages were Algonquian, Choctaw, Dakota, Iroquoian, Muskogean (Creek), Shoshonean, Siouan, and Yuman.

When other people came to America to live, they also spoke different languages.

People from England settled in the East of our country. They spoke English. The people from Spain spoke Spanish. They settled in the South and West. The French settlers in the North spoke French. In other places in America, people spoke Danish, Dutch, German, and Swedish.

Many of the names of places in the United States are words from Native American languages and from the languages of early settlers.

Working It Through

A. Use the map to answer the questions.
  1. Native Americans lived in many places. In the North, the Algonquins named the city of Chicago. What 8 other names of places on the map came from the languages of the Native Americans?
  2. Boston was named by English settlers. What 3 other places were named by the English?
  3. The French named 2 cities near the Great Lakes. What are they? What 3 other places did the French name?
  4. The Spanish people named the city of St. Augustine. What are 2 other places they named?

B. Use the chart to find out the language each place name comes from.
  1. Al lives in Dubuque.
  2. Los Angeles is big.
  3. My aunt likes living in Worcester.
  4. I live in Des Plaines.
  5. El Paso is in the West.

Parts of Place Names		
French	**Spanish**	**English**
lac	El	-ton
Des	Los	-land
-eau	Las	-chester
-que	Santa	-boro
-ville	St.	-burg

Trying It Out

Find out how your city and state were named.

English in Australia and America

Most people in America and Australia speak English. Some of the words Australians use have meanings that are different from American words.

Thinking It Through

The place shown in the picture is in Australia. Most of the people who live in Australia speak English. The paragraph below tells about the picture. Look for any words that are used in a way different from the way you might use them.

> The weather suddenly turned cool and wet while Graham and Josie were walking in the bush with their father. He sent them back to the motor car to take off their runners and to get their jumpers and gumboots out of the boot and put them on.

- Which words are used in a way different from American English?
- Use the picture clues to help you figure out the meanings of those words.
- Then turn this page upside-down to see if you are right.

bush means "wooded area"; *motor car,* "car"; *runners,* "sneakers"; *jumpers,* "sweaters"; *gumboots,* "rubber boots"; *boot,* "trunk"

English is the main language in both Australia and America. Some words, such as *jumper* and *sweater*, are different ways of saying the same thing.

Working It Through

A. Find a word that means the same as the underlined Australian word. Write each sentence, using the word you chose.

1. Susie put her arms in the sleeves of her <u>jumper</u>.
2. Wally bought a pair of <u>runners</u> for his track meet.
3. Mr. Wright opened the <u>boot</u> of the car with a key.
4. Pippa wears her <u>gumboots</u> when it rains.
5. Many wild animals live in the <u>bush</u>.

sneakers
trunk
lake
rubber boots
sweater
wooded area
hat
house

B. Find a word to replace each underlined Australian word. Write each sentence, using the word you chose.

1. Lorna touched the wool of the <u>jumbuck</u>.
2. A man who works for a <u>station</u> is a <u>jackeroo</u>.
3. I saddled the <u>moke</u> for a ride.
4. Chopping wood is <u>yakka</u>.
5. We buy <u>tucker</u> at the grocery store.

ranch
ranch hand
hard work
food
sheep
horse

Trying It Out

Josh lives in Australia and wants to tell his American friend Maria about his home. Rewrite Josh's sentences so that Maria will understand them.

I live on a station near the bush. We raise jumbucks. A jackeroo helps us.

In the morning, I put on my jumper and runners to go to school. If it is raining, I put on my gumboots. When I get home, I ride my moke.

Using Directions to Find Places

When you read, write, or listen to directions about how to find a certain place, pay close attention to the names of landmarks and to the turns that you must make.

Thinking It Through

A person who gives you directions will usually say something like, "To get to the museum, turn right at Mulberry Street. You can't miss the street. There's a Gulp Gas Station on the corner there."

● Why would the person mention the gas station if that isn't where you are going?

The gas station is a place that is easily seen which can help you find your way. Such places are called <u>landmarks</u>.

● What did the person say to do at Mulberry Street?

● What might happen if you turned left, not right?

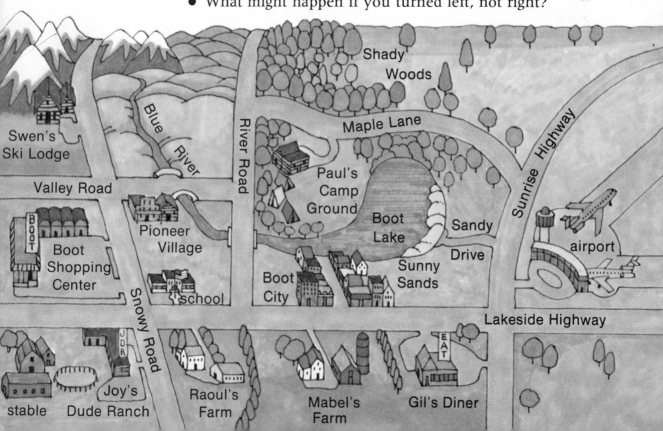

When using directions, it is important to pay close attention to words like *left* and *right* and to the names of landmarks that will help you find your way.

Working It Through

The map shows the country around Boot City. Notice the names of the roads and the landmarks that might help strangers find their way.

A. Begin at the airport, and follow these directions. Imagine yourself walking or riding so that you'll make your left and right turns correctly.

When you leave the airport, turn left onto Sunrise Highway. The first street you'll reach will be Lakeside Highway. You'll see an orange diner across the street. Turn right onto Lakeside Highway. Keep going until you see a little school on the corner. It's where Snowy Road crosses Lakeside Highway. Turn right onto Snowy Road. After you cross Valley Road, stop at a big cabin close to the mountains. The cabin will be on your left. Where will you be?

B. Give directions to go the opposite way—from the lodge to the airport.

1. Put yourself in the place of the person who will follow the directions so that you will get your left and right turns straight.
2. Be sure to name a couple of helpful landmarks.

Trying It Out

Listen to some different directions that begin at Swen's Ski Lodge. Keep these ideas in mind as you listen.

1. Imagine you are traveling along the roads yourself so that you are sure of what ways to turn.
2. Use the map, and see if you get to the right place.

31

Lesson 4 Writing Limericks

A limerick is a funny poem with five lines. It has a special way of rhyming.

Thinking It Through

Read this poem out loud.

Said a restless young person of Yew,
"I will purchase a nice kangaroo;
  I can sit in her pouch
  And pretend it's a couch
And wherever she hops, I will too!"

This poem is a **limerick.** Limericks are easy to recognize because they are funny, and they are always written in the same way.

The following steps tell you how a limerick is written.

1. There are always five lines in a limerick.

2. Each line of a limerick begins with a capital letter.

3. Lines 1, 2, and 5 are the longest lines. Lines 3 and 4 are shorter.

4. Lines 1, 2, and 5 end in words that rhyme. Lines 3 and 4 end in words that rhyme.

5. Lines 3 and 4 are indented.

Read this poem and tell why it is a limerick.

A cheerful old bear at the zoo
Could always find something to do.
  When it bored him to go
  On a walk to and fro
He reversed it and walked fro and to.

Limericks are funny five-line poems written in a special way. Lines 1, 2, and 5 rhyme. Lines 3 and 4 rhyme.

A. Write the missing rhyming word in the last line.

A silly, young, day-dreaming bee
Said, "I'll fly over the sea."
    But it was much too shy
    To take to the sky,
So it sat on a branch in a ____ .

B. Write a last line for this limerick.

There once was a calico cat
Who got exceedingly fat.
    His big tummy grew
    On too much fish stew,

_____ .

C. Write the fourth line of this limerick.

There was a young woman named Fay
Who drove her own bus every day.
    She went here and there

_____ ,

And she always sang songs on the way.

Write your own limericks. Use the steps on page 32 to help
you. Some first lines to get you started are below.

1. *There was a young swimmer from* (your own town or
   city).
2. *There was a young doctor named* (your name).

Do the lines begin with capital letters?
Are lines 3 and 4 indented? Do the last lines of your
limericks have ending marks?

Writing a Post Card

A post card is like a small letter. It tells interesting things. It also has a date, a greeting, a closing, and an address.

Thinking It Through

Writing a post card is like writing a mini-letter.

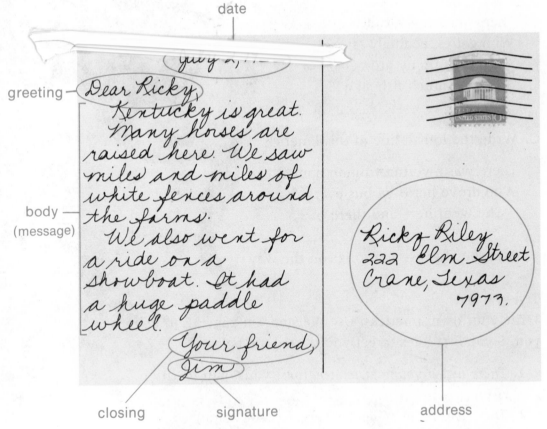

date

greeting —

body — (message)

closing   signature

address

- On what **date** did Jim write the post card? What is capitalized in the date? Where did he use a comma?
- What is Jim's **greeting?** What is capitalized in the greeting? What follows the last word?
- What interesting things did Jim tell Ricky in the **message?** Where did Jim indent his message?

- What is Jim's **closing?** What is capitalized in the closing? What follows the last word?
- Why is a **signature** necessary?
- How did Jim **address** his post card? What is capitalized in the address? What comes between the name of the city and state? What is the zip code?

Working It Through

A. Read all the directions before you do the activity.

1. Read the list of things that Cindy did at camp.

   went fishing

   hiked along the river

   discovered a secret waterfall

   swam in the lake

   had fun living in a tent

   cooked over a campfire

2. Write an interesting message for a post card that Cindy might write to her mom.

3. Be sure to write a date, a greeting, and a closing with the message.

B. Write the names of the following people the way they would appear in an address. Don't forget to use the correct title in each address: *Mr., Mrs., Miss,* or *Ms.* (A title is not usually used with the names of children.)

1. your mother or your father
2. your best friend
3. your aunt and your uncle
4. your teacher

Trying It Out

Write a post card to a friend.

1. Tell interesting things about your city or state.
2. You can also tell about something you have done recently.

Writing a Book Report

A book report tells something about a book. It also identifies the title, the author, and the kind of book.

Thinking It Through

Jane wrote a book report on a card to be placed under the heading *Mysteries* in the class file box.

title

heading

author

Mystery
The Alligator Case was written by William Pène du Bois. It is a funny mystery story about a young detective.
One day the detective sees a stranger in a restaurant. The stranger is popping peas into his mouth. While everyone is watching the stranger, someone robs the cash register. The young detective cleverly solves the crime.

- What is the heading for the kind of book Jane wrote about?
- What is the title of the book?
- Who wrote the book?
- Who or what is the book about?
- What interesting or exciting part did Jane tell about the book?

When you write the title of a book, capitalize the first and last word, and all the important words. Some small words, such as *a, and, the, of,* and *in,* are not capitalized unless they are the first word.

Underline the title of the book when it is part of a sentence in the report.

A. Capitalize the correct words for each title in the following sentences. Underline the title.

1. My favorite book is called charlotte's web.
2. Virginia Burton wrote katy and the big snow.
3. That book's title is the house of sixty fathers.
4. Allen was reading five boys in a cave.
5. I read black beauty last week.

B. What is missing in this book report? Look at the five questions on page 36 for help.

> My book was good. It was written by Joan. It is a story about three girls.
> One girl rode her horse and fell off. Her two friends rescued her in a dangerous canyon.

C. Rewrite the book report in Exercise B. Use the information below.

The Lost Canyon
Joan Foley
Adventure Story

Write a book report on a book you have enjoyed. Be sure to include the information asked for on page 36.

Make sure you capitalized the correct words in the book title. Did you underline the book title in the report?

Review • Writing a Post Card

A. Look at the labels and the information on the post card. Then answer the questions beneath the post card.

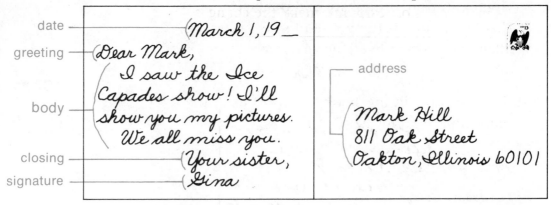

1. Find and name the 6 parts. Explain what each part is used for.
2. What letters are capitalized? Why?
3. Where are commas used? Why?

B. On a piece of paper, write what you would put on a post card to your family. Be sure to include the 6 parts. Tell about something special that has happened to you or why you think they are special people.

C. Answer these questions.
1. Does your post card include a date, greeting, body, closing, signature, and address?
2. Did you capitalize the first word in the date, greeting, and closing? Did you also use capitals for peoples' names, the street, the city, and the state? Did you write the zip code.
3. Did you put a comma between the day of the month and the year, and between the city and state? Did you also put a comma after the greeting and the closing?

For extra practice turn to page 344.

Evaluation • Writing a Post Card

A. Improve the post card below. Find 2 places where commas are needed. Find 6 places where capitals are needed. Write the post card and make the changes.

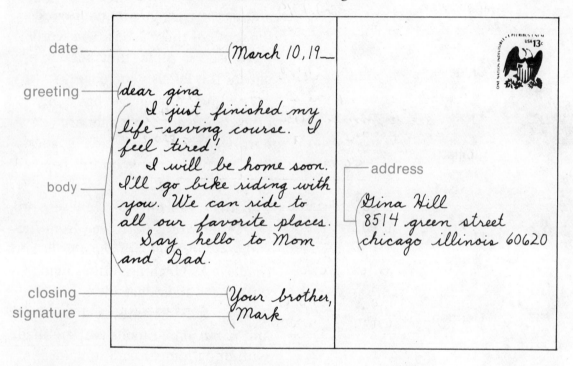

date — March 10, 19__

greeting — dear gina

body —
    I just finished my life-saving course. I feel tired!
    I will be home soon. I'll go bike riding with you. We can ride to all our favorite places.
    Say hello to Mom and Dad.

closing — Your brother,
signature — Mark

address —
Gina Hill
8514 green street
chicago illinois 60620

B. Think about your favorite time of the year.
1. On a piece of paper, write what you would put on a post card to a friend or relative who lives in another city, state, or country.
2. Tell interesting things about your favorite time of the year.
3. Be sure to use capitals and commas where they are needed.

You will be evaluated on completing each part of the post card and using commas and capitals correctly.

Spotlight • Food

Algonquian

Chinese

Italian

Mexican

German

French

Dutch

Native Americans shared some of their favorite foods with the early American settlers. *Squash, succotash,* and *pecan* were Algonquian words for some of these foods. The words were used so often, they became a part of the English language.

The English language has many other words for foods that are borrowed from different languages. The borrowed words on this page all name different kinds of food.

Tea comes from the Chinese word *t'e.* Other words borrowed from the Chinese language are *chow mein* and *chop suey,* which are dishes made with meat and vegetables.

Many Italian words, such as *ravioli* and *pizza,* name foods that are made with dough, meat, and tomatoes. A Mexican *taco* is made with meat and tomatoes too.

The words *noodle, hamburger,* and *pretzel* come from the German language. Some French words for desserts are *crêpe* and *éclair. Cookie* and *waffle* come from Dutch words.

See if you can find the language from which each of these words comes: *tortilla, chili, spaghetti,* and *frankfurter.* A dictionary can help you.

The world is full of people who do many different jobs. You probably know what kinds of jobs a pilot, a doctor, and a teacher do. The underlined words in the paragraphs name other people who do interesting jobs.

Miss María Sánchez is an *architect.* She designs buildings. Copies of her designs are called blueprints. Miss Sánchez makes sure that workers follow the blueprints correctly.

Mr. James Collier is the *curator* of an art museum. He has studied art and knows how to find good art work for the museum. Every week, Mr. Collier tells visitors about the history of the art in the museum.

Mrs. Charyl Bassey is a *correspondent.* She is an American, but she lives in Japan. She writes news stories about people and events in Japan. Newspapers all over the world print Mrs. Bassey's news stories.

Dr. Tom Cohoe is a *marine biologist.* He spends some of his time on a boat, searching for plant life in the ocean. Dr. Cohoe also works in a laboratory. He studies plants, such as seaweed, under a microscope.

Kinds of Sentences

A sentence may be a statement, a question, or an exclamation. Each of these sentences ends with a different punctuation mark.

Thinking It Through

Read the three different kinds of sentences. Notice the ending marks.

> Tim practiced for the track meet every day.
> Will he win the big race?
> He won the race!

The first sentence tells you something.
● Does it end with a period, a question mark, or an exclamation mark?

A sentence that tells something, or states a fact, is called a **statement.** A statement ends with a **period.**

The second sentence asks a question.
● Does it end with a period, a question mark, or an exclamation mark?

A sentence that asks something is called a **question.** A question ends with a **question mark.**

The third sentence shows strong feeling.
● Does it end with a period, a question mark, or an exclamation mark?

A sentence that shows strong feeling or surprise is called an **exclamation.** An exclamation ends with an **exclamation mark.**

There are different kinds of sentences. A statement tells something and ends with a period. A question asks something and ends with a question mark. An exclamation shows strong feeling or surprise and ends with an exclamation mark.

Periods, question marks, exclamation marks, and other marks are called **punctuation.** Punctuation marks help make the meaning of sentences clear.

Working It Through

A. Write each sentence with the correct punctuation mark to show what kind of sentence it is.

1. Do you like to go apple picking
2. I went apple picking with my family yesterday
3. My little brother got stuck in one of the trees
4. He screamed and screamed
5. We got him safely on the ground
6. I put my apples in a basket
7. I tried to carry my basket of apples to the car
8. What do you think happened
9. I tripped and all my apples went rolling away

B. Decide if each sentence is a statement, a question, or an exclamation. Write the kind of sentence it is.

1. I am building a model car.
2. Have you ever built a model?
3. I take great care with every part.
4. Will you pass me the paint?
5. Oh no, the paint fell!
6. Get the cat away from the paint!

Trying It Out

1. Choose 3 subjects from this list.

airports	pillows	game
falling stars	lost pets	snowflakes

2. Write a statement, a question, and an exclamation about each subject.

Simple and Complete Subjects

The subject of a sentence tells who or what the sentence is about. A sentence has a complete subject and a simple subject.

Thinking It Through

The subject of a sentence tells who or what the sentence is about. All the words in the subject are called the **complete subject.** Look at these sentences. The complete subjects are in blue.

> The mountain looked steep.
> Two strong mountaineers climbed up the side.

- What is the complete subject in each sentence?

The most important word in the complete subject is the word that tells who or what the sentence is about. That word is called the **simple subject.** The word *mountain* is the simple subject in *The mountain.*

- What is the simple subject in the other sentence?

The simple subject of a sentence is the word that tells who or what the sentence is about. The other words in the complete subject tell more about the simple subject.

Working It Through

A. Find the complete subject at the right that makes sense in each sentence.

    1. ___ tightened their seat belts.   A child
    2. ___ started to take off.   An airplane
    3. ___ lifted into the plane.   The wheels
    4. ___ stared out of his window.   The passengers

B. Copy the sentences. Underline the complete subject in each sentence. Put a second line under the simple subject.

1. The berries grew in the field.
2. The children picked the berries.
3. A girl wore a sun hat.
4. A boy carried a pail.
5. The family ate the berries.
6. Two bees flew by.
7. A bird sang in a tree.
8. The sunshine felt warm.
9. The day was nice.
10. The family went home.

C. Copy the sentences. Put one line under the complete subject in each sentence. Put a second line under the simple subject.

1. The old road cracked open from the heat.
2. The town mayor hired some workers.
3. Several strong workers built the new road.
4. A big machine paved the road.
5. A careful painter drew yellow lines.
6. Four tall people put up street lights.

Trying It Out

Each of these phrases, or groups of words, describes an action that could happen at a circus.

rode bicycles
blew horns
flew in the air
sold popcorn
went through a hoop

1. Turn each phrase into a sentence by adding a complete subject that has more than one word.
2. Write the sentences.
3. Put one line under the complete subject. Put a second line under the simple subject.

Take Another Look

Did you begin each sentence with a capital letter? Did you end each sentence with a period?

Simple and Complete Predicates

A predicate usually tells what the subject does. A sentence has a complete predicate and a simple predicate.

Thinking It Through

The predicate of a sentence usually tells what the subject does. All the words in the predicate are called the **complete predicate.** Look at these sentences. The complete predicates are in red.

> Ned's Water Show started at noon.
> Two porpoises leaped in the air.

● What is the complete predicate in each sentence?

The most important word in the complete predicate is the verb that usually tells what action the subject does. The verb is called the **simple predicate.** *Started* is the simple predicate in *started at noon.*

● What is the simple predicate in the other sentence?

The simple predicate of a sentence is the verb that usually tells what action the subject does. The other words in the complete predicate tell more about the simple predicate.

Working It Through

A. Find a complete predicate at the right that makes sense in each sentence.

1. A bee ＿＿＿.   drank water at the fountain
2. A thirsty child ＿＿＿.   rode on the bike trail
3. Three bikers ＿＿＿.   buzzed by in the air
4. A jogger ＿＿＿.   waved to the children
5. A squirrel ＿＿＿.   grabbed some acorns
6. The balloon man ＿＿＿.   bounced in the lake
7. A rowboat ＿＿＿.   sold big red balloons

B. Copy the sentences. Underline the complete predicate in each sentence. Put a second line under the simple predicate.

1. The Tully family visited a restaurant.
2. They ordered four sandwiches.
3. The waiter balanced the food.
4. He tripped over a carpet.
5. The plates sailed across the room.
6. They landed perfectly on the Tullys' table.
7. Tim Tully clapped his hands.
8. Teresa Tully laughed for three minutes.
9. Mrs. Tully thanked the waiter.
10. The Tully family enjoyed their sandwiches.

Trying It Out

Mark took these photographs at band practice. Read the subjects Mark wrote under the pictures.

The drummer

The flute players

The conductor

1. Turn each subject into a sentence by adding a complete predicate that has more than one word.
2. Write the sentences.
3. Underline each simple predicate.

Working with Sentences

A complete sentence has a subject and a predicate.

Thinking It Through

Laura found a note from her older brother on the
refrigerator door.

> Laura,
>   I had to go to swimming
> practice. Needs its cat medicine
> right away. The box on the table.
> I'll be home soon. The red bicycle.
>   Tom

Laura is confused.
- Does the orange cat or the black cat need medicine?
- Is the box on the table for Laura?
- Where is the red bicycle?

Sentences that are missing a subject or a predicate are
incomplete and don't make sense. A sentence must have a
subject and a predicate to be complete.
- Which sentences are incomplete in Tom's note?
- How would you complete each sentence?

Working It Through

A. There are 4 incomplete sentences in the paragraph.
Find them and add a subject to make each sentence
complete.

> Our school put on a play. Forgot their lines. Broke
> and there was no music. Pepe got the most applause.
> Had a good time. Liked the play.

B. There are 4 incomplete sentences in the paragraph. Find them and add a predicate to make each sentence complete.

> The yard was filled with snow. Our gloved hands. The red sled and the blue sled. The sun came out and melted the snow. The yard. The next day.

C. Tell whether the missing part of each incomplete sentence is a subject or a predicate. Complete each sentence.

> Went to the beach for a picnic. The red dune buggy. A large sand castle. Was warm enough to swim in. Was shining all day. Went home tired.

Trying It Out

The fourth-grade pupils played a game in their room. Help the class describe the game by adding a subject or a predicate to any sentence that needs one.

> The name of the game. The whole class played. Thought of an item in the room. Everyone else tried to guess what it was. Guessed the map on the wall. She was wrong. Asked for another clue. The clue. The right answer. Won the game.

Take Another Look Reread your sentences to make sure each one has a subject and a predicate.

Combining Sentences

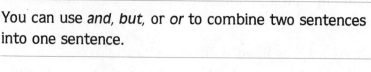

You can use *and*, *but*, or *or* to combine two sentences into one sentence.

Thinking It Through

You can often combine two short sentences to make one longer sentence.

Eric paints walls.
He likes blue paint.

> Eric paints walls, <u>and</u> he likes blue paint.

Enrico paints walls too.
He likes yellow paint.

> Enrico paints walls too, <u>but</u> he likes yellow paint.

Eric and Enrico must be careful.
They could get green walls.

> Eric and Enrico must be careful, <u>or</u> they could get green walls.

- In each sentence at the right, what word was used to combine two short sentences?
- Where was a comma added?

You can often combine two short sentences by placing *and*, *but*, or *or* between them. Put a comma before *and*, *but*, or *or* when you combine sentences.

Working It Through

A. Place a comma where it belongs in each sentence.
1. The zoo has a new cub and Jane wants to see it.
2. Jane goes to the zoo but it starts to rain.
3. The cub must go inside or it will get wet.
4. Jane goes inside or she won't see the cub.
5. Jane sees the cub but she doesn't see its father.
6. The cub growls and it looks tired.

B. Use the word in parentheses to combine the two sentences. Place commas where they belong.

1. Ben was ten. He was sailing to America.   (and)
2. It was his first voyage. He wasn't afraid.   (but)
3. The ship needed wind to fill its sails. It could not move.   (or)
4. For three days there was no wind. The captain was worried.   (and)
5. They must reach land soon. They would run out of food.   (or)
6. Ben couldn't feel any wind. The ship began to move slowly.   (but)

Trying It Out

Combine each pair of sentences with the word in parentheses. Then write the 5 sentences.

The astronaut traveled for days.
She was tired.   (and)

Then the astronaut landed on Zylo.
She was excited.   (and)

She thought no one lived there.
Then she saw a house.   (but)

The house looked strange.
The house also looked
   interesting.   (but)

She could walk to the house now.
She could wait for another astronaut
   to go with her.   (or)

Take Another Look   Be sure you placed a comma before *and*, *but*, or *or* when you combined sentences.

51

Taking Sentences Apart

When a sentence has too many ideas, break it into shorter sentences.

Thinking It Through

This sentence has too many ideas. One idea runs into the next one.

> *I cleaned my goldfish bowl last night and one goldfish almost fell on the floor and next time I'll be more careful.*

The sentence should be taken apart and made into shorter sentences. Notice how the proofreader's marks show the changes to be made.

> *I cleaned my goldfish bowl last night and one goldfish almost fell on the floor and next time I'll be more careful.*

Proofreader's Marks

≡ Make a capital letter.

⊙ Add a period.

℮ Take out.

- What word must be taken out in two places to break the long sentence into short sentences?
- What proofreader's mark was used to show that the word should be dropped?
- What other changes are marked?
- What proofreader's mark shows that a period should be put at the end of each new sentence?
- What mark shows that the first word in each new sentence should begin with a capital letter?

When a sentence runs on and on, it should be taken apart and made into shorter sentences. Drop unnecessary *ands*. Use the right punctuation at the end of each sentence. Capitalize the first word in the next sentence.

Working It Through

A. Rewrite each long sentence as two or three short sentences.

   1. Our house has a big yard and I rake the leaves in the fall and in the summer I pull the weeds.
   2. I planted some vegetables once and they were delicious and everyone wanted more.
   3. There are flowers in the front yard by the porch and I like to pick them and they look beautiful in my room.

B. Rewrite the paragraphs. Each paragraph should have 4 sentences.

   I have an old alarm clock and my dad offered to get me a new clock and I decided to keep my old clock and the ticking puts me to sleep.

   Rosita likes to get up early and she listens to music and sometimes she writes in her diary and she has kept a diary for two years.

Trying It Out

   1. Read over a paper you have written. You might read the book report you wrote for Lesson 6. Look for sentences that run on and on.
   2. Use the marks on page 52 to show the changes you need to make.
   3. Rewrite the sentences, and make the changes you marked.

Review • Sentences

A. Copy each sentence. Add a period, a question mark, or an exclamation mark to show what kind of sentence it is.

1. Have you ever visited Sequoia National Park
2. The park is in California
3. The sequoia trees are very big and very old
4. They are really giants
5. Did you know their bark may be two feet thick
6. Have you seen trees forty feet wide
7. Think of living for 3,500 years

B. Copy each sentence. Put one line under the complete subject. Put a second line under the simple subject.

1. Two red cardinals looked for food one winter.
2. The cold wind ruffled their feathers.
3. A noisy bluejay swooped down on the cardinals.
4. A frisky squirrel jumped over a snowdrift.
5. A heavy snowfall covered the ground.
6. Some worried people got some birdseed.
7. The hungry birds cracked the seeds.
8. A cottontail rabbit ate some of the seeds.

C. Copy each sentence. Put one line under the complete predicate. Put a second line under the simple predicate.

1. Adela stepped off the school bus.
2. She hurried to her room in the farmhouse.
3. Adela changed her clothes.
4. She ran to the pasture.
5. Her horse rubbed its nose against her shoulder.
6. Adela saddled the horse.
7. She rode the horse down the path.
8. They trotted briskly into the woods.

For extra practice turn to page 336.

Evaluation • Sentences

A. Write the letter of the punctuation mark that should come at the end of each sentence.

   1. Did you ask Judy to come
    a. ⊙   **b.** ?   **c.** !

   2. Dinner isn't quite ready
    a. ⊙   **b.** ?   **c.** !

   3. Look out for that wet paint
    a. ⊙   **b.** ?   **c.** !

   4. Don't fall
    a. ⊙   **b.** ?   **c.** !

   5. Swimming is good exercise
    a. ⊙   **b.** ?   **c.** !

   6. Why did she leave so early
    a. ⊙   **b.** ?   **c.** !

B. Write the letter of the response that tells what the underlined part of each sentence is.

   1. A red <u>bird</u> flew to the feeder.
    a. complete subject
    b. simple subject

   2. <u>The hungry cat</u> ate all the food.
    a. complete subject
    b. simple subject

   3. <u>The girls</u> gave Kim a baseball.
    a. complete subject
    b. simple subject

   4. The tiny <u>plants</u> grew like weeds.
    a. complete subject
    b. simple subject

   5. <u>Our aunt</u> went to Hawaii today.
    a. complete subject
    b. simple subject

   6. All the <u>cowboys</u> galloped away.
    a. complete subject
    b. simple subject

C. Write the letter of the response that tells what the underlined part of each sentence is.

   1. We <u>play ball after school.</u>
    a. complete predicate
    b. simple predicate

   2. My dad <u>needs</u> some new boots.
    a. complete predicate
    b. simple predicate

   3. A squirrel <u>jumped onto the roof.</u>
    a. complete predicate
    b. simple predicate

   4. The young man <u>built</u> a boat.
    a. complete predicate
    b. simple predicate

   5. The reckless driver <u>sped away.</u>
    a. complete predicate
    b. simple predicate

   6. She <u>rode</u> the horse every day.
    a. complete predicate
    b. simple predicate

Spotlight • Activities to Choose

1. Find out about place names. Find or draw a map of your state. Use the chart on page 27 to help you find out what languages the names of some cities, lakes, and rivers came from. Label each place with the name of the language. Here is one way to do it with thumbtacks and yarn.

2. Draw a map. Show the streets in your neighborhood. Put in your house, the school, and a few landmarks. Give the map to a friend. Have your friend listen as you give directions from one place to another. Your friend should be able to follow the directions to find out where you are going.

3. Start a file for book reports. Use file cards and a box to file the cards in. At the top of each card, write down the heading that tells the kind of book you read. For example, the heading could be *adventure, mystery,* or *science fiction.* Write the title and name of the author on the first line. After you write your book report, file your card in the box alphabetically by the book title. Put it under the correct heading.

4. Find sentences. Look through old magazines or newspapers for some of your favorite advertisements. Write down some sentences you find. Underline each subject with one line. Put two lines under each predicate. Make a poster with some of your sentences. Title it "Sentences in Advertising."

If you find any incomplete sentences, make a poster of these. Title it "Incomplete Sentences in Advertising."

5. Make a proofreader's chart. Make a chart showing the proofreading marks you have learned. Be sure to tell what they mean. Lesson 12 will help you.

Spotlight • Books to Read

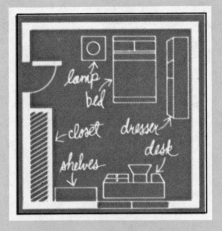

Looking at Maps
by Erich Fuchs

Maps can help you get to places near and far—to the street where your new friend lives, to a city nearby, or to another planet in the universe. With this book you can learn about maps of the moon, weather maps, road maps, and even a map of a child's room.

The Alligator Case
by William Pène du Bois

What do two robberies, three strangers, and a circus have in common? Find out as a boy detective tracks down puzzling clues to one of the most mysterious cases of his career. The young detective is always cleverly disguised, and he's as smart as he is determined.

What Can She Be? An Architect
by Gloria Goldreich and Esther Goldreich

As an architect, Susan Brody designs buildings. She draws plans for their construction and makes sure they are carried out. The plans tell builders, plumbers, and electricians where everything must go. Imagine how exciting it must be to watch a building *you* designed take shape.

Unit Three

Words can be a source of fun. Read this verse and see.

Do you carrot all for me?
My heart beets for you,
With your turnip nose
And your radish face.
You are a peach.
If we cantaloupe,
Lettuce marry;
Weed make a swell pear.

Author unknown

If you listened to someone else read this verse, it would probably sound all right. When you read it, you can see that some of the words are used in a funny way.

In this unit, you will be learning many surprising things about words. You will discover that some words can sound alike, look alike, or be spelled alike. "Lettuce" look inside.

Lesson 1 **Learning About Words in a Dictionary**

Dictionaries can help you learn how to pronounce and use words correctly.

Thinking It Through

You have learned that a guide word, an entry word, and a definition are parts of a dictionary. You also know that entry words are placed in alphabetical order.

There are other helpful parts in a dictionary. An **entry** includes the entry word and all the information after the entry word. A **pronunciation** usually follows an entry word. A **pronunciation key** is a list of pronunciation symbols that stand for letter sounds. Each symbol is followed by a key word that has that sound in it.

Guide words are the first and last entry words on a page.

The *pronunciation key* is a list of pronunciation symbols to help you say a word.

An *entry word* is a word listed in a dictionary, usually in heavy black type.

A *definition* is what a word means.

An *entry* is the entry word and all the information listed after it.

A *pronunciation* is how the word is said.

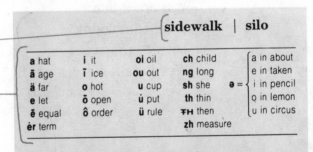

sidewalk | silo

a hat	**i** it	**oi** oil	**ch** child	a in about
ā age	**ī** ice	**ou** out	**ng** long	e in taken
ä far	**o** hot	**u** cup	**sh** she	ə = i in pencil
e let	**ō** open	**u̇** put	**th** thin	o in lemon
ē equal	**ô** order	**ü** rule	**ŦH** then	u in circus
ėr term			**zh** measure	

side walk (sīd′wôk′), place to walk at the side of a street, usually paved.
sigh (sī), **1** let out a very long, deep breath because one is sad, tired, or relieved: *We heard her sigh with relief.* **2** act or sound of sighing: *a sigh of relief.* **3** make a sound like a sigh: *The wind sighed in the treetops.* **4** wish very much; long: *He sighed for home.*
sight see ing (sīt′sē′ing), going around to see objects or places of interest: *a weekend of sightseeing.*
sig na ture (sig′nə chər), **1** a person's name written by that person. **2** signs printed at the beginning of a staff to show the pitch, key, and time of a piece of music.
si lo (sī′lō), an airtight building or pit in which green food for farm animals is preserved. *plural* **si los.**

60

- What information is in the entry for the word *silo?*
- How do you pronounce *sigh?*
- Which word in the pronunciation key helped you pronounce *sigh?*

Working It Through

A. Use the dictionary sample on page 60 to help you answer the questions. Tell the part of the dictionary sample you used.

1. What does the entry for the word *sidewalk* include?
2. Which of the entry words has the sound /ô/?
3. Look at the symbol /e/. Pronounce its key word *let.* Which of these words has the sound /e/?

   bat   bet   but   bit
4. What key words help you pronounce the word *silo?*

B. Tell what part or parts of a dictionary you would use to
1. say the word *catsup.*
2. find out what *catkin* means.
3. find out what page *cattail* is on.
4. find out all the information about the entry word *catfish.*

Trying It Out

1. Look at the pictures and notice the pronunciations of the words.
2. Use the pronunciation key on page 60 to help you pronounce the words.
3. Decide which word below goes with each picture.

   ant   crab   deer   lamb   ox   squid   wasp
4. Write a paragraph about visiting a zoo. Make sure you use each word in the picture at least once.

Lesson 2   Some Words Have Several Meanings

A word can have more than one meaning. Context clues and a dictionary can help you find the meaning you want.

Thinking It Through

Read each paragraph below.

● Can you find what *hot* means in each paragraph?

illustrative sentence

hot (hot), **1** much warmer than the body; having much heat: *That fire is hot. The sun is hot today. That long run has made me hot.* **2** having a sharp, burning taste: *Pepper and mustard are hot.* **3** fiery: *a hot temper, hot with rage.* **4** new; fresh: *a hot scent, a hot trail.* **5** following closely: *We were in hot pursuit of the runaway horse. adjective,* **hot ter, hot test.**

Sue stirred the bowl of chili. She added some salt, more chili powder, and some pepper. Then she tasted it. "This is hot!" she yelled.

The sun had been burning down all day. The fan broke at noon. Sticky air hung in the kitchen. The cook sweated over the stove. "It's hot!" he groaned.

The other words in a sentence or paragraph that help you know the meaning of a word are **context clues.** In the first paragraph, *chili, chili powder, pepper,* and *tasted* are context clues for the meaning of *hot.*

● What context clues in the second paragraph help you know the meaning of *hot?*
● Does *hot* have the same meaning in both paragraphs?
● Which definition of *hot* is used in the first paragraph? in the second paragraph?
● Which illustrative sentences helped you know how *hot* is used?

If a word has more than one meaning, context clues will help you recognize which meaning was used. If you are still not sure, use a dictionary.

Working It Through

A. What does each underlined word mean? Use the context clues to help you.

1. The football game ended in a tie with a score of 7–7.
   necktie   equal points

2. John wore a tie with his shirt.
   necktie   equal points

3. Iron the shirt and get the wrinkles out.
   metal   press smooth

4. The iron fence is strong.
   metal   press smooth

5. She kept cool and steady in the emergency.
   calm   cold

6. The cool wind blew the snow over the icy street.
   calm   cold

7. She has a gift for gymnastics.
   talent   present

8. I got a gift for my birthday.
   talent   present

B. Read the entry for *season*. Write a sentence to answer each question.

1. What is your favorite season of the year?

2. What do you do during a holiday season?

3. What do you season your soup and salad with?

sea son (sē′zn), **1** one of the four periods of the year; spring, summer, autumn, or winter. **2** any period of time marked by something special: *the holiday season, the harvest season.* **3** improve the flavor of: *Season your egg with salt.* 1,2 *noun,* 3 *verb.*

Trying It Out

Read all the directions before doing the activity.

1. Think of more than one meaning for each word on the right. Use a dictionary, if necessary.

2. Write sentences that show two meanings of each word.

3. Try to include context clues in your sentences so people will know the meaning of the word.

cold
train
field
point
chair

Lesson 3 Homonyms

Words called homonyms sound alike and have the same spellings, but they have different meanings.

Thinking It Through

In Lesson 2, you learned that one word can sometimes have several different meanings. Sometimes two or more words sound alike and may even be spelled alike, but have different meanings.

Read the joke below.

> George asked, "Did you put the bat away with the baseball?"
>
> Sue answered, "No, I couldn't catch the bat."

- How did George use the word *bat?*
- What meaning did Sue use?
- Did you know that *bat* is really two different words?

Read the dictionary entry.

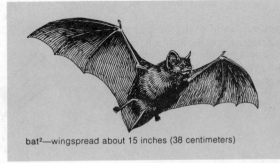

bat¹ (bat), **1** a stout wooden stick or club, used to hit the ball in baseball, cricket, and similar games. **2** hit with a bat; hit: *He bats well. I batted the balloon with my hand.* **3** a turn at batting: *Who goes to bat first?* 1,3 *noun,* 2 *verb,* **bat ted, bat ting.**
bat² (bat), a flying mammal with a body like that of a mouse and wings made of thin skin. Bats fly at night. Most of them eat insects but some live on fruit and a few suck the blood of other mammals. See picture. *noun.*

bat²—wingspread about 15 inches (38 centimeters)

- Do the words *bat¹* and *bat²* sound the same?
- Are *bat¹* and *bat²* spelled the same?
- What is the first meaning of *bat¹*?
- What is the meaning of *bat²*?

Words like *bat¹* and *bat²* are called **homonyms.** They sound alike and are spelled the same, but they have different meanings.

Working It Through

A. Read the dictionary entries. Which homonym, *pile¹*, *pile²*, or *pile³*, is used in each sentence? Use each of the three homonyms in a sentence of your own.

> **pile¹** (pīl), many things lying one upon another in a more or less orderly way: *a pile of wood.* *noun.*
> **pile²** (pīl), a heavy beam driven upright into the ground or the bed of a river to help support a bridge, wharf, or building. *noun.*
> **pile³** (pīl), a soft, thick nap on velvet, plush, and many carpets: *The pile of that rug is almost half an inch long. noun.*

1. That pile of books is overdue.
2. That carpet has a deep pile.
3. They have driven in the piles for the bridge.

B. In each joke below, the underlined word has two different meanings. See if you can figure out both meanings.

1. "How are dogcatchers paid?"
   "By the <u>pound</u>."
2. "Did your pig break his <u>pen</u>?"
   "That's right. Now he has to type his letters."
3. "Did you <u>tip</u> the waiter?"
   "No, he fell over by himself."
4. "I have a <u>case</u> of measles."
   "Well, don't open it until you've had a shot."

Trying It Out

Read all of the directions below before you begin the activity.

1. Write down what these words mean to you and what they would have meant to a knight. Use a dictionary if necessary.

   page   foil   mail

2. Write two sentences for each homonym above. One sentence should show what the word means to you. The other sentence should show what the word would have meant to a knight.

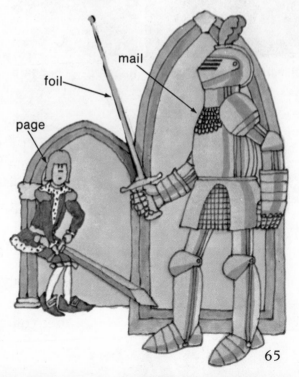

mail

foil

page

Learning New Words

Learning new words can help you describe things more exactly.

Thinking It Through

Look at the pictures. Read the captions, or titles, below the pictures. Then read the dictionary entries.

eerie—an **eerie** face   haggard—a **haggard** expression   **placid—placid** water

eer ie or **eer y** (ir′ē),
strange; weird; causing fear.
adjective, **eer i er, eer i est.**

hag gard (hag′ərd), looking
worn from pain, fatigue,
worry, or hunger; worn by
care. *adjective.*

plac id (plas′id), pleasantly
calm or peaceful; quiet: *a
placid temper. adjective.*

Use the pictures, captions, and definitions to answer these questions.

- Which word would best describe a monster?
- Which word would best describe a worried parent?
- Which word would best describe a calm rainfall?

When you learn new words like *eerie, haggard,* and *placid,* you can describe things that you write or talk about more exactly.

Working It Through

A. Use the words *eerie, haggard,* and *placid* to tell exactly what is happening in each group of sentences.

1. There were no waves on the lake. The water did not move. The lake was _____.
2. The wolf's howl was frightening. The howl was an _____ sound in the night.
3. The old prospector had traveled a long way. He was tired and worn out. His face was _____.

B. Choose one of the entry words at the right to use instead of the underlined word in each sentence.

1. We played inside on such a <u>hot</u> day.
2. We found some <u>unusual</u> hats in the attic.
3. One of the hats was <u>bright</u> red.
4. Risha let out a <u>loud</u> laugh.
5. She thought the hats were <u>funny</u>.

bois ter ous (boi′stər əs), noisily cheerful: *The room was filled with boisterous laughter.* *adjective.*
hi lar i ous (hə ler′ē əs *or* hə lar′ē əs), very merry; very funny; noisy and cheerful: *a hilarious party. adjective.*
out land ish (out lan′dish), not familiar; strange or ridiculous; odd: *an outlandish hat. adjective.*
tor rid (tôr′id), very hot: *July is usually a torrid month. adjective.*
viv id (viv′id), strikingly bright; brilliant; strong and clear. *adjective.*

Trying It Out

Read the definition. Then look at the picture and caption. Write a short paragraph about something incredible.

in cred i ble (in kred′ə bəl), seeming too extraordinary to be possible; beyond belief: *The racing car rounded the curve with incredible speed. adjective.*

incredible—The boy thought the stunt was **incredible.**

Take Another Look
Does each sentence begin with a capital letter? Do your sentences end with the correct punctuation?

Lesson 5 **Writing a Descriptive Paragraph**

Using exact words and specific details in a paragraph will help make your description clear and interesting.

Thinking It Through

Notice how the author has used exact words and specific details to make the following paragraph clear and interesting. The paragraph describes a boy looking down the street.

It's sure empty today. There's practically no one on the street in the five or six blocks from the subway station to the aquarium. But it's not quiet. There are a few places open—merry-go-rounds and hot-dog shops—and tinny little trickles of music come out of them, but the big noise is the wind. All the signs are swinging and screeching. Rubbish cans blow over and their tops clang and bang rolling down the street. The wind makes a whistly noise all by itself.

- What setting, or place, is the author describing?
- How do the words "tinny little trickles" help you hear the music?
- What other exact words help you see or hear what is going on in the street?
- How does the detail about swinging and screeching signs add to the description?
- What other specific details help you see or hear what is going on in the setting?

Remember that the first line of a paragraph is usually indented. A paragraph tells about just one idea, such as a description of a street. Exact words and specific details about what you can see, hear, or taste will make your description clear and interesting.

Working It Through

A. Make a list of what you see in the picture. Use exact words and specific details. Answer questions like these to help make your list.

1. How does each child feel about eating the food?
2. How do the foods taste and smell?
3. How do the foods sound when you eat them?
4. How do the foods feel when you touch them?
5. What size, shape, and color is each food?

B. Turn the items on your list into complete sentences.

Trying It Out

A. Think about the street where you live. Make a list of items to describe it. Use exact words and specific details. Answer these questions.

1. What do you see? a fireplug? a cracked sidewalk? smoke from chimneys? trees?
2. What do you hear? a baby crying? noise from cars? children playing? birds singing?
3. What do you smell? trees or flowers? fumes from cars or industry?

B. Write complete sentences about 5 of the items from your list.

C. Make your sentences into a paragraph about your street. Remember to indent the first line.

Lesson 6 Improving Your Writing

Checking your paragraphs for exact words and specific
details will improve your writing.

Thinking It Through

You can use proofreader's marks to show the changes you
want to make in your writing. Look at the marks on the
left and read what they stand for.

Ann used proofreader's marks to improve her story.
Read the story and note the changes she wanted to make.

Proofreader's Marks

≡   Make a capital letter.

⊙   Add a period.

ℓ   Take out.

∧   Put in one or more words.

> At the circus, I could smell dry sawdust and hot buttered popcorn. I loved the clowns, lion tamers, and huge, clumsy elephants. and my favorite performers were the trapeze artists. I was scared when one of them flipped in a somersault twenty feet through the air.

- Why did Ann add *dry* before "sawdust" and *huge, clumsy* before "elephant"?
- What specific details did she use to describe the popcorn? to describe the somersault?
- What changes did Ann want to make?
- Which proofreader's mark did she use for each change?

Checking your writing for exact words and specific
details improves your writing. Proofreader's marks show
the changes you want to make.

Working It Through

A. Rewrite the paragraph on page 70. Make the changes that are marked.

B. Add exact words and specific details to the paragraph below. Use the picture to help you. Write the paragraph.

> I like the leaves in the fall. The leaves are brown. They are different shapes. The leaves are on the ground. They smell nice. I have some in my arms.

C. Proofread your paragraph. Use the proofreader's marks on page 70 to show changes you want to make. Rewrite your paragraph, and make the changes you marked.

Trying It Out

A. Reread the paragraph you wrote in Lesson 5 or write a new paragraph. Think of changes you can make to improve it. Ask yourself these questions to help find mistakes.

  1. Did I describe one idea?
  2. Did I use exact words?
  3. Did I include specific details?
  4. Did I indent the first line?

B. Use proofreader's marks to show the changes you want to make in your paragraph. Rewrite the paragraph, making the changes you marked.

Review • Using Exact Words

A. Read the sentences. Notice the underlined words used to describe the dancers. Then answer the questions that follow.

> The <u>agile</u> dancers moved easily.
> She made <u>powerful</u> leaps.
> He <u>twirled</u> in the air.
> They were <u>extraordinary</u> dancers.

1. Which word helps you know that the dancers moved easily?
2. Which word tells you that the female dancer put great strength in her leaps.
3. Which word tells you how the male dancer moved?
4. Which word tells you the dancers were very good?

B. Replace the underlined word in each sentence with a more exact word. Write the sentences.

1. We <u>laughed</u> at the joke.
2. I <u>like</u> peanut butter.
3. I have a <u>bad</u> stomach ache.
4. Act as <u>though</u> you're asleep!
5. That is a <u>big</u> bowl of soup.
6. Why do you look so <u>sad</u>?
7. Todd <u>ate</u> the popcorn.
8. Colette is a <u>nice</u> friend.
9. You <u>look</u> happy.
10. The <u>little</u> insect chased Alex.
11. Let's <u>make</u> a treehouse.
12. A <u>good</u> friend is rare.

C. Answer the questions.

1. Which of your exact words do you like best? Why?
2. Which underlined word was the hardest for you to replace? Why?
3. Did you start each sentence with a capital letter?
4. Did you write complete sentences?
5. Does each sentence have end punctuation?

Evaluation • Using Exact Words

A. Choose one of the words at the right to replace the underlined word in each sentence. Make the meanings more exact. Write the sentences.

bril liant (bril′yənt), **1** shining brightly; sparkling: *brilliant jewels, brilliant sunshine.* **2** splendid; magnificent: *The singer gave a brilliant performance.* **3** having great ability: *She is a brilliant musician. adjective.*

ma jes tic (mə jes′tik), grand; noble; dignified; stately. *adjective.*

pleas ant (plez′nt), **1** that pleases; giving pleasure: *a pleasant swim on a hot day.* **2** friendly; easy to get along with: *She is a pleasant person.* **3** fair; not stormy: *a pleasant day. adjective.*

sym pa thet ic (sim′pə thet′ik), **1** having or showing kind feelings toward others; sympathizing: *She is an unselfish and sympathetic friend.* **2** approving; agreeing: *The teacher was sympathetic to the class's plan for a trip to the museum.* **3** enjoying the same things and getting along well together. *adjective.*

thun der ous (thun′dər əs), **1** producing thunder. **2** making a noise like thunder: *The famous actor received a thunderous burst of applause at the end the play. adjective.*

1. I had a <u>good</u> nap.
2. Eric saw a <u>great</u> redwood tree.
3. The waterfall sounds <u>loud</u>.
4. Rosita is a <u>fine</u> pianist.
5. A <u>kind</u> person listens to your troubles.

B. Think about a pleasant experience you had one day, a place you may have gone. Where did you go? Did you ice skate in the park? Did you go fishing? Did you swim at the beach or in a pool? Did you go to an amusement park? Did you play baseball?

Write several sentences about your experience. Include as many exact words as you can. Make your sentences clear and interesting.

You will be evaluated on your choice of exact words and on the following:

    capital letters at the beginning of sentences

    complete sentences

    correct ending marks for the sentences

Long, long ago, there was a battle in an area of Greece called Marathon. The battle was between a Persian army and an Athenian army. The Persians had 100,000 warriors but the Athenians had only 10,000. The Athenians won.

The Athenians wanted to tell the people in their city of Athens that they had won. But Athens was 26 miles or 43.3 kilometers away.

They decided to send a runner named Pheidippides to Athens. Pheidippides ran at top speed to the city. When he got to the market-place, he gasped, "We have won a great victory. The Persians have been driven away." And then he died because of his great effort.

Today we use the word *marathon* to mean a foot-race of 26 miles. In many American cities, people run in marathons. The picture at the left shows some people running in the 1978 Chicago marathon.

Spotlight • Funny Autographs

Jackie was moving to another city, and she wanted to remember her friends. She asked them to write jokes in her autograph book and then sign their names.

The pictures on this page show some of the jokes from Jackie's autograph book. Many of the jokes were made by using words that sound the same but have different meanings. These kinds of jokes are called puns. See if you can find the puns in these jokes.

You might want to think of a funny pun to write in someone's autograph book. Use words that can have more than one meaning, such as *butterflies, kitchen sinks,* or *cereal bowls.*

I'm Cliff
Drop over
sometime.
Cliff D.

Doctor Bell fell down
the well
And broke his collarbone
Doctors should attend
the sick
And leave the well alone.
Barry J.

Don't tell secrets in a cornfield because corn has ears.
Yoriko J.

Remember us till Niagara falls, till the bed spreads, till the barn dances, till the pencil case is solved, and till ice skates.
Randy and Vicky

Nouns and Noun Markers

Words that name persons, places, and things are called nouns. The words *a*, *an*, and *the* are noun markers. They signal that a noun will soon appear in the sentence.

Thinking It Through

Mr. Nemo, gym, and *basketball* are nouns because they name a person, place, and thing. Nouns are often signaled by words like *a*, *an*, and *the*. A word that signals a noun is called a **noun marker.**

In the following sentence, the noun markers *a*, *an*, and *the* are followed by nouns.

● What nouns follow *a?*   What noun follows *an?*   What noun follows *the?*

A is used before a word that begins with a consonant sound, as in *a dress. An* is used before a word that begins with a vowel sound, as in *an umbrella. The* is used before both kinds of words.

Whenever you see a noun marker such as *a*, *an*, or *the* in a sentence, you know that a noun will soon appear.

Working It Through

A. Copy the sentences. Put one line under the noun markers *a*, *an*, and *the* and two lines under the nouns that follow them. You shold find 12 noun markers.

  1. Alice and Uncle Ned went to the lake.

  2. They rowed a boat to an island nearby.

3. They brought a blanket and a camera.
4. With the camera, they took a picture of an animal.
5. They had never seen an animal with an ear, an eye, and a mouth that large.

B. Add either *a* or *an* to the sentences. Write the sentences.

1. Carol is ____ artist.
2. She drew ____ picture of ____ elephant that was ten feet tall.
3. She also painted ____ zebra running through the grass.
4. She painted ____ worm in her picture of ____ apple.
5. Bright red is ____ color she uses often.

C. Add a noun from the list of nouns on the right to the sentences. Then write the sentences.

1. Bob saw a ____ use its four legs to climb up the ____ .
2. It wanted to get an ____ that grew there.
3. A ____ was flapping its wings to protect an ____ in its nest.
4. Bob opened the ____ of bread he brought.
5. Some ants ate the ____ that fell on the ____ .

bird
crumbs
acorn
grass
squirrel
tree
egg
loaf

Trying It Out
Write 6 sentences that tell a story.
Use the nouns below.

anteater   trip
ostrich   peanut
zoo   monkey

Take Another Look   Did you use
a, an, or *the* correctly?

Common and Proper Nouns

A proper noun names a particular person, place, or thing.
All other nouns are common nouns.

Thinking It Through

Notice the underlined nouns in the following sentence.

<u>Abigail Jones</u> was an early <u>settler</u>.

- What is the name of the settler?
- Does each word begin with a small or a capital letter?

Abigail Jones is a proper noun. A **proper noun** names
a particular person, place, or thing. The word *settler*
refers to any settler. It is a **common noun.**

A proper noun can be more than one word. Each word
must begin with a capital
letter.

Look at the common and
proper nouns in the chart.

Common Nouns	Proper Nouns
city	Atlanta
state	Oregon
country	Canada
holiday	Thanksgiving
continent	Africa
region	Midwest
ocean	Atlantic Ocean
lake	Fox Lake
river	Nile River

- Why are the nouns in the
  first list common nouns?
- Why are the nouns in the
  second list proper nouns?
- What kind of letter does
  each proper noun begin
  with?

A word that names a particular person, place, or thing
is a proper noun. All other nouns are common nouns.

Working It Through

A. Proofread the nouns below. Capitalize the proper nouns.

1. new york
2. state
3. city
4. iowa
5. labor day
6. america

B. Read each sentence. Then complete the sentences with a proper noun that names a particular place or thing from the chart on page 78. The underlined common nouns will help you.

1. George lives in a <u>region</u> called the ____ .
2. His favorite <u>lake</u> is ____ .
3. He likes to read about the <u>continent</u> of ____ .
4. He dreamed he sailed down a <u>river</u> named the ____ .
5. When he woke up he was on an <u>ocean</u> called the ____ .

C. Find the common nouns and proper nouns in the sentences. Write the 9 common nouns in one column and the 7 proper nouns in another column.

1. Aunt Carla lives in a region called the South.
2. Her house is near a lake called Clear Lake.
3. The last holiday we visited her was Labor Day.
4. She showed us the pictures of her trip to the continent of Africa.
5. She flew over an ocean called the Atlantic Ocean.
6. She sailed up a river called the Nile River.

Trying It Out

1. Pretend you are a world traveler.
2. Choose a proper noun from each list below.
3. Write 5 sentences telling where you would like to go.

Continent	Region	Ocean	Lake	River
Asia	South	Arctic Ocean	Great Salt Lake	Ohio River
Europe	North	Indian Ocean	Lake Huron	Rio Grande
South America	New England	Pacific Ocean	Reindeer Lake	Seine River

79

Plural Nouns

Most plural nouns are formed by adding *-s* or *-es* to the singular noun.

Thinking It Through
Notice the plural form of each singular noun in the chart.

Nouns	
Singular	**Plural**
cook	cooks
bee	bees
bun*ch*	bunches
fi*sh*	fishes
fo*x*	foxes
walru*s*	walruses
cla*ss*	classes
dais*y*	daisies

- How are *cook* and *bee* made plural?
- How are *bunch, fish, fox, walrus,* and *class* made plural?
- What letters do these singular words end with?
- How is *daisy* made plural? Why?

  Look at these words.   monkey + s = monkeys

- What letter does *monkey* end with?
- Does the *y* in *monkey* follow a vowel or a consonant?
- What letter is added to *monkey* to make it plural?
- How would you spell the plural forms of *boy* and *tray*?

  Most nouns are made plural by adding *-s* or *-es.* In nouns ending in a *y* that follows a consonant, change the *y* to *i* before adding *-es.* In nouns ending in a *y* that follows a vowel, add only *-s* to form the plural.

Working It Through

A. Make each noun plural.

1. plant   **3.** sandwich   **5.** fox
2. house   **4.** brush   **6.** recess

B. Check each noun to see if the *y* follows a consonant or a vowel. Make each noun plural.

1. pony   **3.** city   **5.** subway
2. journey   **4.** hobby   **6.** key

C. Look at the underlined noun in each sentence. Use the plural form to complete the sentence.

1. Sue saw a <u>pony</u> and her brother saw a whole group of ____.
2. John's class finally chose a <u>play</u> after reading three other ____.
3. We visited one <u>city</u>, but the fifth grade visited two ____.
4. We needed one <u>tray</u> for the crackers but four ____ for the juice and glasses.

D. What noun belongs in each sentence? Tell if it is singular or plural.

1. Three (boy, boys) went on a trip.
2. Their (donkey, donkeys) were loaded with packages.
3. They saw a (valley, valleys) and a river.
4. A (monkey, monkeys) chattered in a tree.
5. They were gone for twenty (day, days).

Trying It Out

Write a paragraph of your own about a trip you would like to take to a city. Try to use the plural form of three of the words below.

journey   money
runway   subway

Other Plural Nouns

Some singular nouns are made plural by changing the spelling or by adding letters.

Thinking It Through

Usually -*s* or -*es* is added to a singular noun to make it plural. Some plural nouns do not end with -*s* or -*es*. Look at the chart below.

Nouns	
Singular	**Plural**
chairman	chairmen
chairwoman	chairwomen
eyetooth	eyeteeth
foot	feet
goose	geese
mouse	mice
ox	oxen
grandchild	grandchildren

The spellings of the singular nouns in the chart are changed when the nouns are made plural.

The *a* in *chairman* is changed to *e* to form the plural noun *chairmen*.

- What letter is changed in *chairwoman* to form the plural noun *chairwomen?*
- What letters are changed in *goose* to form the plural noun *geese?*
- What letters were added to *ox* to form the plural noun *oxen?* to *grandchild* to form the plural noun *grandchildren?*

Some nouns are made plural by changing letters within the singular nouns or by adding letters: *foot, feet; mouse, mice; ox, oxen; grandchild, grandchildren.*

Working It Through

A. Make each noun plural.

1. grandchild
2. ox
3. mouse
4. goose
5. foot
6. eyetooth
7. chairwoman
8. chairman
9. tooth
10. woman
11. man
12. child

B. Change each underlined noun to a plural noun.

1. Some <u>man</u>, several <u>woman</u>, and <u>child</u> went to a fair.
2. They took three <u>goose</u> and two pet <u>mouse</u> to sell.
3. Two of the <u>goose</u> ran away.
4. They ran over a peddler's <u>foot</u>.
5. He fell down and broke his <u>tooth</u>.
6. When the peddler felt better, all the <u>child</u> fixed him a feast. (Guess what he had to eat!)

C. What noun belongs in each sentence? Tell if it is singular or plural.

1. Sue took a (blanket, blankets) to the park.
2. Sara brought a picnic basket and some plastic (glass, glasses) for juice.
3. The grass felt good under their bare (foot, feet).
4. They sank their (tooth, teeth) into some delicious (sandwich, sandwiches) from the basket.
5. After lunch, they read a (book, books) and a (magazine, magazines) they had brought with them.
6. At sunset, all the (man, men), (woman, women), and (child, children) left the park.

Trying It Out

Write a story about a veterinarian's office. Tell about the people and the pets they bring in to be treated. Use some of the plural forms you have practiced in this lesson. Use the picture for help in writing your story.

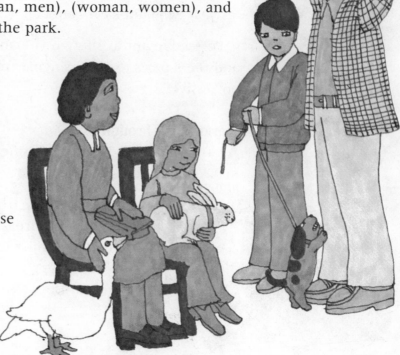

Singular Possessive Nouns

Nouns that show ownership are possessive nouns. Singular nouns have a special form to show possession.

Thinking It Through

An apostrophe and the letter *s* (*'s*) are added to a singular noun to make it show ownership, or possession.

> Ann's sweater is red.
> Tony's new shoes are comfortable.
> The boy's raincoat is lost.

- What belongs to Ann? to Tony? to the boy?
- What was added to each singular noun to make it show possession?

- What nouns show possession in these sentences?

> The turtle's shell is hard.
> John's dog is frisky.
> An elephant's ears are big.

Possessive nouns show ownership. Add an apostrophe and the letter *s* (*'s*) to a singular noun to make it possessive.

Working It Through

A. The underlined words are singular nouns. Add *'s* to make them show possession.

1. <u>Sandy</u> frog was famous.
2. The <u>frog</u> name was Hopper.
3. <u>Hopper</u> legs were made for hopping.
4. Hopper lived in <u>Sandy</u> backyard.

B. Below are lists of things that tell about Joanne, her dog Snowball, and her Uncle Ted. Write out each item as a singular possessive noun. For example: Joanne's bicycle.

Joanne	Snowball	Uncle Ted
bicycle	dish	garden
baseball	leash	umbrella
sweater	bark	suitcase

C. Add an apostrophe and the letter *s* (*'s*) to the singular nouns that should show possession. There should be one singular possessive noun in each sentence.

1. Susan hobby is learning about animals.
2. Her dog health record is on a chart in the kitchen.
3. She also keeps a record of her cat growth on a chart.
4. Her father helps Susan understand an animal habits when they go on nature walks.
5. Susan also learns about animals with her mother help.
6. Her mother is a veterinarian and works at the city new animal hospital.

Trying It Out

Write a story about a surprise party a fourth-grade class gave the teacher. Use the singular possessive form of at least four of the nouns below.

1. class	**3.** principal	**5.** cake	**7.** hat
2. card	**4.** present	**6.** party	**8.** teacher

Take Another Look Did you add *'s* to the singular nouns to show possession?

Lesson 12 — Plural Possessive Nouns

Plural nouns have a special form to show possession.

Thinking It Through

You learned in Lesson 11 that you make a singular noun show ownership by adding an apostrophe and *s* (*'s*).

The dentist's office is closed.

Plural nouns also change form to show possession. Add only an apostrophe (*'*) to a plural noun that ends in *s* to form the possessive.

- What are the nouns that show possession in these sentences?

The knives' handles need fixing.
The girls' houses were freshly painted.
The ponies' heads were covered with mud.

Add an apostrophe and *s* (*'s*) to a plural noun that does not end in *s* to form the possessive.

- What are the plural possessive nouns in these sentences?

Mom asked me to clean the mice's cage.
The men's club cooked the pancake breakfast.
The women's group won the race.

Add an apostrophe (*'*) to a plural noun that ends in *s* to form the possessive. Add an apostrophe and *s* (*'s*) to a plural noun that does not end in *s* to form the possessive.

Working It Through

A. The underlined words are plural nouns that end in *s*. Change the plural nouns to show possession.

1. the <u>wolves</u> cave
2. the <u>dwarves</u> home
3. the <u>ladies</u> team
4. the <u>boys</u> bicycles
5. the <u>girls</u> jackets
6. the <u>dogs</u> leashes

B. The underlined words are plural nouns that do not end in *s*. Change the plural nouns to show possession.

1. the <u>men</u> chorus
2. the <u>geese</u> food
3. the <u>women</u> meeting
4. the <u>mice</u> tails
5. the <u>cattle</u> pastures
6. the <u>children</u> books

C. Add ' or 's to the underlined plural nouns to show possession in these sentences.

1. The <u>fireworks</u> brightness lit up the sky.
2. The <u>women</u> letters were a week early.
3. The <u>boxes</u> covers are lost.
4. The <u>geese</u> honking awakened us.
5. The <u>scissors</u> blades needed to be sharpened.
6. The <u>children</u> toys were scattered on the floor.

Trying It Out

Rewrite the advertisement for the dude ranch. Add ' or 's to five plural nouns to show possession.

Come to the Bar B Q Ranch. Our three cooks chili is delicious. Our horses stables are near the ranch house. Children riding lessons are free.

See our two ranchers roping tricks. Hear the wolves howls at night.

Welcome! Bar B Q Ranch

Review • Nouns

A. Copy the following sentences. Write the plural form of each noun in parentheses.

1. I saw two huge ____.   (bee)
2. We ran two ____.   (mile)
3. They saw some ____.   (daisy)
4. He raises ____.   (turkey)
5. Babies do not have ____.   (tooth)
6. Three ____ ran past us.   (fox)

B. Copy the following sentences. Capitalize all proper nouns. Underline the common and proper nouns. You should find 14 nouns. Ten of them will be proper nouns.

1. George lives in a cabin in the south.
2. Hawaii is in the pacific ocean.
3. Paris is a city on the continent of europe.
4. A lake in africa is lake victoria.
5. The rhone river runs through switzerland.

C. Copy the following sentences. Complete each with the possessive form of the noun in parentheses. There are 3 plural possessives.

1. The ____ edges were curled up.   (leaves)
2. A ____ eyes are black and beady.   (mouse)
3. See the decoration on the ____ handles!   (knives)
4. This is ____ house.   (Tony)
5. Are these the ____ shirts?   (men)

For extra practice turn to pages 337–338.

Take Another Look   Copy the sentence. Put one line under the complete subject. Put two lines under the simple subject.

The little lake lay high in the mountains.

Did you underline <u>The little lake</u> once and <u>lake</u> twice?

For more practice turn to Exercise B on page 67.
Underline each complete subject once and each complete predicate twice.

Evaluation • Nouns

A. The plural forms of nouns are not correct in 7 sentences.
Write the letters of those sentences.

1. **a.** How many inchs long is it?
   b. These are the new calendars.
   c. All of my tooth hurt!
2. **a.** The cabin's stood in a row.
   b. We laughed at the monkies.
   c. Here are three new brushes.

3. **a.** Two oxes pulled the wagon.
   b. The bell gave two rings.
   c. She ate four of the cookeys.
4. **a.** They took along two boxes.
   b. We have two recesses.
   c. I lost all my pennys.

B. Write the letters of the underlined words that should
begin with capital letters. If none of the underlined words
in a sentence needs to be capitalized, write the letter for
"None of these."

1. The first <u>thanksgiving</u> took
               a
   <u>place</u> in the <u>east</u>. <u>None of these</u>
   b   **c**   **d**

2. Joe <u>flew</u> over the <u>pacific</u>
       a   **b**
   <u>ocean</u> to <u>africa</u>. <u>None of these</u>
   c   **d**   **e**

3. Ali <u>lives</u> by <u>red</u> <u>lake</u> in
       a   **b** **c**
   <u>carson</u>, <u>texas</u>. <u>None of these</u>
   d   **e**   **f**

4. He went to <u>see</u> the <u>Avon</u> <u>River</u>
                a   **b**   **c**
   in <u>England</u>. <u>None of these</u>
      d   **e**

C. The possessive form of the noun is not correct in 8 of
the sentences below. Write the letters of those sentences.

1. **a.** Here are the two girls caps.
   b. The bird's beak is yellow.
   c. We went to Anns house.
   d. Both boys' dogs were waiting.
2. **a.** A robins breast is orange.
   b. Here are two robins nests.
   c. The geese's feet are webbed.
   d. The mens club won the race.

3. **a.** The people's houses were red.
   b. The trees' leaves fell off.
   c. The mices tails are long.
   d. Tony's ax was gone.
4. **a.** Look at the pumpkins teeth!
   b. The elves coats were torn.
   c. The puppy's feet were muddy.
   d. The two cats' fur was wet.

Spotlight • Activities to Choose

1. Make a picture book. Cut out pictures of things from magazines or newspapers. Paste them in a book. Write a sentence for each picture, telling who the owner is. Use a possessive in each sentence. Lend the book to classmates for reference when they write possessives.

These are Mary's mittens.   These are the girls' bikes.

2. Start a file of new words. When you read a new word, write it on a card. Then write the definition and make up a sentence using the word. Put the card in alphabetical order in a file box. Try to use the words in your writing and speaking.

3. Illustrate homonyms. Draw pictures that show the different meanings of homonyms. Use the homonyms listed below or your own. Use a dictionary to help you with the different meanings. Show your pictures to your classmates. See if they can guess what homonyms you pictured.

| scale | palm | mail |
| bank | heel | bill |

4. Play a proper noun game. With classmates, make a list of proper nouns. Include at least two names from each of these groups: rivers, continents, holidays, regions, lakes, states, cities, oceans, streets, girls' names, and boys' names. Choose teams. One person, who does not play, gives the words from the list. The others spell the proper nouns, remembering to say *capital* before each capital letter. Each team earns one point for a correct spelling.

5. Paint a mural for the bulletin board or wall. Paint pictures of buildings that are found in a city, like a bank or a department store. Then list things found inside the buildings. Use the words *a*, *an*, and *the* before the nouns. For example, you could list *the vault* for a picture of a bank.

Puns, Gags, Quips and Riddles: A Collection of Dreadful Jokes
by Roy Doty

These puns are especially fun to read and tell. Each pun has its own delightful picture. The jokes and riddles will have your family and friends asking for more—or less.

The Street of the Flower Boxes
by Peggy Mann

When a new family plants flowers in a window box, a group of tough boys pulls them up saying, "Who plants flowers on this crummy street?" But Carlos finds a way to keep flowers on the street. The wonderful thing about the book is that part of this story is true.

The Make-it, Play-it Game Book
by Roz Abisch and Boche Kaplan

Here's a book that tells how to turn such things as drinking straws, shoelaces, cotton balls, and paper towel rolls into games. The twenty-three indoor and outdoor games are as much fun to make as to play!

Unit Four

Action words are exciting, lively words. Look at the action words in this poem.

The Acrobats

I'll swing
By my ankles,
She'll cling
To your knees
As you hang
By your nose
From a high-up
Trapeze.
But just one thing, please,
As we float through the breeze—
Don't sneeze.

Shel Silverstein

You may not be an acrobat, but your days are full of action too. That's what most of this unit is about—action and words that show action.

Expressing Action in Different Ways

You can show action with your body when you pantomime. You can also express action with words when you write or talk.

Thinking It Through

When you act out a situation without using words, you are **pantomiming.** The man in the picture is Marcel Marceau, the famous mime. Notice how he "speaks" with his body. He uses his body instead of words to express action.

● What do you think Marceau is doing in the picture?

Read the paragraph below and think what you would do to act out the scene.

The horse and rider *chase* the calf. The horse *gallops* steadily. The cowboy *grips* his saddle with one hand as he *twirls* his lasso faster and faster. He *aims* his lasso. It *whistles* through the air. He *ropes* the calf.

● Which words in the paragraph help you see the action?

There are different ways to express action. You can express action in pantomime by using your body. You can express action in writing or speech by using good action words, such as *chase, gallop,* and *twirl.*

Working It Through

A. Marcel Marceau is pretending to be a pilot. What action words could be used to describe what happens during his flight?

The pilot is *(1)* through the air. Suddenly, the engine *(2)*. He *(3)* the control wheel as the plane *(4)* through the air. He *(5)* for a place to land. Finally, he *(6)* an empty field and *(7)* the plane down.

B. Pantomime the pilot.

C. Choose a partner and pantomime the scene below.

A girl is pretending to land on the moon. She is weightless. She is having trouble walking. A "moon person" is trying to help her.

Trying It Out

1. Write a brief description of an activity you enjoy. You could pretend you are playing catch, roller skating, or riding a bicycle. Use good action words in your description.
2. Pantomime the activity you wrote about. Have your classmates guess what you are pantomiming.

Showing Action Words in Poetry

You can use your voice to express action words in poetry.

Thinking It Through

Some poems have good action words. Read this poem about making things with clay. Notice the action words.

Clay

all   Oh, so many things to make.
         A dog and a basket, a cat and a snake:
           I'm rolling,
           I'm pushing,
           I'm squeezing,
           I'm squishing,
eight solos   I'm poking,
           I'm pinching,
           I'm twisting,
           I'm wishing
all   a piece of clay into a ring,
               a face,
two solos   a flower—
all   everything!

Myra Cohn Livingston

- What does the person in the poem want to make from clay?
- What action words does the person in the poem use?
- What action words tell how you work with clay?

You can read this poem aloud by yourself or in a group. The poem will be more exciting if you use your voice to express the action of the words.

Working It Through

A. Use the following guidelines to help you say the poem aloud.

1. Read the poem to yourself several times until you know it well.
2. Practice saying the poem aloud.
3. Pay special attention to the action words: *rolling, pushing, squeezing, squishing, poking, pinching,* and *twisting.* Can you say each of them in a way that suggests its meaning?

B. Use these guidelines if you wish to say the poem in a group.

1. Decide with your group, or class, which lines should be said by everyone and which lines should be said by one person, or as solos. Look at page 96 for one way to do this.
2. Practice all the parts aloud. Speak clearly. Say your line or lines promptly when it is time for you to speak.
3. When your group knows the poem, practice saying it to someone else. Ask for suggestions to improve your speaking.

Trying It Out

A. Now that you have learned to say the poem aloud, you may wish to present it to other classrooms.

B. You may want to learn to say aloud the poems that begin Units 1, 2, and 3 of this book. Use the guidelines in this lesson to help you learn the poems. You may want to use pantomime when you say the poems aloud.

Lesson 3 **Using Action Words in Sentences**

You can help people see and hear what you're writing about by using interesting action words.

Thinking It Through

The photographs on this page show people taking part in actual sports events. Look at the photographs closely. Read the two sentences below each picture.

1. Lou Brock <u>reaches</u> second for another stolen base.
2. Lou Brock <u>slides</u> into second for another stolen base.

1. Nadia Comaneci, champion gymnast, <u>goes</u> through the air.
2. Nadia Comaneci, champion gymnast, <u>flies</u> through the air.

Both sentences under each photograph explain what the athlete is doing. But one of the sentences in each case is more interesting and exact.

- Why is *slides* a better action word than *reaches* to describe Lou Brock's actions?
- Why is *flies* a better action word than *goes* to describe the action of Nadia Comaneci?

If you use exact action words, people will be able to see and feel the action you are writing about.

Working It Through

A. Choose a good action word from the list at the right to replace the underlined word in each sentence.

1. Thunder <u>came</u> in the west.
2. Lightning <u>appeared</u> in the sky.
3. Rain <u>fell</u> on the roof.
4. Wind <u>blew</u> through the trees.
5. When the storm was over, Enrico <u>walked</u> through the deep mud puddles.

flashed
whipped
roared
trudged
pounded

B. Think of a better action word for the 5 underlined words.

   Deborah's grocery bag <u>broke</u>. The pickle jar <u>fell</u> to the ground. The waxy milk carton <u>came</u> out of her hand. Then the apples <u>dropped</u> on the sidewalk. Groceries <u>went</u> in all directions.

C. Write a sentence for each idea below. Use a colorful action word instead of the underlined word.

1. <u>hit</u> the ball
2. <u>fell</u> out of bed
3. <u>shut</u> the door
4. <u>said</u> to the umpire
5. <u>went</u> up the hill

6. <u>flew</u> in the sky
7. <u>ran</u> into the curb
8. <u>broke</u> the mirror

Trying It Out

Look at the picture of a forest fire. Write at least 5 sentences about the fire. Make sure you use good action words to describe what is happening. You can use the sentence under the picture as an example.

The flames leaped as high as the trees.

Using Topic Sentences in Paragraphs

You can write your sentences in a paragraph. Sometimes the paragraph has a topic sentence that states the main idea of the paragraph.

Thinking It Through

One sentence in a paragraph can tell the main idea of the paragraph. Find a sentence like that in this paragraph from *The Trumpet of the Swan* by E. B. White.

> The day Sam Beaver visited the Philadelphia Zoo was the turning point in his life. Up until that day, he had not been able to decide what he wanted to be when he grew up. The minute he saw the zoo, all his doubts vanished. He knew he wanted to work in a zoo. Sam loved every living thing, and a zoo is a great storehouse of living things—it has just about every creature that creeps or crawls or jumps or runs or flies or hides.

- Which sentence tells the main idea?
- Are all of the other sentences about that idea?

When a sentence tells the main idea of a paragraph, it is called the **topic sentence.** A topic sentence is very often the first sentence in a paragraph, but it can come in different places. All the other sentences in the paragraph tell about the topic sentence.

Working It Through

A. Find the topic sentence in each paragraph. Are all the other sentences about that idea?

1

It was a very wet day. The rain began in the early morning. Puddles soon became small ponds. Street gutters gurgled with water. When the rain stopped, everything dripped for hours.

2

I can't hit a baseball very hard or knock a tennis ball into the court. My sister can beat me at running. My dad wins most of our checker games. I hardly ever win at anything.

B. Write a topic sentence for each of these paragraphs.

1

_____. Each morning we practice archery and go horseback riding. In the afternoon we swim. Then a camp counselor teaches us songs and games.

2

The minute I stepped into the boat I felt sick. The seat was full of splinters and too small to sit on. The oars were hard to use. _____.

Trying It Out

1. Think of a topic you would like to write about.
2. Write a topic sentence about your topic, or choose one of the sentences below.
   My pet is smarter than many other pets.
   A funny thing happened to me.
   Friends are important.
3. Write a paragraph at least 4 sentences long about your topic.

Take Another Look Did you indent the first line of your paragraph? Did your topic sentence state the main idea of your paragraph? Were all the other sentences in the paragraph about that idea?

101

Keeping to the Subject

When you write a paragraph, all of the sentences in the paragraph should be about the main idea.

Thinking It Through

Read the paragraph. Answer the questions below the paragraph.

When cars were invented, most people thought that cars were better than horses. I always wanted to ride a horse. Cars seemed cleaner than horses. Cars were easier to take care of. My grandmother took care of the horses on her farm when she was young. Cars didn't have to be kept in stables. They didn't have to be fed and watered every day.

- What is the main idea or subject of the paragraph?
- Which sentences tell about the main idea?
- Which sentences do not?

A paragraph is about one main idea. If a sentence does not keep to the main idea, the sentence does not belong in the paragraph.

Working It Through

A. Which two sentences do not belong in a paragraph about music?

1. I enjoy soft music.
2. Al likes magic.

3. I like to sing to music.
4. It's fun to paint.

B. Find the main idea in each paragraph. Find any sentences that do not keep to the subject.

1

Airplanes can cause problems. My baby brother can cause problems too. Airplanes cause dirty air. Cars make air dirty. Another problem with airplanes is the noise they make. Supersonic airplanes cause a loud booming noise. Their booms even cause damage to big buildings.

2

Each year, more highways are built for cars. The United States today has about four million miles of roads. I like to travel by boat. The sand, gravel, and stone that has been used in roads is enough to build a wall fifty feet high around the whole world. I want to go around the world when I grow up.

C. Write 2 sentences that tell about each main idea. Be sure to keep to the subject.

1. People will live on space stations in the future.
2. I do several chores to earn my allowance.
3. It is important to listen to others.
4. Takeo decorated his gym shoes last night.
5. My friends and I just finished building our clubhouse.

Trying It Out

1. Think of a subject to write about, or choose one of the subjects below.

| My Favorite Breakfast | Fingerprints | Puppets |
| Ghost Towns | Marching Bands | Hiking |

2. Write a topic sentence about your subject.
3. Add at least 4 sentences about the subject.
4. Be sure every sentence keeps to the subject.

Improving Your Writing

Keeping to the main idea in a paragraph will improve your writing.

Thinking It Through

The proofreader's marks on the left will help you when you make changes in your writing.

Read Jeff's paragraph about baskets to see if he keeps to the main idea. Then answer the questions.

Proofreader's Marks

☰ Make a capital letter.

⊙ Add a period.

℮ Take out.

∧ Put in one or more words.

> *Baskets*
>
> Baskets have many different uses. grocers use baskets ^to hold berries and fruits. (Strawberries are red.) Many people use baskets to carry laundry, kitens, toys, and food ^for picnics (and) some baskets have a hoop and a net. They are used for basketball. (I like soccer better than basketball.)

- What is the main idea of Jeff's paragraph?
- Why did he want to take out two sentences?
- What other changes did Jeff want to make?
- Why do you think he wanted to make the changes?
- What marks did he use to show each change?

Remember that keeping to the main idea in a paragraph improves your writing.

Working It Through

A. Rewrite Jeff's paragraph on page 104. Make the changes that are marked.

B. Use the paragraph at the right to write answers for these questions.

1. What is the main idea of the paragraph?
2. Which sentences should be taken out? Why?
3. What mark would you use to show that a sentence should be taken out?
4. Where would you use the mark $\equiv$? the mark ⊙?
5. What word is missing in the last sentence?
6. What mark do you use to put in the missing word?

> Sally Murray has a newspaper route. She puts the newspapers on her bicycle Her bicycle is red. sally rides to each house on her route. She also rides her bicycle to school. She makes sure everyone gets newspaper every day

C. Rewrite the paragraph about Sally. Use the answers from Exercise B to help you.

Trying It Out

A. Read over the paragraph you wrote for Lesson 5, or write a new paragraph. Ask yourself questions like these to decide where to make changes in your paragraph.

1. Did I keep to the main idea in each sentence of the paragraph?
2. Did I use the right ending mark for each sentence?
3. Did I capitalize the first letter of each proper noun?

B. Use the proofreader's marks from page 104 to show the changes you need to make.

C. Rewrite the paragraph and make the changes you marked.

Review • Using Action Words

A. Read the sentences and notice the underlined words. Then answer the questions below the sentences.

Kim loves to play the banjo, and she <u>goes</u> to her
lesson every Saturday.
Kim loves to play the banjo, and she <u>races</u> to her
lesson every Saturday.

Often Mr. Bach <u>walks</u> through the park after dinner.
Often Mr. Bach <u>strolls</u> through the park after dinner.

1. Why is <u>races</u> a better action word than <u>goes</u> in the first pair of sentences?
2. Why is <u>strolls</u> a better action word than <u>walk</u> in the second pair of sentences?

B. Replace the underlined word in each sentence with a more interesting action word. Write the sentences.
1. The pirates <u>found</u> an old treasure chest.
2. They opened the chest and <u>looked</u> at the silver inside.
3. One pirate <u>put</u> some silver coins in his pocket.
4. The pirates <u>talked</u> about what to do with the treasure.
5. They <u>hid</u> the treasure chest in a hole in the ground.
6. Then the pirates <u>went</u> toward their boat.
7. They <u>kept</u> the treasure on the island.

C. Answer the questions.
1. In which sentence do you think you wrote the best action word? Why?
2. Which sentence was the hardest for you to do? Why?
3. Did you start each sentence with a capital letter?
4. Did you write complete sentences?
5. Does each sentence have end punctuation?

Evaluation • Using Action Words

A. Improve the following sentences. Choose one of the action words at the right to replace the underlined word in each sentence. Write the sentences.

1. At the library, we <u>read</u> many things about firefighting.
2. At airports, firefighters <u>use</u> chemicals on a burning plane instead of water.
3. Sometimes firefighters <u>go</u> to a fire by boat.
4. Firefighters <u>get</u> people trapped by fire.
5. Once I saw water <u>come</u> out of a hydrant.

rush
rescue
discovered
gush
spray

B. Write 5 sentences about the picture. Make sure you use good action words to describe what is happening.

You will be evaluated on your use of good action words and on the following:

capital letters at the beginning of your sentences
complete sentences
end punctuation

Spotlight • The Days of the Week

The Norse people have lived in the land we call Norway for a long time. Long ago, they named the days of the week for gods, goddesses, and things they saw in the sky. What two days are named after the sun and the moon?

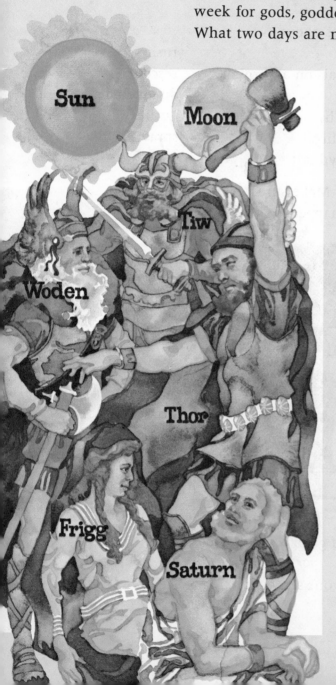

Tuesday is Tiw's day. Tiw was a Norse god. He lost one of his hands when he saved the gods from a ferocious wolf.

Wednesday is Woden's day. Woden was the chief god of the Norse. He watched over the world and decided who would win battles.

Thursday is Thor's day. Thor was a son of Woden. He was huge and very strong. Thor had a powerful, magical hammer. He made thunder when he drove his chariot across the sky.

Friday is Frigg's day. Frigg was the Norse goddess of motherly love. She loved the people of the earth and knew everything that happened to them. If she was happy with what she saw, the sunset would be full of beautiful colors. If she was sad, the sunset would be gray.

Saturday is Saturn's day. It is the only day named for an ancient god of the Romans. Saturn was the Roman god of agriculture, or farming.

Spotlight • Names of Hobbyists

Do you have a hobby? Some people who have hobbies have special names.

Ben West's hobby is coin collecting. He has coins from ten different countries. He knows the history of each coin. Ben is a *numismatist*.

Ms. Anderson collects postage stamps. She has old and new stamps from several countries. Ms. Anderson is a *philatelist*.

Mr. Ralph Sands has an aquarium. He has several colorful and unusual fish in his tank. He knows how to feed and take care of each one. Mr. Sands is an *aquarist*.

María Cruz likes to collect post cards. She has post cards with pictures of cars, mountains, and buildings. She has post cards from all over the world. María is a *deltiologist*.

Many children and adults love movies. They watch many movies and like to read about the history of the cinema. A person who loves movies is a *cineast*.

109

Lesson 7　Action Verbs

Verbs are words that can show action in a sentence.

Thinking It Through

A verb can show what action is taking place in a sentence. A verb can show if the action is happening in the present or if it happened in the past.

Look at the pictures and sentences to see what Diego is doing now and what Diego did yesterday.

Diego <u>sews</u> a red patch now.　　Diego <u>sewed</u> a yellow patch yesterday.

- What is the verb in each sentence?
- Why are they verbs?
- Which sentence tells what Diego is doing now?
- Which sentence tells what Diego did yesterday?
- How did the verb change form to show action that happened in the past?

Words like *sews* and *sewed* that show action are **action verbs.** They can show if action is happening in the present or in the past.

Working It Through

A. Tell which verb belongs in each sentence.

1. Diego (washes, washed) his jacket now.
2. He (washes, washed) it yesterday also.
3. Diego (likes, liked) his jacket now.
4. He (likes, liked) it yesterday too.

B. Choose an action verb from the Verb Box for each sentence. Write the sentence.

1. Maria ____ a bag of oranges home.
2. She ____ the skin off one orange.
3. She ____ into the orange.
4. Juice ____ out of the orange.

Verb Box
peels
bites
squirts
carries

C. Choose an action verb from the Verb Box for each sentence. Write the sentence.

1. A dog ____ at John's kitten.
2. The kitten ____ up a tree.
3. The kitten ____ in the tree all day.
4. Then John ____ his kitten down.

Verb Box
called
stayed
scrambled
growled

D. Think of an action verb for each sentence. Show past action in sentences **1-3**. Show action that is happening now in sentences **4-6**.

1. Kim ____ her room yesterday.
2. She ____ the windows.
3. She ____ the floor.

4. Today Kim ____ her closet.
5. She ____ her shoes neatly on the floor.
6. She ____ her clean closet to her mother.

Trying It Out

Write 2 sentences for each picture below. Use these action verbs to help you: cries, cried; laughs, laughed; washes, washed.

Lesson 8 Linking Verbs

A linking verb links, or joins, the subject to a word or words in the predicate.

Thinking It Through

Some verbs do not show action. Verbs like *am, is, are, was,* and *were* are linking verbs. A **linking verb** links, or joins, the subject to a word or words in the predicate. Read the paragraph below.

I <u>am</u> a potter. My sister Kara <u>is</u> a potter too. Her clay bowls <u>are</u> interesting. Last year, her best bowl <u>was</u> brown and orange. Her mugs <u>were</u> black.

● Which words are linking verbs?

Look at the chart of linking verbs on the left.

● What verb forms do you use to tell about the present?
● What verb forms do you use to tell about the past?
● Use some of the verb forms in the chart in sentences. Use the names of people, places, or things for your subjects. For example: Bob is tall.

Present	Past
I am	I was
You are	You were
He is	He was
She is	She was
It is	It was
We are	We were
You are	You were
They are	They were

An action verb shows what action is taking place in a sentence. A linking verb does not show action. A linking verb links, or joins, the subject to a word or words in the predicate.

Working It Through

A. Copy the sentences. Underline the linking verbs.

1. My family is happy.
2. We are in an old country store.
3. The smells are delicious.
4. The taffy apples were huge.
5. The apple cider was spicy.
6. A peanut butter machine was interesting to see.
7. I am eager to go back next week.

B. Choose the linking verb that goes with each subject.

1. I (am, are) a crocodile.
2. My mother (were, is) a crocodile too.
3. We (are, was) starved.
4. We (was, were) famished yesterday too.
5. Our friend, Sluggish Turtle, (are, was) full.
6. Sluggish (is, are) good at finding food.

C. Choose a linking verb for the blank in each sentence. Use the chart on page 112 to help you. Copy the sentences.

1. I ____ in a play today.
2. You ____ in the play too.
3. It ____ a play about some wild horses.
4. They ____ in the desert.
5. We ____ the ranchers.
6. I ____ happy with our play last year too.

Trying It Out

Pretend you found a puppy. Tell about the puppy. Write a sentence using a linking verb to answer each question.

1. Where was the puppy when you found it?
2. What were the puppy's eyes like when you found it?
3. What is the puppy's name?
4. What are the puppy's eyes like now?
5. Are you happy you found the puppy?

Lesson 9 **Tenses of Verbs**

A verb can tell when the action takes place in a sentence. A verb can be in the present, past, or future tense.

Thinking It Through
Look at each picture and read the sentence beneath it.

1. Jake <u>skates</u> at the pond now.

2. Jake <u>skated</u> at the pond last night.

3. Jake <u>will skate</u> at the pond soon.

- What verb in the first sentence tells what Jake does now, in the **present?**
- What verb in the second sentence tells what Jake did last night, in the **past?**
- What verb in the third sentence tells what Jake will do soon, in the **future?**

Verbs have different **tenses** to tell whether something happens in the present, past, or future. The verb *skate* is in the present tense. The verb *skated* is in the past tense. The verb *will skate* is in the future tense.

A. Complete the sentences. Use the verbs in the Verb Box
to help you. Choose the correct tense of each verb.

   1. Julie ____ her shoes now.
   2. Julie ____ her shoes yesterday.
   3. Julie ____ her shoes again tomorrow.

   4. The cat ____ that tree now.
   5. It ____ the tree all next week.
   6. The cat ____ the tree last week too.

Verb Box		
Present	**Past**	**Future**
ties	tied	will tie
climbs	climbed	will climb
cooks	cooked	will cook

   7. Suzanne and Hal ____ dinner last night for their
      aunt.
   8. Hal ____ lunch right now.
   9. Suzanne and Hal ____ another dinner tomorrow.

B. Write the verb in each sentence. Then write *present*,
past, or *future* to tell the tense of the verb.

   1. We will paint next week in art class.
   2. We will tape our pictures on the wall.
   3. George uses bright paint.
   4. He likes the colors.
   5. He used yellow in every picture last week.
   6. He signed his pictures in the corners.

Write three paragraphs.

   1. The first paragraph should tell
      about something that you did in
      the past.
   2. The second paragraph should
      tell about something you do
      now.
   3. The third paragraph should tell
      about something you will do in
      the future.

Using Verbs

The verbs *buy*, *catch*, *bring*, and *teach* do not end in *-ed* to show past tense.

Thinking It Through

Notice the underlined verbs in each paragraph.

Sandy and her father buy tickets for many shows. They catch the bus to get to the shows. Sandy brings her new camera and film. Her father teaches Sandy how to use the camera.

Last year, Sandy and her father bought tickets for the Old West Show. They brought their old camera and film. One cowboy caught a horse with a lasso. Another cowboy taught Sandy how to twirl a lasso.

- Which paragraph shows action that is happening now?
- Which verbs are in the present tense?
- Which paragraph shows action that happened in the past?
- Which verbs are in the past tense?

The verbs *buy, catch, brings,* and *teaches* show action that is happening now. They are in the present tense.

The verbs *bought, brought, caught,* and *taught* show action that happened in the past. These verbs do not end in *-ed* to show past tense.

Working It Through

A. Tell whether each sentence shows action that happened in the past or action that is happening now.

1. Joe bought a red scarf.
2. Allen buys a red scarf.
3. A receiver catches the football.
4. A running back caught the football.

B. Complete each sentence with verbs from the Verb Box. Write sentences **1-4** to show action that is happening in the present. Write sentences **5-8** to show action that happened in the past.

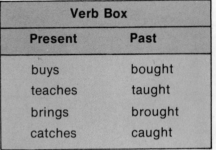

Verb Box	
Present	**Past**
buys	bought
teaches	taught
brings	brought
catches	caught

1. Janis _____ fifty cents to the store.
2. She _____ a ball and jacks there.
3. Lois _____ Janis how to play jacks.
4. Janis _____ the ball with one hand.

5. Lois _____ her dog along.
6. The dog _____ the ball and ran away.
7. Lois _____ Janis a new ball.
8. The children _____ the dog not to take the ball.

C. Complete each sentence with the correct form of the verb in parentheses.

1. Ms. Solomon _____ my class now.   (teach)
2. When she walks into the room, she _____ interesting things.   (bring)
3. Ms. Solomon _____ arithmetic yesterday.   (teach)
4. She _____ a cardboard grocery store then.   (bring)
5. We used play money and _____ groceries.   (buy)
6. We _____ the bus home after the bell rang.   (catch)

Trying It Out
A. Write a paragraph about buying a kite, catching fish, or teaching someone to play marbles. Use the past tense of the verbs.

B. Write a second paragraph, telling someone how to buy a kite, catch fish, or teach the game of marbles. Use the present tense of the verbs.

Take Another Look   Did you use the past or present form of each verb correctly? Did you indent each paragraph?

Using Other Verbs

The verbs *hear, tell, tear, sell,* and *wear* do not end in *-ed* to show past tense.

Thinking It Through

Notice the underlined verbs as you read the paragraphs.

> I <u>hear</u> John telling about the Farmers' Market. As he <u>tells</u> us about it, he <u>tears</u> the husks from some corn. People <u>sell</u> fresh vegetables there. Often John <u>wears</u> a backpack so he can carry the vegetables he buys.

> I <u>heard</u> John telling about the Farmers' Market yesterday. As he <u>told</u> us about it, he <u>tore</u> an advertisement for the market from a newspaper. He said people <u>sold</u> crafts and leather goods there too. Yesterday, John <u>wore</u> a belt he got at the market.

- Which paragraph shows action that is happening now?
- Which verbs are in the present tense?
- Which paragraph shows action that happened in the past?
- Which verbs are in the past tense?

The verbs *hear, tells, tears, sell,* and *wears* show action that is happening now. They are in the present tense.

The verbs *heard, told, tore, sold,* and *wore* show action that happened in the past. These verbs do not end in *-ed* to show past tense.

Working It Through

A. Tell whether each sentence shows past or present action.

1. Sally wears blue boots today.
2. Kristin wore red boots last winter.

3. Today Ms. Brown tells us about how to take care of boots.

4. Yesterday, she told us about old-fashioned boots.

B. Choose the verb in each sentence that shows present action. Use the Verb Box to help you.

Verb Box	
Present	**Past**
hear	heard
sells	sold
wears	wore
tell	told
tears	tore

   1. Mrs. Larson (sells, sold) materials to repair things in her store.

   2. She always (wears, wore) a blue jacket and a name tag.

   3. I bring my broken clock to Mrs. Larson and she (tells, told) me how to fix it.

   4. When I get home, I (tear, tore) the clock apart to fix it.

   5. Each morning, when I (hear, heard) my alarm, I remember fixing the clock.

C. Choose the verb in each sentence that shows past action. Use the Verb Box to help you.

   1. Sue (tell, told) me about the carnival yesterday.

   2. I (hear, heard) about the games and music at the carnival.

   3. At the door, a teacher (tears, tore) the tickets in half.

   4. The fourth grade (sells, sold) taffy apples at its booth.

   5. Sue got taffy on the new pants she (wear, wore).

   6. Tom (tells, told) ghost stories.

   7. Alicia (sells, sold) candy.

Trying It Out

   1. Pretend you are on a deserted island. Write a paragraph about it and use the present tense of these verbs: *hear*, *wear*, and *tear*.

   2. Pretend you were rescued and wrote a book about your experiences. Write a paragraph about it and use the past tense of these verbs: *hear*, *sell*, and *tell*.

Lesson 12 Subject-Verb Agreement

The subject and the verb in a sentence must agree.

Thinking It Through

The subject and the verb in a sentence must agree. Look at the sentences below.

Singular	Plural
A spider spins.	Spiders spin.
A caterpillar crawls.	Caterpillars crawl.
A moth eats.	Moths eat.
A frog hops.	Frogs hop.

- Which subjects are singular?
- With what letter do the verbs end that go with a singular subject?
- Which subjects are plural?
- Do the verbs that go with the plural subjects end with -s?

When the noun in the subject is singular, the verb has an -s ending. When the noun in the subject is plural, the verb does not have an -s ending.

Working It Through

A. Choose the verb that agrees with the noun in the subject in each sentence. Use the Verb Box to help you. Write the sentences.

1. The picnic basket ____ at the top.
2. Thermos bottles ____ juices.
3. Sandwiches ____ on paper plates.
4. Watermelon slices ____ on people.
5. The ant ____ the picnic.

Verb Box	
opens	open
holds	hold
sits	sit
drips	drip
likes	like

120

Evaluation • Verbs

A. Write the letter of the response that tells what tense the underlined verb in each sentence is.

1. Angela <u>puts</u> on her skis.
   a. present tense
   b. future tense
2. The birds <u>were</u> hungry.
   a. present tense
   b. past tense
3. Benita <u>will cook</u> dinner.
   a. past tense
   b. future tense
4. The kittens <u>climbed</u> in the box.
   a. present tense
   b. past tense

5. Sam <u>combed</u> his hair.
   a. past tense
   b. future tense
6. The cereal <u>was</u> crunchy.
   a. present tense
   b. past tense
7. The jackets <u>are</u> warm.
   a. present tense
   b. past tense
8. Sally <u>is</u> a happy baby.
   a. present tense
   b. past tense

B. Write the letter of the past tense verb that completes each sentence correctly.

1. I _____ a kite last week.
   a. buy   **b.** bought
2. She _____ me here yesterday.
   a. brought   **b.** brings
3. Mr. Sims _____ gym last year.
   a. teaches   **b.** taught

4. Ed _____ me a joke yesterday.
   a. told   **b.** tells
5. I _____ my bike last Saturday.
   a. sold   **b.** sell
6. She _____ her hat last winter.
   a. wears   **b.** wore

C. Write the letter of the response that completes each sentence correctly.

1. Both Sue and Sam
   a. hear
   b. hears
   the song.

2. The dog
   a. catch
   b. catches
   the stick.

3. Many children
   a. wear
   b. wears
   jackets.

4. Fred
   a. teach
   b. teaches
   us a game.

Spotlight • Activities to Choose

1. Pick a Pantomime. Act out a pantomime for the class. You could pantomime practicing for a basketball game, making a pizza, or hiking through a thick forest. Make sure you pantomime the action words clearly so your classmates can guess what you are doing.

2. Try saying different poems. Try to find poems with happy rhythms, like songs. Think of different ways to say them, and decide which is best. A tape recorder can help you. In working with "The Acrobats" on page 93, you and some classmates might try saying two lines each, and then saying the final line together. See how it sounds!

3. Play a verb game. Write the present and past tenses of the verbs you learned in Lessons 10 and 11 on one side of some cards. Divide into teams. A person on Team A holds a card up to Team B. A person on Team B must give a sentence using a different tense from the one on the card.

4. Find a verb. Write sentences such as the ones below on a large sheet of construction paper.

  1. Jacob ____ my best friend.
  2. We ____ at the zoo now.
  3. I ____ happy to see the animals today.
  4. We ____ here last week too.
  5. The elephant ____ grumpy last week.

Put the paper on the bulletin board. Then write on three different sets of cards these linking verbs: *am, is, are, was, were.* Put all the cards in a container, like a fishbowl. Invite a classmate to draw a card from the container. He or she must match the linking verb on the card to one of the sentences and then tack the card in the blank. The same linking verb can be on more than one card and may fit more than one sentence. Score a point for each correct match.

Spotlight • Books to Read

An Eskimo Birthday
by Tom D. Robinson

What do you do on your birthday? At Eeka's birthday party, the children eat caribou soup and cake. In this book, you can discover what modern life is like for Eeka in Point Hope, Alaska. You can also share her grandfather's stories about Alaska before it was a state.

The Marcel Marceau Counting Book
by George Mendoza

Can you pantomime a miner, pirate, artist, or astronaut? The famous mime, Marcel Marceau, uses only hats and movements to show many occupations. You'll see how he does it in colorful photographs. Count the hats as you look at the pictures.

The Days of the Week
by William R. Keyser

The myths, or old stories, in this book tell the adventures of the ancient gods and goddesses for whom our days are named. You can find out why the great father of these gods and goddesses, Odin, sent two ravens to fly over the world each morning before breakfast.

125

Unit Five

Did you ever look closely at a little insect? Did you ever hear anything like this bee song?

A Dragon-Fly

When the heat of the summer
Made drowsy the land,
A dragon-fly came
And sat on my hand,
With its blue jointed body,
And wings like spun glass,
It lit on my fingers
As though they were grass.

Eleanor Farjeon

Bee Song

Bees in the late summer sun
Drone their song
Of yellow moons
Trimming black velvet,
Droning, droning a sleepysong.

Carl Sandburg

In this unit, you'll be learning about ways to describe the many kinds of things that you see, hear, or feel.

Using Synonyms from a Thesaurus

Synonyms are words that have the same or nearly the same meaning. A thesaurus can help you find synonyms so you can use the exact words you need.

Thinking It Through

How many different ways can you walk?

entry word ——	**walk**	*Walk* means move along on foot.
illustrative sentence ——	march	*March* means walk steadily, with a regular step.
		Bands *march* by walking to the beat of drums.
	tiptoe	*Tiptoe* means to walk on your toes.
	stalk	*Stalk* means walk stiffly and perhaps angrily. It can also mean walk cautiously when hunting— in order to follow or catch something. Cats *stalk* mice.
synonyms	stroll	*Stroll* means walk easily and probably slowly, for fun. People *stroll* on a warm evening.
	hike	If you *hike*, you take a long walk for fun or for exercise.
	trudge	*Trudge* means walk when walking is very hard. People *trudge* through sand on the beach.
	shuffle	*Shuffle* means walk without raising the feet. A very tired person sometimes *shuffles* down the street.

All the words listed under *walk* mean about the same as *walk*. A word that has the same or about the same meaning as another word is a **synonym.**

A thesaurus lists synonyms. From the list of synonyms, you can find the exact word you need. This will help you avoid repeating the same words and it will make your writing more interesting.

Working It Through

A. Use the synonyms for *walk* shown on page 128 to answer these questions.

1. How would a group of soldiers move in a parade?
2. How might someone leave a room after an argument?
3. How would someone walk through deep mud?
4. How would you walk if you were afraid your shoes were going to fall off?

B. Replace *walked* in each sentence with the best synonym from page 128 so the sentences are more interesting.

1. Ramona *walked* quietly into her baby sister's room.
2. The campers *walked* five miles a day.
3. Dave and Rob *walked* five miles a day.
4. The mayor *walked* at the front of the parade.
5. We *walked* through the deep snow after the storm.
6. John looked tired and weak as he *walked* down the hall.
7. After the debate, Karen *walked* out of the room.

Trying It Out

Write a paragraph about the picture. Use the synonyms below to describe what each person in the picture is doing.

laugh
smile
giggle
guffaw
howl

Using Antonyms from a Thesaurus

An antonym is a word that means the opposite of another word. A thesaurus can help you find antonyms, so that you can use the exact word you need.

Thinking It Through

An **antonym** is a word that means the opposite of another word. A word may have more than one antonym. You can often find antonyms listed at the end of a thesaurus entry.

Read the entry for *hot* from this part of a thesaurus.

hot	*Hot* describes something that feels warmer than things around it.
burning	*Burning* describes something hot enough to be painful—the *burning* sand on the desert.
warm	*Warm* means just hot enough to be comfortable or to give comfort. A *warm* coat feels good.
	ANTONYMS: cool, cold, icy, mild

- What are the synonyms listed for *hot?*
- Can you think of an antonym—a word that means the opposite—of *hot?*
- What are the antonyms listed for *hot?*
- Which antonym means "not quite cold"? "the opposite of hot"? "covered with ice"? "neither hot nor cold"?

An antonym is a word that means the opposite of another word. A thesaurus often lists antonyms. From the list of antonyms, you can find the exact word you need.

Working It Through

A. Write an antonym for each word.
 1. dangerous   **3.** happy   **5.** fast
 2. clean   **4.** quiet   **6.** little

B. Write the pair of antonyms in each sentence.
 1. At the furniture store, we saw some tables made of light wood and some made of dark wood.
 2. Some felt rough, and others felt smooth.
 3. We saw old and new styles of furniture.
 4. Some of the rugs were thin and some were thick.
 5. One man was pleasant, and another was grouchy.

C. Think of an antonym for the underlined word in each pair of sentences. Add the antonym to the second sentence in each pair. Write the sentences.
 1. The pancakes were <u>hot</u>. The milk was ____.
 2. The <u>warm</u> breeze felt pleasant. The ____ water felt nice.
 3. The <u>icy</u> cider tasted good. The ____ chili tasted even better.
 4. It was <u>mild</u> today at the beach. Yesterday we had ____ weather.

Trying It Out

Rewrite the paragraph. Replace each underlined word with an antonym. Use the illustration to help you. You may also use a thesaurus or dictionary if you need help.

   Every morning, even in <u>hot</u> or <u>dry</u> weather, Mr. Phillips walks to work. He always wears a <u>large</u> hat and a <u>light</u> jacket. He carries his <u>empty</u> briefcase and his <u>old</u> umbrella. He has a <u>fast</u> walk and a <u>loud</u> voice. He gives everyone he passes a <u>sad</u> greeting.

Using Comparisons in Sentences

You can use the words *like* and *as* to help you describe more exactly what you mean.

Thinking It Through

Have you ever felt as restless as leaves rustling in the wind or as lonely as a tree without leaves? One way to tell how you feel is to compare your feelings to something else. The words *like* and *as* can help you.

Read this poem and notice how the author uses *like* to describe her feelings.

Lemons and Apples

One day I might feel
Mean,
And squinched up inside,
Like a mouth sucking on a
Lemon.

The next day I could
Feel
Whole and happy
And right,
Like an unbitten apple.

Mary Neville

- How does the author feel in the first part of the poem? in the second part?
- What are the author's feelings compared to?

Notice how *as* is used to compare feelings with other things in these two sentences.

I feel as sour as a lemon.
I feel as fresh as a ripe apple.

One way to tell how you feel is to compare your feelings to something else. The words *like* and *as* can help you.

Working It Through

A. Complete each comparison by using a word at the right.

1. The kite fluttered to the ground like a ____.   rainbow
2. The dancer whirled around like a ____.   leaf
3. The store window was as colorful as a ____.   ice
4. Her hands were as cold as ____.   spinning top

B. Copy each sentence. Underline the two things compared in each sentence. Was *like* or *as* used to compare the two things?

1. The snow sparkled like diamonds.
2. Donna's eyes were as bright as glowing coals.
3. She scurried like a mouse to the park.
4. Donna knew her sled was as fast as the wind.

C. Think of a word or words to complete each comparison. Then write each comparison in a sentence.

1. as hot as ____   4. as happy as ____
2. as gloomy as ____   5. as free as ____
3. as quiet as ____   6. as lazy as ____

Trying It Out

A. Pretend you are at the sledding party in the picture.

1. How does going down an icy hill make you feel?
2. How does it feel to be near the fire?
3. How does it feel to be out by the trees?

B. Write a paragraph about the sledding party. Include comparisons using *like* or *as*.

Lesson 4 Writing a Paragraph About Likenesses

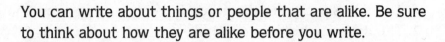

You can write about things or people that are alike. Be sure to think about how they are alike before you write.

Thinking It Through

Rosa and her best friend, Marta, have new jackets. Rosa wanted to write about how the jackets are alike. Look at the pictures.

The first thing Rosa did was make a list. She wrote down all the things about the jackets that were alike. Here is the list she made.

> blue outside
> fuzzy orange lining inside
> zipper in front
> two pockets

Next Rosa wrote a topic sentence. Her topic sentence was *My best friend Marta and I have jackets that are alike.*

Then Rosa turned her notes into sentences. She added these sentences to the topic sentence when she wrote her paragraph.

● Read Rosa's paragraph about the jackets.

> My best friend, Marta, and I have jackets that are alike. Both of our jackets are blue outside. Marta's jacket has a fuzzy orange lining and mine does too. There is a zipper in the front of each of our jackets. There are two big pockets on my jacket. Marta's jacket has two big pockets also.

When you write about two things or people that are alike, be sure to think about the ways they are alike before you write.

Working It Through

A. Read the list below that shows some of the ways the sheriffs look alike. Think of 5 more ways they look alike. Write the complete list.

> long, curly mustaches
> gold teeth
> red plaid shirts
> black gloves with fringe

B. Decide which of the following sentences would be the best topic sentence for a paragraph about the sheriffs.

1. Sheriff Tumbleweed and Sheriff Fumbleweed have gold teeth.
2. Both of the sheriffs have scars on their faces.
3. The sheriffs have the same badge.
4. Sheriff Tumbleweed and Sheriff Fumbleweed look alike.
5. Sheriff Tumbleweed and Sheriff Fumbleweed both have black vests.

C. Write a paragraph about how the sheriffs look alike. Be sure to begin with the topic sentence that you chose in Exercise B. Make sentences from the completed list in Exercise A before you write the paragraph.

Trying It Out

Write a paragraph about how two things or people are alike. You could use one of the topic sentences below.

> My sister and I are alike in many ways.
> My old house and new house are alike.

Take Another Look

Did you list how the things or people are alike before writing the paragraph? Does your topic sentence tell what the paragraph is about? Did you indent the first line of the paragraph?

Writing a Paragraph About Differences

You can write about things or people that are different. Be sure to think about how they are different before you write.

Thinking It Through

Burt and Tim have different kinds of rooms. Burt wanted to write about how the rooms are different. First he made a list of all the things about the rooms that are different.

My room	Tim's room
yellow walls	green walls
striped curtains	white shutters
table	desk
brown rug	wood floor

Then Burt wrote a topic sentence. His topic sentence was *Tim and I have different kinds of rooms.*

Next Burt turned his notes about the rooms into sentences. He added his sentences to the topic sentence to make a paragraph.

● Read Burt's paragraph about the rooms.

> Tim and I have different kinds of rooms. Tim's room has green walls. My room has yellow walls. Tim put white shutters on his tall windows. My windows have striped curtains. Tim has a desk in his room. I have a table. Tim's room has a wood floor. Mine has a brown rug.

When you write about two things or people that are different, make sure you think about the ways they are different before you write.

Working It Through

A. Alicia and Martha have different kinds of boots. Read the lists that show how the boots are different. Think of 3 more ways they are different.

Alicia's boots	Martha's boots
red	brown
slide on and off easily	hard to get on and off
plastic	leather

B. Decide which of these sentences would be the best topic sentence for a paragraph about Alicia's and Martha's boots.

1. Alicia has red boots, and Martha has brown boots.
2. Alicia's boots have laces, but Martha's don't.
3. Alicia and Martha have different kinds of boots.
4. Alicia has plastic boots, and Martha has leather boots.
5. Alicia's boots have a soft lining, but Martha's boots have no lining.

C. Write a paragraph about how Alicia's and Martha's boots are different. Begin your paragraph with the topic sentence you chose in Exercise B. Before you write the paragraph, make sentences from the completed lists in Exercise A.

Trying It Out

Write a paragraph about how two things or people are different. You could use one of these topic sentences:

My friend and I are different in many ways.
A farm and a city are different kinds of places.

Take Another Look Did you list how the things or people are different before writing the paragraph? Does your topic sentence tell what the paragraph is about? Did you indent the first line of the paragraph?

Improving Your Writing

When you write about things that are alike or things that are different, be sure you think about what you want to say before you write.

Thinking It Through

Use the proofreader's marks to help you make changes in your writing.

Sara and Al like to make the same kind of sandwich. But they like to have different kinds of drinks. Read the lists that show the likenesses and differences.

Proofreader's
Marks

= Make a capital letter.

⊙ Add a period.

ℓ Take out.

∧ Put in one or more words.

Sandwiches	Drinks	
Sara and Al both like:	Sara likes:	Al likes:
whole wheat bread	hot drinks	cold drinks
peanut butter	no straws	straws
slices of banana	warm cider	orange juice

Notice how the lists were turned into a paragraph about likenesses and a paragraph about differences.

Sara and Al like to make the same kind of sandwich. They both use whole ∧wheat bread, peanut butter, and slices of banana. ~~Sara likes tuna fish sandwiches too.~~

Sara and Al like different kinds of drinks. Sara likes hot drinks, but al likes cold drinks. Al likes to drink through a straw, but Sara doesn't. Their little sister likes to drink milk. Sara's favorite drink is warm cider, and Al's is orange juice.

- Which paragraph is about likenesses? about differences?
- What is the topic sentence of the first paragraph? the second paragraph?

- Why is the last sentence of the first paragraph being taken out?
- Which sentence should be taken out of the second paragraph? Why?
- What other changes were made in the paragraphs?
- What marks were used to show the changes?

When you write about things that are alike or things that are different, be sure you think about what you want to say before you write.

Working It Through

A. Rewrite both paragraphs on page 138. Make the changes that are marked.

B. Read the topic sentences and the lists. Write a paragraph about how the pens are alike. Write another paragraph about how the kites are different.

My pen and your pen are alike.
    yellow
    blue tops
    red ink

My kite and your kite are different.
    paper   plastic
    white string red string
    long tail   short tail

Trying It Out

A. Read the paragraph you wrote for Lesson 4, for Lesson 5, or use one from Exercise B. Ask yourself questions like these to decide where to make changes.

1. Did I make a list of likenesses or differences before I wrote the paragraph?
2. Did I write a topic sentence?
3. Does every sentence tell about the likenesses or differences?

B. Use the proofreader's marks from page 138 to show the changes you need to make.

C. Rewrite the paragraph, making the changes you marked.

Review • Likenesses and Differences

A. Read the lists. Notice how the lists were turned into a paragraph about likenesses and a paragraph about differences.

School		
Tony and Marta both like:	Tony likes:	Marta likes:
band practice	softball	soccer
Spanish class	hockey	basketball
new friends	football	tennis

Tony and Marta like school. They both play in the school band and take Spanish. Tony and Marta enjoy making new friends at school.

Tony and Marta like different kinds of sports. Tony likes softball, but Marta likes soccer. Marta enjoys basketball, but Tony enjoys hockey. Tony's favorite sport is football, and Marta's is tennis.

1. Which paragraph is about likenesses? about differences?

2. What is the topic sentence of the first paragraph? of the second paragraph?

B. Look at the picture. Write one list about how the cars are alike and one list about how they are different. Turn each list into a paragraph. Write a topic sentence for each paragraph.

C. Answer the questions.

  1. Did you write a topic sentence for each paragraph?

  2. Did you indent the first line of each paragraph?

Evaluation • Likenesses and Differences

A. Improve the paragraphs. Ask yourself the questions below to decide where to make changes. Rewrite the paragraphs.

My shirt and Tim's shirt are alike. They are both red with white stripes. Tim's shirt has blue stripes too, but my shirt doesn't.

Tim's shirt is itchy, but mine is soft. My shirt has the letter *B* on the front, but Tim's has a *T*. Both shirts are warm.

1. Does each paragraph have a topic sentence?
2. Does each sentence in the first paragraph tell about likenesses?
3. Does each sentence in the second paragraph tell about differences?

B. Write a paragraph about how the scarecrows are alike. Write another paragraph about how the scarecrows are different. Make lists to help you.

You will be evaluated on whether the sentences in your paragraphs tell only about the likenesses or differences and the following:

using a topic sentence in each
  paragraph
indenting the first line of each
  paragraph

141

Spotlight • One Idea Said in Three Ways

The same idea can be said with different words, using different forms of writing.

Poem

I loved my friend.
He went away from me.
There's nothing more to say.
The poem ends
Soft as it began—
I loved my friend.

Langston Hughes

Old Saying

A friend is a present you give yourself.

Robert Louis Stevenson

Song Lyrics

If you ever lose your mind,
    I'll be kind.
If you ever lose your shirt,
    I'll be hurt.
If you're ever in a mill and get
    sawed in half,
      I won't laugh!
It's friendship, friendship,
Just a perfect blendship . . .
When other friendships are up the
    crick,
      Ours will still be slick!

Cole Porter

The poem, the saying, and the song lyrics all describe the warm feeling of friendship.

Spotlight • The Pledge of Allegiance

You may often say the Pledge of Allegiance and you may know it by heart. But did you ever think about what some of the words mean? Notice the underlined words.

I pledge allegiance to the flag of the United States of America and to the Republic for which it stands, one Nation under God, indivisible, with liberty and justice for all.

Pledge means "promise."
Allegiance means "loyalty."
Republic means "a nation in which the government is run by persons the people elect."
Indivisible means "cannot be divided."

If the Pledge of Allegiance were written using other words, it might read this way:

I promise loyalty to the flag of the United States of America and to the nation in which we elect people to run the government, one Nation . . ., that cannot be divided, with liberty and justice for all.

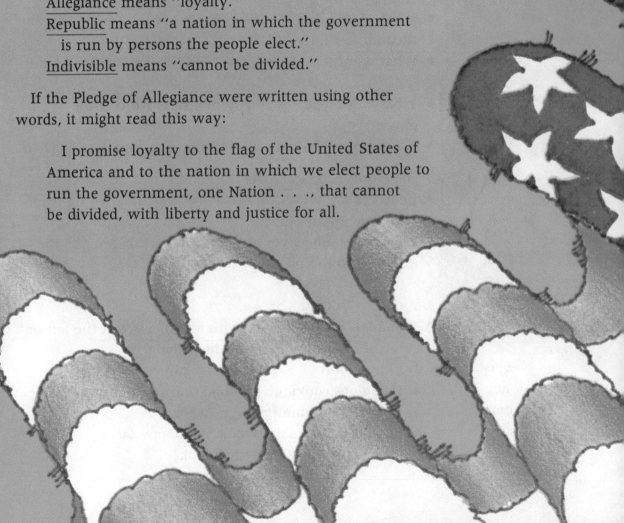

Lesson 7 **Adjectives**

Some words describe nouns by telling what kind or how many. These words are called adjectives.

Thinking It Through

Read the paragraph and notice some of the words that describe nouns.

> Rodney and his <u>two</u> friends went to a <u>scary</u> monster movie. <u>Several</u> monsters were in the movie. All of them had <u>green</u> skin.

- What word tells how many friends went with Rodney to the monster movie?
- What word tells what kind of monster movie they went to?
- What word tells how many monsters were in the movie?
- What word tells what kind of skin the monsters had?

The words *two, scary, several,* and *green* are adjectives. **Adjectives** are words that describe nouns by telling what kind or how many.

- What other adjectives can you think of to describe the monsters in the picture?

Working It Through

A. Complete each sentence with an adjective at the left or use one of your own that tells how many.

every
one
some
few
ten

1. I know only _____ person who can cook well.
2. He enjoys cooking _____ food you can imagine.
3. He can fix hamburger _____ ways.
4. He makes _____ salads look like happy faces.
5. He has written a _____ cookbooks.

B. Complete each sentence with an adjective at the right, or use one of your own that tells what kind.

1. One ____ evening Jay walked along the beach.
2. The waves lapped at his ____ feet.
3. He heard some ____ birds overhead.
4. Jay found an ____ seashell.
5. Some girls had caught a ____ fish nearby.
6. One girl wore a ____ sweater.

noisy
summer
bare
huge
green
unusual

C. What adjective describes the underlined noun?

1. Robin and Pablo played a new <u>game</u>.
2. Pablo moved his marker three <u>spaces</u>.
3. Robin won several <u>prizes</u> when she spun the wheel.
4. Pablo pulled the wrong <u>card</u> from the pile.
5. He had to go back to the first <u>square</u>.
6. Robin had a proud <u>feeling</u> when she won.

D. Choose an adjective that tells how many and an adjective that tells what kind to describe each noun.

For example—*one green bike, dozen new pennies.*

1. bike
2. leaves
3. pennies
4. eggs
5. nose
6. hat
7. morning
8. milk
9. shoes
10. onions

Adjective Box	
How Many	**What Kind**
one	new
some	large
few	green
dozen	bright
ten	cold

Trying It Out

1. Take a close look at your classroom.
2. Write several sentences, describing some of the things you see, such as the desks, posters, lights, books, and windows.
3. Use adjectives that tell what kind and how many.

Adjectives in the Complete Subject

The complete subject of a sentence often has a noun marker, an adjective, and a noun.

Thinking It Through

Notice how the three words in each subject are labeled.

Noun Marker	Adjective	Noun	
The	fluffy	cloud	floated by.
A	few	clouds	floated by.

- What is the label for each word in the subject, *The fluffy cloud? A few clouds?*

The and *A* are noun markers. A noun marker signals that a noun will soon appear in the sentence.

Cloud and *clouds* are nouns. A noun is a word that names a person, place, or other thing.

Fluffy and *few* are adjectives. *Fluffy* tells what kind of cloud is floating by. *Few* tells how many clouds are floating by. Adjectives often come between noun markers and nouns.

The complete subject of a sentence often has a noun marker, an adjective, and a noun.

Working It Through

A. Complete each sentence with an adjective from the Adjective Box.

Adjective Box	
What Kind	**How Many**
frisky	few
hungry	dozen
tired	single

1. The _____ man sat on the bench.
2. A _____ pigeons chattered around him.
3. A _____ squirrel sniffed at his bag of crumbs.
4. The _____ birds waited hopefully for food.
5. The _____ pigeons waited.
6. The _____ birds ate all the crumbs.
7. Not a _____ crumb was left.

B. Read each sentence below. Choose a noun from the box on the right that makes sense in the sentence. Then choose an adjective to describe the noun. Put a noun marker before the adjective. Write the sentences.

1. _____ _____ _____ covered the sun.
2. _____ _____ _____ began to fall.
3. _____ _____ _____ flew away.
4. _____ _____ _____ swirled in the wind.
5. _____ _____ _____ was left on a tree.

Noun Marker	Adjective	Noun
A	single	rain
An	cold	clouds
The	orange	leaves
	dark	birds
	dozen	leaf

C. Copy the sentences. Draw a line between the complete subject and predicate. Then label each word in the subject, using the letters **NM** for *Noun Marker*, **A** for *Adjective*, and **N** for *Noun*. For example:

```
NM   A     N
The pink lizard | ate worms.
```

1. A strong wind shook the shutters.
2. A single owl hooted in the darkness.
3. A few floorboards groaned loudly.
4. An icy chill filled the air.
5. The wild storm raged outside.
6. The dark night didn't scare me.
7. The rickety house wasn't really haunted!

Trying It Out

Read both directions before starting the activity.

1. Write at least five sentences about the haunted house.
2. Begin each sentence with a noun marker, followed by an adjective, followed by a noun.

147

Adjectives in the Complete Predicate

The complete predicate of a sentence often has a noun marker, an adjective, and a noun.

Thinking It Through

The complete subject of a sentence often has a noun marker, an adjective, and a noun. The complete predicate can also have a noun marker, an adjective, and a noun. Notice how each word in the complete predicate is labeled.

	Verb	Noun Marker	Adjective	Noun
The purple moose	ate	the	green	grass.
The fat cat	ate	a	dozen	onions.

- Which words in the complete predicates are verbs?
- Which words are the noun markers?
- What does a noun marker tell you?
- Which words are the nouns?
- What kind of word can come between a noun marker and a noun?

Like the complete subject of a sentence, the complete predicate can have a noun marker, an adjective, and a noun.

Working It Through

A. Use a different adjective between the noun marker and noun in each blank below. Use the kind of adjective shown in parentheses.

1. Mr. Cowley is a _____ clown. (what kind)
2. He always puts on a _____ face. (what kind)
3. He wears an _____ hat. (what kind)
4. Often he trips in the _____ shoes. (what kind)
5. He performs a _____ times each week. (how many)
6. He waves to the _____ children. (what kind)

B. Complete each sentence. First choose a noun from the box on the right. Then choose an adjective to describe the noun. Put a noun marker before each adjective.

Noun Marker	Adjective	Noun
a	adorable	~~candles~~
an	~~birthday~~	~~party~~
the	~~ten~~	~~game~~
	~~guessing~~	puppy

1. Sue and I went to ____ ____ ____.

2. We played ____ ____ ____.

3. Our friend blew out ____ ____ ____.

4. He got ____ ____ ____.

C. Copy the sentences. Draw a line between the complete subject and the complete predicate. Then label each word in the predicate, using the letters **NM** for *Noun Marker*, **A** for *Adjective* and **N** for *Noun.* For example:

```
              NM  A    N
Peter │ liked the cold weather.
```

1. Peter opened an old box.
2. He found the black skates.
3. Peter felt the dull blades.
4. He saw the broken laces.
5. But they were the best skates.

Trying It Out

Rewrite the story about Ruler. Make Ruler a different kind of animal. Change each underlined group of words. Be sure you have a noun marker, an adjective, and a noun that describes your animal.

Ruler is <u>a giant bear</u>. She prowls through <u>the thick forest</u> all day. She devours <u>the wild fruit</u> she finds. She also eats <u>a dozen fish</u> each day. Ruler growls at <u>the pesty insects</u> that tease her. At night, she sleeps in <u>a small cave</u>.

Lesson 10 Combining Sentences

Sentences with adjectives that describe the same noun can often be combined. Use commas to separate the adjectives when they are in a series.

Thinking It Through

Notice the adjectives in these sentences.

> The car is <u>old</u>.
> The car is <u>noisy</u>.
> The car is <u>red</u>.

- What is the adjective in each sentence?
- What noun does each adjective describe?

You can often combine sentences that have adjectives that describe the same noun.

> The car is <u>old</u>.
> The car is <u>noisy</u>.   >   The car is <u>old</u>, <u>noisy</u>, and <u>red</u>.
> The car is <u>red</u>.

The adjectives are now in a series, coming one right after the other in the sentence.
- How are the adjectives separated in the series?
- What word is added before the last adjective?

Sentences with adjectives that describe the same noun can often be combined. If there are three adjectives in a series, use a comma after the first two adjectives.

Working It Through

A. Copy each sentence. Use commas where they are needed.
1. The puppies are small cute and playful.
2. That house is huge quiet and mysterious.
3. These books are old heavy and valuable.
4. The summer was short hot and sticky.

150

B. Combine each group of sentences. Separate the adjectives in a series with commas. Remember to add the word *and*.

   1. The hike through the forest was fun. It was interesting. It was unusual.
   2. The bridge was long. It was narrow. It was dangerous.
   3. The path was muddy. It was grassy. It was slippery.
   4. The berries were small. They were red. They were round.
   5. After the hike, we were tired. After the hike, we sleepy. After the hike, we were hungry.

C. Write 5 sentences with three adjectives to describe something.

The boy's hair is short, black, and curly.

Trying It Out
Rewrite the paragraph by combining sentences that have adjectives that describe the same noun.

   Doug's orange-juice stand was tall. It was wooden. It was sturdy. Doug's orange juice was always cold. It was sweet. It was delicious. Joy bought some juice because she was hot. She bought some juice because she was tired. She bought some juice because she was thirsty. When Doug sold all his orange juice, he was happy. When he sold all his orange juice, he was excited. When he sold all his orange juice, he was relieved.

Take Another Look
When you combined sentences, did you use commas with the adjectives in a series? Did you remember to put *and* before the last adjective?

Special Titles Before Names

Some special titles before names are abbreviated. The abbreviations begin with a capital letter and end with a period.

Mr. Ray Cobb

Thinking It Through

Notice the titles that are abbreviated in the chart below. The chart also tells you who uses each title.

Ms. Joy Gray   Mrs. Kay Smith   Dr. Joe Green

Mr.	title used before a single or married man's name
Ms.	title that may be used before a single or married woman's name
Mrs.	title often used before a married woman's name
Dr.	title used before the name of a doctor or dentist
Supt.	title of a person who manages something or someone
Lt.	title of an officer
Gov.	title of an official elected to carry out state laws
Pres.	title of the chief officer of a company, club, or country

Supt. Kiyo Tamura   Lt. Oscar Perez   Gov. Matt Howard

- What does each abbreviation begin and end with?
- What does each abbreviation stand for?

Some titles are often not abbreviated, such as *Governor* and *President*. Titles that are abbreviated begin with a capital letter and end with a period.

Pres. Stacy Adams

Working It Through

A. Write the abbreviated title before the name for each person below.

1. Carol Ladd, our superintendent
2. Jacob Scott, our police lieutenant
3. Suzanne Forest, our new class president
4. Adam Walker, the governor of our state

B. Write an abbreviation for each title. Write one of the names below after each abbreviated title.

1. Doctor   Bray K. Leg
2. President   Ike N. Lead
3. Governor   Della Ware
4. Lieutenant   Ima Soldier
5. Superintendent I. C. All

C. Use the abbreviations at the right in these sentences.

1. ____ Jeff Foster is our family doctor.
2. ____ Tony Marzetti is a lieutenant in the army.
3. ____ Julia Ray is the new superintendent of our schools.
4. ____ Gordon Hines is the president of our club.
5. ____ Daisy King is the governor of our state.
6. ____ Rita Moore is your sister.
7. ____ Delores Riley is your aunt.
8. ____ Joe Willis lives on my block.

Mr.
Dr.
Ms.
Supt.
Mrs.
Pres.
Gov.
Lt.

Trying It Out

Look at the picture. Write a sentence about each person. Give each person a name and a title. Use these abbreviations in your sentences.

Dr.   Ms.   Pres.   Supt.
Mrs.   Mr.   Lt.   Gov.

Homophones

Some words called homophones sound alike, but they have different meanings and spellings.

Thinking It Through

Some words called **homophones** sound alike when you say them, but they have different meanings and spellings. See if you can figure out which underlined words go with the definitions in the balloons.

as long as

one more than three

more than enough

one more than one

in the direction of

in or at this place

belonging to them

in or at that place

a contraction for they are

listen to

The <u>four</u> of us are going <u>to</u> the art fair Sunday in Woodside. We will walk <u>for</u> <u>two</u> hours, looking at pictures. If it gets <u>too</u> crowded, we'll come home. We'll probably <u>hear</u> music on the streets and buy balloons to bring back <u>here</u> with us. The pictures will be on display when we get <u>there</u>. The artists will be selling <u>their</u> works. <u>They're</u> sure to sell many of them.

Homophones are words that sound alike, but they have different meanings and spellings: *for* and *four*; *to*, *too*, and *two*; *here* and *hear*; *there*, *their*, and *they're*.

154

Working It Through

A. Write a definition for each word below. Use the definitions on page 154 to help you.

1. for
2. four
3. there
4. their
5. they're
6. here
7. hear
8. to
9. too
10. two

B. Complete each sentence with the correct word in parentheses.

1. We went (to, too, two) the airport (for, four) the skywriting contest.
2. Every spring, we see the contest (here, hear) at the airport.
3. When we got (there, their, they're), we saw (to, too, two) planes on the ground and (for, four) in the air.
4. We could (here, hear) the announcer list the names of the pilots and the numbers on (there, their, they're) planes.
5. They are good pilots, but (there, their, they're) poor spellers.

Trying It Out

John has trouble with homophones. Rewrite his paragraph, correcting the misspelled words.

I went <u>two</u> a camp in Yellowstone Park for <u>for</u> weeks last summer. I saw <u>too</u> eagles <u>they're</u>. They glided <u>four</u> a long time without flapping <u>there</u> wings. I couldn't <u>here</u> them make any noise. <u>Their</u> beautiful birds. There aren't <u>to</u> many eagles left. You don't see eagles <u>hear</u> in the city.

Review • Adjectives

A. Copy the sentences. Underline the adjectives. Circle the noun each adjective describes. Write whether each adjective tells *what kind* or *how many*.
1. We slid down several hills.
2. There was a blue cover on the box.
3. In the field we saw six horses.
4. The horse had a white star on the forehead.

B. Copy the sentences. Write **NM** above each noun marker, **A** above each adjective, and **N** above each noun.

1. A laughing clown waved.
2. The thin man cried.
3. An orange snake disappeared.
4. The fat groundhog ate.
5. A clumsy elephant tripped.
6. An odd noise woke me.

C. Copy the sentences. Put in commas correctly.
1. The cave was cool   damp   and dim.
2. They walked down a quiet   shady   and narrow path.
3. Pedro felt happy   relieved   and tired.
4. I saw an old   rundown   and unpainted shack.

D. Copy the sentences. Complete each one with the correct word in parentheses.
1. That book belongs ____ in my room.   (hear, here)
2. I hope ____ happy.   (their, there, they're)
3. Can you ____ that cardinal singing?   (hear, here)
4. Lou gave an apple ____ me.   (to, two, too)
5. Kim has ____ kittens.   (for, four)

For extra practice turn to pages 341–343.

Take Another Look   Copy the sentence. Choose the correct tense of the verb in parentheses.

Gus ____ his shirt yesterday.   (tear, tore)

Did you use *tore*?

For more practice turn to page 339 in the Handbook.

Evaluation • Adjectives

A. Write the letter of the response that tells what the
underlined word in each sentence is.

1. Sue has a <u>red</u> coat.
   a. noun   **b.** adjective
2. Dad has a beautiful <u>smile</u>.
   a. noun   **b.** adjective
3. Can you eat a <u>dozen</u> carrots?
   a. noun   **b.** adjective
4. I have <u>ten</u> marbles.
   a. noun   **b.** adjective
5. Carolyn made a <u>delicious</u> soup.
   a. noun   **b.** adjective
6. Mark has a brown <u>hat</u>.
   a. noun   **b.** adjective

7. <u>A</u> heavy box fell off the truck.
   a. noun marker   **b.** adjective
8. Only a <u>few</u> people ever come here.
   a. noun   **b.** adjective
9. The telephone gave a <u>loud</u> ring.
   a. noun marker   **b.** adjective
10. The horse wore a new <u>saddle</u>.
    a. noun   **b.** noun marker
11. A little <u>bird</u> cheeped loudly.
    a. noun   **b.** adjective
12. Phil is <u>the</u> best friend I have.
    a. noun marker   **b.** adjective

B. Write the letter of each word that should be followed
by a comma.

1. The loaf is small soft and hot.
   a b c d e f g
2. He is happy quiet and nice.
   a b c d e f
3. The ant was tiny red and busy.
   a b c d e f g

4. The hat is red gold and blue.
   a b c d e f g
5. My key is old bent and rusty.
   a b c d e f g
6. The fox was old wise and sly.
   a b c d e f g

C. Write the letter of the response that gives the correct
word for the blank in each sentence.

1. I have _____ friends.
   a. for   **b.** four
2. I can't _____ you.
   a. here   **b.** hear
3. My books are over _____.
   a. there   **b.** they're

4. That is _____ new garage.
   a. there   **b.** their
5. Please sit _____.
   a. here   **b.** hear
6. Tom gave a dog _____ his brother.
   a. too   **b.** to

Spotlight • Activities to Choose

1. Fish for an adjective. Ask some classmates to each take two cards and write an adjective on each card. Then put all the cards into a shoe box or a bowl. Have each person take turns and draw, or fish for, two cards from the box or bowl. Use the cards to complete one of these sentences.

The _____ tree is _____.
The _____ dog is _____.

You may end up with a funny sentence like this: The orange dog is tall. Draw a picture to illustrate the sentence, and put it on the bulletin board.

2. Make a class scrapbook. Describe yourself by finishing these sentences.

I am as tall as _____.
I am as old as _____.
I am like a _____.
I feel like a _____.

Write your sentences on a piece of construction paper. Then draw a picture of yourself. Put your picture in a class scrapbook.

3. Find likenesses and differences. Think of and draw two pictures of one thing, like your room, a book, or a pet. Then show your pictures to a classmate. Ask her or him to tell three ways the pictures are alike and three ways they are different.

4. Homophone tongue twisters. Make up a sentence using each word in one of these sets of words:

for, four
to, two, too
here, hear
there, their, they're

For example, Tom told Ted to travel *to* the *two* tan tents *too*. Then say your tongue twister to a classmate. See if he or she can spell the homophones in your tongue twister.

Spotlight • Books to Read

Marian Anderson
by Tobi Tobias

This is the life story of Marian Anderson, from her childhood in a poor section of Philadelphia to the time she became known as one of the world's finest singers. Her courage, pride, and hard work make this a wonderful book to read.

Funny Number Tricks: Easy Magic with Arithmetic
by Rose Wyler and Gerald Ames

You can be a magician by learning the tricks and stunts in this book. You can surprise your friends by always picking the "right" card and by predicting how a game of dominoes will end. Only simple props, such as coins, are needed.

Getting Something on Maggie Marmelstein
by Marjorie Weinman Sharmat

In the first sentence of this story, Thad says, "My mother told me that I should never hate anybody, so I guess that I only dislike Maggie Marmelstein very, very, very, very, very much." Thad and Maggie just can't keep from teasing each other or from trying to outdo each other. How do they become friends?

Unit Six

Have you ever found something special? Read the poem to find out what special things some children found.

Discovery

In a puddle left from last week's rain,
    A friend of mine whose name is Joe
    Caught a tadpole, and showed me where
    Its froggy legs were beginning to grow.

Then we turned over a musty log,
    With lichens on it in a row,
    And found some fiddleheads of ferns
    Uncoiling out of the moss below.

We hunted around, and saw the first
    Jack-in-the-pulpits beginning to show,
    And even spotted under a rock
    Where spotted salamanders go.

I learned all this one morning from Joe,
But how much more there is to know!

Harry Behn

An encyclopedia is a good place for discoveries—to learn something new, or to learn more about a subject you already know a little about. Asking questions such as when, where, and how something happened will also lead you to interesting discoveries.

Lesson 1 **An Encyclopedia**

An encyclopedia is a book or set of books that gives you information on many kinds of subjects.

Thinking It Through

The picture shows an encyclopedia. An **encyclopedia** contains short articles on many kinds of subjects. Each book, or **volume,** has a number.

● How many volumes does this encyclopedia have?

It's easy to find the information you want because the volumes and the subjects inside the volumes are in alphabetical order. If the subject is a person, look up the person's last name to find information about that person.

● Which volume would you use to find out about cyclones? about hornets? about Abraham Lincoln?

If you can't find what you want in an article, try to think of another subject to look up. If an article on *Music* doesn't give much information on folk singing, look up *Folk Singing* or *Folk Music.*

Subjects in an encyclopedia are arranged in alphabetical order. Sometimes you will have to look up more than one subject to find the information you want.

Working It Through

A. In what volume would you look to learn about these subjects? Give the volume number. Use the picture of the encyclopedia on page 162 to help you.

1. Railroads
2. Emily Dickinson
3. Kangaroos
4. Benjamin Franklin
5. Glassmaking
6. Whales
7. England
8. Harriet Tubman
9. Trees
10. Thomas Edison

B. What other volume should each of these people use? Give the volume number. Use the picture of the encyclopedia on page 162 to help you.

1. Pearl wanted to write about owls. She could find only a picture of a barn owl in the article on birds in volume 2.
2. Laszlo loved music. He looked up information about jazz in volume 11.
3. Henrietta wanted to write about tennis champion Chris Evert. She looked up *Tennis* in volume 16.
4. Joel wanted to write a report about volcanoes in Hawaii. He looked up *Volcanoes* in volume 17.
5. Greg wanted to learn more about the different ways George Washington Carver found to use peanuts. He looked up *Peanuts* in volume 13.
6. Rita wanted to know the different kinds of foods the Pilgrims and Native Americans ate at the first Thanksgiving at Plymouth Colony. She looked up *Native Americans* in volume 12.

Trying It Out

List several subjects you want to know more about. Write the volume numbers where you would find the subjects. Use the volumes on page 162 to help you.

Using an Encyclopedia

You can use guide words and entry words to find information in an encyclopedia.

Thinking It Through

Articles in an encyclopedia are called **entries.** The title of an article is called an **entry word,** even if it is more than one word. An entry word is printed in heavy type so that it will be easy to find on a page.

At the top of encyclopedia pages are **guide words.** The guide word on the left-hand page tells what entry word is the first on that page. The guide word on the right-hand page tells what entry word is last on that page. All the entries on those two pages will come between the two guide words. The entries are in alphabetical order.

To look up the entry about stilts, take the volume labeled *S.*

- If you turned to pages with the guide words **sponge** and **spring,** would the entry word *stilts* be on one of those two pages? Why or why not?
- Should you turn further toward the front or the back of volume *S?* Why?
- When you reach the guide words **stick** and **sting ray,** stop. Why?

The alphabetical order of guide words and entry words helps you find information in an encyclopedia.

Working It Through

A. Answer the questions and tell why you answered as you did.

1. Could you find the entry word *dandelion* between the guide words **dancing** and **daniel?**

2. Could you find the entry word *Gila Monster* between the guide words **glider** and **globe?**

3. Could you find the entry word *Volga River* between the guide words **volcano** and **volleyball?**

B. Would you turn further to the front or further to the back of the volume if you were looking for an entry for

1. *Scarlet Fever,* and you open the volume to the guide words **saturn** and **sand?**

2. *Cabbage,* and you open the volume to the guide words **calcium** and **calico?**

3. *O. J. Simpson,* and you open the volume to the guide words **shreveport** and **shrimp?**

Trying It Out

In your own words, write three things you learned from this entry about stilts.

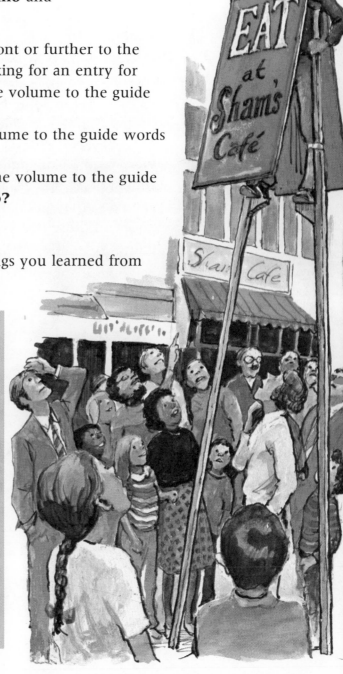

STILTS are two long poles that allow a person to walk with his feet some distance above the ground. Each stilt has a footrest fastened to it. Stilt walkers stand on the footrests, keep the top of the stilts in their armpits, and grip the stilts with their hands. With each step they move a stilt forward with their hands. Some stilt walkers strap their legs to the stilts so they can use the motion of their legs to operate the stilts.

Stilts are used chiefly for amusement. Children like to walk on them. Some circus performers entertain by walking on stilts.

No one knows when stilt walking began. Hundreds of years ago, people in some areas used stilts to walk above water during floods. A legend dating from the 1600's tells of soldiers using stilts in Namur, Belgium. Some farmers in parts of Gascony, France, once used stilts to wade in marshland and cross streams. They could run on stilts with remarkable speed and ease.

Choosing a Topic

A topic you write about should not be too small or too big.

Thinking It Through

Choosing a topic for a report can be like Goldilocks choosing a chair. Some topics are too small. Some topics are too big. But some topics are just right.

When Enrique decided to write about Native Americans, he knew the topic was too big. There would be too many things to tell about Native Americans for one report. He also knew that the topic "When Did Chief Crazy Horse Die?" was too small. There would not be enough to write about.

Enrique thought about some of the things he wanted to know more about. He wrote these questions.

> How did the Native Americans make birchbark canoes?
> How did the Native Americans hunt buffalo?
> What are some Native American songs and dances?
> Who is Maria Tallchief?

The answer to any one of these questions would make a good report. There would be enough to write about, but not too much.

When you choose a topic, be sure it is not too small or too big. Questions about a big topic will help you choose a topic that is easier to write about.

Working It Through

A. In each example, tell which topic would be easier to write about.

1. Pets	2. Sports	3. Thomas Jefferson
My Turtle	Diving	U.S. Presidents

4. Daisies
   Flowers
5. Mexico
   Mexican Food

6. Cars
   The Zoom 230
7. My Tenth Birthday
   Birthdays

8. San Francisco
   Cities
9. School
   Fourth Grade

B. Think of at least one more question about each topic.

1. Musical Instruments
   How is a guitar made?
2. Food
   How is peanut butter made?
3. The Planets
   What is the surface of the moon like?
4. Insects
   What makes a firefly glow?
5. Boats
   What were the showboats like?
6. Hobbies
   How do you begin a coin collection?
7. Holidays
   Why do we celebrate Halloween?
8. Vegetables
   How do you grow tomatoes?
9. First Aid
   What should a first-aid kit contain?
10. Toys
   What were the first toys like?

Trying It Out

Are you interested in guitars, airplanes, pottery, square dancing, or photography? Choose a topic you would like to write about. Write at least two questions about your topic.

Taking Notes

Taking notes will help you remember the important ideas you read.

Thinking It Through

Enrique chose "Who Is Maria Tallchief?" as the topic for his paragraph. When he read about Maria Tallchief, he needed to take notes to remember the important ideas. His teacher gave him some steps for taking notes.

Steps for Taking Notes

1. Read to find information about your topic.
2. Choose the important information you want to include in your report.
3. Don't copy the information. Write it down in your own words.
4. Read your notes to see if they make sense.
5. Check your notes to be sure they are correct.
6. Write the name of the book, the author, and the page where you found your information. If you use an encyclopedia, write the name of the encyclopedia, the volume letter and number, and the page number.

- Why should you choose only the important information when you take notes?
- Will taking notes in your own words help you understand what you read? Why or why not?
- Why should you read your notes after you've written them?
- What should you remember to record when you get your information from a book? from an encyclopedia?

Working It Through

Enrique found an article on Maria Tallchief in an encyclopedia. Read the article and the notes he took.

TALLCHIEF, MARIA (1925-   ), is an American ballerina often praised for her superb technical discipline and command of style. As one of the first American ballerinas to gain international fame, she showed that American ballet dancing could equal European dancing in quality.

Maria Tallchief was born in Fairfax, Okla., the daughter of an Osage Indian father and a Scottish-Irish mother. She danced with the Ballet Russe de Monte Carlo from 1942 to 1947, but her career has been associated chiefly with the New York City Ballet. She danced with this company from 1947 to 1960. She was once married to New York City Ballet director George Balanchine. She created roles in many of Balanchine's ballets, including *Orpheus* (1948) and *Scotch Symphony* (1952).

Who Is Maria Tallchief?
1. Maria Tallchief is a famous American dancer.
2. She showed that American ballet dancing could equal European dancing in quality.
3. Maria Tallchief's mother was an Osage Indian and her father was Scottish - Irish.
4. From 1947 to 1960
World Book, Vol. T, 19, pps. 20-21.

1. Which note did Enrique forget to complete? Why should he complete it? Write the note correctly.

2. What mistake did Enrique make in the third note? Write the note correctly.

3. Which note did he forget to put in his own words? Write it in your own words.

Trying It Out

Find and read information on the topic you chose in Lesson 3. Take notes, using the steps for note taking. Keep your notes for the next lesson.

Take Another Look
Did you put each note in your own words? Did each note have all the information you need? Are your notes correct?

Turning Your Notes into a Paragraph

You can turn your notes into a paragraph. State the main idea of your paragraph in a topic sentence.

Thinking It Through

Enrique turned his notes on Maria Tallchief into a paragraph for a report. Read his notes and then read the paragraph Enrique wrote.

Who is Maria Tallchief?
1. Maria Tallchief is a famous American dancer.
2. She showed that Americans could dance as well as Europeans.
3. Maria Tallchief's father was an Osage Indian and her mother was Scottish—Irish.
4. From 1947 to 1960, she danced with the New York City Ballet.
World Book, Volume T, 19, pps. 20-21.

Who Is Maria Tallchief?
Maria Tallchief is a famous dancer. She taught the world that Americans can dance as well as Europeans. Maria Tallchief's father was an Osage Indian and her mother was Scottish—Irish. From 1947 to 1960, she danced with the New York City Ballet.

- What is the title of Enrique's report?
- What is the topic sentence of his paragraph?

When you turn your notes into a report, decide which notes belong in a paragraph. Then write the main idea in a topic sentence. Write the other notes in sentences. Make sure every sentence tells something about your topic.

Working It Through

A. Read the notes on cork. One note tells the main idea about cork. Which note is it?

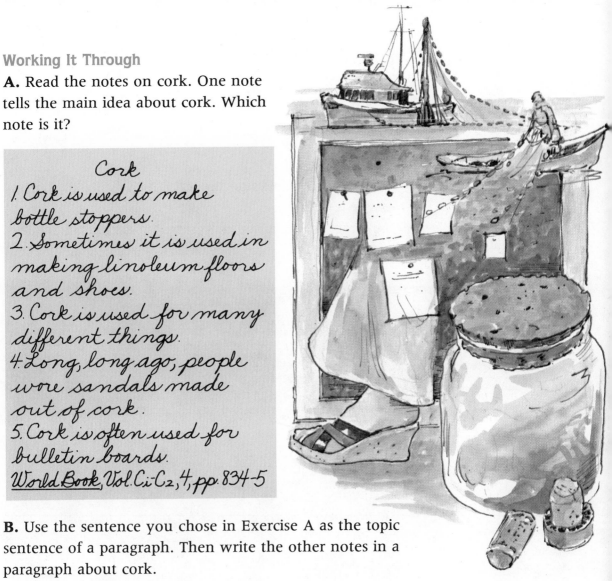

Cork
1. Cork is used to make bottle stoppers.
2. Sometimes it is used in making linoleum floors and shoes.
3. Cork is used for many different things.
4. Long, long ago, people wore sandals made out of cork.
5. Cork is often used for bulletin boards.
World Book, Vol. Ci-Cz, 4, pp. 834-5

B. Use the sentence you chose in Exercise A as the topic sentence of a paragraph. Then write the other notes in a paragraph about cork.

Trying It Out

Use the notes you wrote in Lesson 4 to write a paragraph. Decide what the main idea is, and write a topic sentence. Then add the other sentences to tell more about the main idea.

Take Another Look   Did you capitalize any proper nouns? Did you indent the first line of your paragraph?

Improving Your Writing

When you write a paragraph, use a topic sentence and keep to the main idea.

Thinking It Through

The proofreader's marks on the left help you make changes in your writing.

Read Carl's paragraph about grasshoppers and notice the changes he marked.

Proofreader's Marks

≡ Make a capital letter.

⊙ Add a period.

ℓ Take out.

∧ Put in one or more words.

> Grasshoppers
>
> Grasshoppers are interesting insects. They have five eyes and six legs. ~~Ants have six legs too.~~ Grasshoppers eat the leaves of plants. Sometimes they destroy farmers' crops. ~~and~~ grasshoppers are great at jumping. If you could jump as far as a grasshopper, you would be able to jump 40 yards.

- What is the topic sentence of Carl's paragraph?
- Why did he want to take out the third sentence?
- What other changes did he want to make?
- What marks did Carl use to show each change?

When you write a paragraph, remember to write a topic sentence. Make sure each sentence in the paragraph tells something about the topic.

Working It Through

A. Rewrite Carl's paragraph. Make the changes that are marked.

B. Answer the questions about the paragraph below. Then write the paragraph, making the changes.

    1. Where would you use the mark |≡ ? the mark ⊙ ?

    2. Which sentence should be taken out? Why?

    3. Is there a topic sentence? If not, what should the sentence say?

> Many people wear hats all year. In cold weather, people wear fur hats or wool hats. They also wear mittens and boots. in hot weather, people wear hats with big brims to keep off the sun. In other kinds of weather, people wear cloth hats and hats to keep off the rain

Trying It Out

A. Read the paragraph you wrote for Lesson 5 or write another paragraph. Then answer these questions to decide where to make changes in your paragraph.

    1. Have I written a topic sentence?

    2. Do all the sentences tell about the main idea?

    3. Did I indent the first line?

    4. Did I use the right ending mark after each sentence?

    5. Is all the information correct?

B. Use the proofreader's marks from page 172 to show the changes you need to make.

C. Rewrite the paragraph and make the changes you marked.

Review • Using an Encyclopedia

A. Nancy decided to look in an encyclopedia to learn about alligators. Write answers to the questions below to help her find the information.

1. What is the letter of the volume Nancy should use to find the entry for *alligator?* Why?

2. When Nancy opened volume A, she noticed the guide words **astronaut** and **atlanta.** Would she find the entry for *alligator* between those guide words? Why or why not? Should she turn farther toward the front or the back of volume A?

3. On the next pages she turned to, Nancy saw the guide words **algae** and **aluminum.** Would she find the entry for *alligator* between these guide words? Why or why not?

B. Write the answers to these questions to see how well you can use an encyclopedia.

1. What is the letter of the volume you would use to find out about your state?

2. What kind of animal would you like to find out about? What is the letter of the volume you would use to find information about it?

3. Pretend your name is an entry in an encyclopedia. What guide word might come before your name? after your name?

C. Look at page 165 and take notes on the history of stilts. Decide which notes belong in a paragraph about the history. Which note states the main idea?

Evaluation • Using an Encyclopedia

A. Pretend you need to find information about inventions.

1. What is the letter of the volume you would use to find out about inventions?

2. Would you find the entry for *inventions* between **iceland** and **indiana?** Why or why not?

3. Would you find the entry for *inventions* between **insect** and **iowa?** Why or why not?

B. Read the encyclopedia entry for *papier-mâché*. Then answer the questions.

1. What is the letter of the volume in which you would find the entry?

2. Between which pair of guide words might you find the entry? **paint** and **panther** or **paper** and **parachute**

C. Read the entry on the right. Write 3 notes about what you learned from the entry. Make sure you use your own words. Then turn your notes about papier-mâché into a paragraph.

    You will be evaluated on using your own words and on the following:

    writing facts correctly

    stating the main idea in a
       topic sentence

    indenting the first line of your
       paragraph

    PAPIER-MÂCHÉ, *PAY pur muh SHAY,* is a French term meaning *pulped paper.* Papier-mâché can be made by churning newspaper in water until the fibers are well separated. The excess water is then squeezed out, glue is added, and the soft material is molded into any desired form. It later hardens and becomes fairly durable.

    Papier-mâché pulp can be mixed with clay, sand, lime, salt, or borax to give it body. Sodium phosphate makes it fireproof. Halloween masks, doll heads, toy helmets, and picnic plates are a few of the many things made of papier-mâché. When pressed and waterproofed, it is used for making such things as water buckets. Children can create dolls and puppets by gluing strips of newspaper onto a bottle and then decorating the paper after the strips dry.

Spotlight • Do Animals Communicate?

Have you ever sat quietly and listened to or watched the animals, birds, and insects around you? Did you wonder if they were "talking" to each other? You might be right! Animals do not use words, but they communicate in many ways.

Bees communicate by moving in a special way. When a bee finds a good supply of sweet nectar in flowers, it flies back to the hive. Then the bee does a special dance to tell the other bees about the nectar. The dance tells in what direction and just how far the nectar is.

Ants have a special way of communicating too. They leave a trail of scent. The trail leads the other ants to something sweet. Sometimes ants must travel far to get food. Then they follow the trail of scent to get home.

Look at the picture of the dog and cat, and see if you can tell how they communicate. What is the cat "telling" the dog? Does the dog understand what the cat is "telling" it? How do you know?

Spotlight • Words That Sound Like Fun

Notice the underlined words in the conversation below.

"Boys! Enough of this chitchatting," said Mother. "You'll be late for school."

Greg and Steven got up from the breakfast table and started to get their books together. Then Greg began looking around the kitchen.

"Greg, stop dillydallying," said Steven.

"Fiddlesticks!" said Greg. "I can't find the thingamajig I was going to take to school for science."

"Do you mean this?" asked Mother holding up a funnel.

"Yes, that's what I was looking for," answered Greg.

Then both boys skedaddled off to school.

The underlined words in the story are fun to use. They sound lively when you read them aloud. They add zest to both writing and talking.

Try to spice up your writing and conversation with some interesting words like the ones on this page.

Lesson 7 Adverbs

An adverb tells more about a verb. Adverbs tell when, where, or how.

Thinking It Through

Each of the underlined words in the school notice tells when, where, or how.

> ### School Trip
>
> We will go <u>tomorrow</u> to TUBE television studio. The bus will leave <u>early</u> in the morning.
>
> At the studio, we will gather <u>inside</u>, walk to the escalator, and go <u>up</u>.
>
> Talk <u>politely</u> and <u>clearly</u> when you ask your questions. We will come <u>back</u> on the bus.

- Which words in the notice answer the question *when? where? how?*
- Which verb does each adverb tell more about?

An **adverb** is a word that tells more about a verb by telling when, where, or how.

Working It Through

A. Complete each sentence with an adverb that will tell more about the underlined verb. The adverb you use should answer the question following each sentence.

1. Linda <u>went</u> to the attic ____ this morning.   (When?)
2. Linda <u>found</u> a drum ____.   (Where?)
3. Linda <u>played</u> the drums ____ all morning.   (How?)
4. ____ her father <u>came</u> to hear her play.   (When?)
5. She <u>put</u> the drums ____.   (Where?)

B. Choose an adverb for each sentence from the list at the right. Write the sentences.

1. Our summer vacation starts ____.
2. We are going ____ to camp.
3. We will pack our things ____.
4. We will wake up ____ in the morning.
5. We will eat breakfast ____.
6. We will wait ____ for the bus.
7. Our dog will watch ____ as we leave.

carefully
sadly
tomorrow
back
cheerfully
quickly
outside

C. Write the sentences. Underline the adverb in each sentence that answers the question following the sentence. You should find 7 adverbs.

1. Paco sent for some funny masks yesterday.   (When?)
2. The masks never came.   (When)?
3. Paco sat down and wrote a letter to the company. (Where?)
4. He told them politely and firmly, "My money or my masks!"   (How?)
5. Finally, Paco got the masks.   (When?)
6. Paco didn't think the company did business fairly. (How?)

Trying It Out
Write a story about the picture. Use at least 5 of the adverbs below to help you.

When	Where	How
now	here	quietly
early	outside	happily
today	there	loudly

Take Another Look   Does your story have adverbs that tell when, where, and how?

Lesson 8 Adverbs or Adjectives

An adverb tells more about a verb, and an adjective tells more about a noun.

Thinking It Through

Notice the adverbs and adjectives in these sentences.

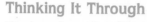

Verb   Adverb

Beth drew happily all day.

Adjective   Noun

Beth drew a happy face.

- Is *drew* a verb or a noun?
- What word tells more about *drew*?
- Is *happily* an adverb or an adjective?
- What are the last two letters in *happily*?
- Is *face* a verb or a noun?
- What word tells more about *face*?
- Is *happy* an adverb or an adjective?

Use adverbs to tell more about verbs and adjectives to tell more about nouns. Note that adverbs often end in -*ly* as in *happily*.

Working It Through

A. Decide if the underlined word is a verb or a noun. Write an adverb or adjective for each sentence. Copy the sentences.

1. Roger likes ____ movies.
2. He ____ finished his work so he could watch TV.
3. Roger's ____ actor was in the movie.
4. Roger laughed ____ at the movie.
5. He ate ____ peanuts.
6. ____ he was asleep.

180

B. Decide if the underlined word is a verb or a noun. Then choose the correct adverb or adjective for each sentence.

1. Dan wanted to add some (new, newly) <u>stamps</u> to his collection
2. When he looked through his drawer, the stamps <u>were</u> not (green, there).
3. Dan <u>solved</u> the mystery (quick, quickly).
4. (Sudden, Suddenly), he <u>noticed</u> some letters on his desk.
5. The stamps were (neat, neatly) <u>pasted</u> on the envelopes.

C. Copy the sentences. Decide if the underlined word is a verb or a noun. Then draw a line under the adverb or adjective that tells more about the underlined word.

1. Sandy <u>read</u> a book about clocks yesterday.
2. The first <u>clock</u> was a sundial.
3. As the sun <u>moved</u> slowly in the sky, it cast a shadow on the dial.
4. Sandy wondered how people told time on cloudy <u>days</u>.
5. She eagerly <u>went</u> for another book about clocks.

Trying It Out

Write a paragraph about the picture. Use some of the adverbs and adjectives below and some of your own to describe the sailboats and how they sail.

Adverbs	Adjectives
quickly	many
smoothly	red
slowly	yellow
here	sharp
soon	narrow

Contractions

A verb and the word *not* can be put together to form a contraction. An apostrophe shows that a letter or letters have been left out when the contraction was made.

Thinking It Through

Notice the contractions below.

1. is not	isn't		**7.** has not	hasn't
2. are not	aren't		**8.** have not	haven't
3. was not	wasn't		**9.** had not	hadn't
4. were not	weren't		**10.** can not	can't
5. does not	doesn't		**11.** will not	won't
6. do not	don't			

- What verb is put together with *not* in number 1? What is the contraction?
- What is used in place of the letter *o* in *not*?
- What verbs are put together with *not* in numbers 2-11 to form each contraction? What are the contractions?

Many contractions are formed by combining a verb and the word *not*. An apostrophe shows where a letter or letters have been left out. Sometimes a spelling change is made when a verb is combined with *not,* such as the change of *will not* to *won't*.

Working It Through

A. Write the contractions for these words.

1. are not

2. have not

3. do not

4. will not

5. can not

6. does not

7. had not

8. was not

9. has not

10. were not

11. is not

B. Write the two words that were used to make the underlined contraction in each sentence.

1. Mr. Brass <u>doesn't</u> know if he should still have band practice.
2. Sabrina <u>isn't</u> feeling well.
3. Peter and Larry <u>can't</u> find their instruments.
4. Yoko <u>wasn't</u> going to be on time for band practice.
5. Joey <u>hasn't</u> returned from his vacation in Canada.
6. The music room <u>won't</u> be open for another hour.

C. Replace the underlined words in each sentence with a contraction. Rewrite the sentences.

1. Myra and I <u>are not</u> happy today.
2. We <u>have not</u> any money.
3. I <u>do not</u> know how to get the money.
4. Myra <u>does not</u> have any ideas either.
5. We <u>had not</u> known it was our friend's birthday.
6. We <u>were not</u> able to buy a gift, so we made our friend a card.

Trying It Out
Look at the picture. Write sentences telling about each thing that is wrong in the picture. Use at least 6 of the contractions listed in Thinking It Through on page 182 in your sentences.

Take Another Look Did you remember to put an apostrophe in place of the letter *o* in each contraction?

Using Any and No

To make a sentence mean "no," use only one word that means "no."

Thinking It Through

A word like *not* means "no." A contraction formed from a verb and *not* means "no" too. You should use only one "no word" in a sentence. Notice how many "no words" are in these sentences.

> There *isn't no* bread left.
> There *isn't any* butter.
> There *is no* jam.

- What are the two "no words" in the first sentence? Why is the sentence incorrect?
- What is the "no word" in the second sentence? Why is the sentence correct?
- Is the third sentence correct? Why or why not?

Look at the sentences in the chart.

Incorrect—Two "No Words"	Correct—Only One "No Word"
There aren't no apples.	There aren't any apples. There are no apples.
There wasn't no milk.	There wasn't any milk. There was no milk.
Jim hasn't no food.	Jim hasn't any food. Jim has no food.

- What two "no words" are in each sentence on the left?
- Why are these sentences incorrect?
- How have the sentences on the right been corrected?

Use the word *no* when there is no contraction formed from a verb and *not*. Many times the word *any* can be used with a contraction instead of the word *no*.

Working It Through

A. Choose the correct word in parentheses. Write the sentence.

1. There was (any, no) pen on the desk.
2. There wasn't (any, no) pencil either.
3. There are (any, no) sheets of paper in the drawer.
4. There aren't (any, no) stamps.
5. Carla has (any, no) envelopes.
6. There is (any, no) store nearby.
7. Carla hasn't (any, no) news to tell her friend.
8. There isn't (any, no) way she can write a letter now.

B. There are 6 sentences in which *no* is used incorrectly. Find and correct the 6 sentences.

1. Mr. Green hasn't no squash in his garden.
2. There is no sign of Chico at the skating rink.
3. There wasn't no way for us to get home.
4. There aren't any people in the building.
5. There isn't no time for Sandra to take a nap before dinner.
6. There aren't no trains leaving town today.
7. There isn't no hockey game tomorrow.
8. David hasn't no book about snakes.

C. Write a sentence with each group of words.

1. wasn't any
2. are no
3. isn't any
4. hasn't any
5. was no
6. has no
7. is no
8. aren't any

Trying It Out

Look at the signs. Write a sentence telling about the letters or words that are missing from each sign. Use some of the groups of words in Part C of Working It Through.

Using Good and Well

The word *good* is used to describe nouns. The word *well* is used to describe verbs.

Thinking It Through

Notice the words *good* and *well* in the sentences.

       Verb Adverb
John ran *well* at the track meet.

       Adjective Noun
He beat the other *good* runners.

- Is *good* or *well* used with the verb ran?
- Which word is used with the noun runners?

The adverb *well* tells how John ran. The adjective *good* tells what kind of runners the others were. Notice the underlined words and the words *good* and *well* in these sentences.

    Carole jumped *well* at the meet.
    She had worn her old shoes for *good* luck.

- Are *good* and *well* used correctly in each sentence? Why or why not?

The word *good* is used to describe nouns. The word *well* is used to describe verbs.

Working It Through

A. Complete each sentence with *good* or *well*.
  1. Even if we have _____ weather, the trip will be long.
  2. The roads are not paved _____.
  3. The route is not marked _____.
  4. And _____ camels are hard to find.

B. Decide whether each underlined word is a noun or a verb. Then decide whether *good* or *well* fits in each sentence.

1. Catherine <u>writes</u> (good, well).
2. Betsy is a (good, well) <u>writer</u> too.
3. They have (good, well) <u>ideas</u> in their stories.
4. Catherine and Betsy both <u>draw</u> (good, well).

C. Write the sentences. In each sentence, underline *good* and the noun it modifies or *well* and the verb it modifies.

1. Christopher Columbus was a good sailor.
2. His brother, Bartholomew, sailed well too.
3. They planned well for their trip, but it took much longer than they thought it would.
4. They had good ships, but small ones compared to ships today.
5. Columbus was treated well when he returned to Spain after the discovery.

Trying It Out

Write a sentence for each noun and each verb listed below. Use either *good* or *well* in each sentence. The first two sentences are done for you.

Nouns	Verbs
singer	sings
baker	bakes
speaker	speaks
catcher	catches

I try to be a good singer.
Suzy always sings well.

Commas with Yes and No

The word *yes* or *no* at the beginning of an answer to a question is followed by a comma.

Thinking It Through

On the first day of school, Lucy had to fill out a form. Read the questions and answers below.

> **1.** Is this your first year at Elk School?
>
> *No, it is my second year.*
>
> **2.** Do you walk to school?
>
> *No, I ride the bus.*
>
> **3.** Do you bring your lunch to school?
>
> *Yes, I bring my lunch to school.*

- What is the first word of each answer Lucy wrote?
- What punctuation mark follows *yes* or *no*?

When *yes* or *no* is the first word of an answer, it is followed by a comma.

Working It Through

A. Write a complete sentence to answer each of these questions. Begin each sentence with either *yes* or *no*.

1. Did you have a nice weekend?
2. Can you wiggle your nose?
3. Will you take a vacation on the moon next summer?
4. Did you get to school on time today?
5. Is spinach your favorite vegetable?
6. Have you ever seen a rhinoceros stand on its head?
7. Do you like to play checkers?
8. Would you like to fly airplanes some day?

B. Ms. Felheim asked several pupils if they enjoyed their last vacation from school. Write the answers the children gave, adding the correct punctuation.

1. Yes I liked it very much.
2. No the weather was bad.
3. Yes but it wasn't long enough.
4. No I like school better.
5. Yes we went on a trip.
6. No my dog got sick.

C. Hal answered his mother's questions when he got home from the grocery store. Rewrite each sentence that is incorrect. Make the necessary corrections.

1. Yes, I went to the grocery store.
2. No I couldn't find everything you wanted.
3. Yes, the store had bananas.
4. No, I couldn't find any turnips.
5. No I didn't buy myself a treat.
6. Yes I did find a jar of pickles.
7. No, I didn't mean to drop the jar on the way home.

Do you have any bananas?

Trying It Out

Joel wanted to ask a sheep dog these questions. Pretend you are the sheep dog. Answer Joel's questions. Write complete sentences for all the questions. Begin your answers with either *yes* or *no*.

1. Do you like having the name Shag?
2. Can you see through the hair on your face?
3. Have you thought about getting a haircut?
4. Would you like to wear bows in your hair?
5. Do you like taking a bath?
6. Do you like children?
7. Do you have many brothers and sisters?

Review • Adverbs, Contractions, Commas

A. Copy each sentence. Circle the verb and underline the adverb. Write *when, where,* or *how* to show what the adverb tells about the verb.

1. She waited patiently for Jo.
2. I went yesterday.
3. The big tree fell heavily.
4. Pink flowers bloomed outside.
5. He soon returned with the box.
6. We all sleep downstairs.

B. Copy each sentence. Choose the correct word in parentheses to complete it. Write *adjective* or *adverb* above the word you choose.

1. She skates ____. (good, well)
2. Your shoes have a ____ shine. (good, well)
3. Sam ran ____ at the track meet. (good, well)
4. Dawn did a ____ job painting. (good, well)

C. Copy each sentence. Complete it with a contraction of the two words in parentheses.

1. Cecilia ____ ready to go to the game. (is not)
2. Amy ____ like rice. (does not)
3. Uncle Ed ____ go. (can not)
4. Dr. Polaski ____ be in today. (will not)

D. Copy each sentence. Put in commas correctly.

1. Yes   we went apple picking.
2. No   you can't paint today.
3. No   he isn't at home.
4. Yes   please bring sandwiches.

For extra practice turn to pages 342–344.

Take Another Look   Copy the sentence. Write **NM** above the noun marker, **A** above the adjective, and **N** above the noun.

　　The tall tree dwarfed everything below.

Did you write NM above *The*, A above *tall*, and N above *tree?*

For more practice turn to page 321 in the Handbook.

Evaluation • Adverbs, Contractions, Commas

A. Write the letter of the underlined word that is an adverb. Then write whether the adverb tells *when, where,* or *how.*

1. We are going soon.
   a   b   c   d

2. She spoke sharply to the dog.
   a   b   c   d e   f

3. He didn't go early.
   a   b   c   d

4. We played ping-pong inside.
   a   b   c   d

B. Write the letter of the response that gives the correct word for the blank in each sentence.

1. Emilio is a ____ artist.
   a. good   **b.** well

2. I don't feel ____.
   a. good   **b.** well

3. Judy can sing ____.
   a. good   **b.** well

4. You did a ____ report.
   a. good   **b.** well

5. Aunt June slept ____.
   a. good   **b.** well

6. That is a ____ umbrella.
   a. good   **b.** well

C. Write the letter of the response that is the same as the underlined contraction in each sentence.

1. I don't like rain.
   a. does not   **b.** do not

2. She hasn't been here today.
   a. has not   **b.** have not

3. They haven't seen Max.
   a. have not   **b.** has not

4. Marian can't come over.
   a. can not   **b.** could not

5. The boat won't float.
   a. was not   **b.** will not

6. Josie doesn't like to sing.
   a. do not   **b.** does not

7. The dog can't reach the cat.
   a. could not   **b.** can not

8. Ellen isn't here yet.
   a. is not   **b.** I will

D. Write the letter of the word that should be followed by a comma.

1. Yes you can go.
   a   b   c d

2. No my brother isn't home.
   a   b   c   d   e

3. No I can't find it.
   a   b c   d   e

4. Yes I can be there soon.
   a b   c   d   e   f

Spotlight • Activities to Choose

1. Make an encyclopedia. Collect the report you wrote in this unit, any other reports you've written, and your classmates' reports. Put the reports in alphabetical order by topic. Draw pictures on the pages to illustrate the entries. Put the pages in a folder. To help locate information, put guide words and page numbers on all the pages.

2. Make a contraction collage. Find contractions in advertisements from newspapers and magazines. Try to find as many of the eleven contractions you learned in Lesson 9 as possible. Paste the advertisements on paper or cardboard to make a collage. Underline the contractions. Put your collage on the wall or bulletin board as a reference for spelling and writing.

3. Write a mystery. Write a paragraph in which you describe some object or living thing, but don't tell what it is. Use at least five adverbs in your paragraph. Here is an example:

It gurgles softly and smells sweet. It sleeps soundly for many hours each day. It smiles often and claps its hands clumsily.

Then read your paragraph to classmates. See if they can guess what you've described.

4. Photograph an "interview." With a camera, take pictures of your classmates, two-at-a-time. If you do not have a camera, cut out from old magazines pictures of two people talking. Underneath the pictures, write the questions and answers of an interview. Have some questions that require *yes* and *no* answers, along with explanations. For example,

Q: Do you like hats?
A: No, I think they taste terrible.

Find a place to display your interview.

What Is That Alligator Saying? A Beginning Book on Animal Communication
by Ruth Belov Gross

How does an alligator communicate with another alligator? This book explains how many kinds of animals can communicate through sight, sound, smell, and touch. The information may be hard to believe, but it's all true.

Paper Science
by Harry Milgrom

Did you know that you can perform experiments with paper? This book has step-by-step instructions on how you can use paper to clean muddy water and detect air currents. You can make things with paper— a helicopter, for example. Cartoon pictures and some paper games are also included in the book.

The Spider, the Cave, and the Pottery Bowl
by Eleanor Clymer

Each summer Kate stays with her grandmother in a village. This summer her grandmother is unhappy because there is no clay for the pottery. Kate makes a discovery that helps her grandmother. Kate's family and friends keep the fine ways of the Native American past as they live in the present.

Unit Seven

Have you ever heard your echo? How did it sound?

Echo

Hello!
 hello!

Are you near?
 near, near.

Or far from here?
 far, far from here.

Are you there?
 there, there

Or coming this way,
Haunting my words
Whatever I say?

Halloo!
 halloooo

Listen, you.
Who are you, anyway?
 who, who, whoooo?

Sara Asheron

Listening to your echo can be like having a dialogue, or
conversation, with yourself. In this unit, you will find out about
dialogues in plays. You will also learn how to put on a play.

Lesson 1 **Learning About Plays**

Every play begins with a list of characters and a description of the opening scene. A play also has stage directions, and gives words for the characters to speak.

Thinking It Through

The **characters** are the people in a play. The **scene** tells you where the play takes place. The characters and the scene are usually listed at the beginning of a play. The **stage directions** are instructions. They tell the characters how to speak or move. The **dialogue** is what the characters say to each other.

Read the following play. Notice the characters, the scene, the stage directions, and the dialogue.

Operation Satellite
by Bernice Wells Carlson

Characters:

GRAND WIZARD	OLDROT
SLOWCUM	WITCHES AND WIZARDS
HATTRAP	

Scene: *Meeting place of witches and wizards.* GRAND WIZARD *stands behind a big black pot, placed center stage.* HATTRAP *sits on a carton to the right of the pot.* OLDROT *sits on a box to the left of the pot. Other witches and wizards are grouped around the* GRAND WIZARD.

GRAND WIZARD: Where is Slowcum? Every witch and every wizard is here except Slowcum.

HATTRAP: You need a strong chant to bring back Slowcum.

GRAND WIZARD: Why do we need a strong chant to bring back Slowcum?

HATTRAP: Because, sir, Slowcum has young ideas.

GRAND WIZARD: Young ideas? Whoever heard of a witch with young ideas? (*Other witches and wizards look at each other, shake heads, and say, "I don't know. Not me."*)

GRAND WIZARD: (*to* HATTRAP) Do you know what young idea Slowcum is trying?

HATTRAP: Yes, sir. Slowcum broke her broom.

GRAND WIZARD: I know, I know. She came to me—to me, the Grand Wizard—and asked, "What shall I do?"

HATTRAP: And you said?

GRAND WIZARD: I said, "Don't bother me. Go fly a kite!"

HATTRAP: Slowcum is doing what you told her to do.

GRAND WIZARD: Oh, no! Slowcum flying through the air on a kite? "Go fly a kite" is just an expression.

HATTRAP: To a witch, sir, flying a kite is a means of travel.

GRAND WIZARD: (*pacing floor, wringing hands*) Oh, no! Not Slowcum on a kite! Well, we'll just have to try and bring Slowcum back. Is everybody ready?

WITCHES AND WIZARDS: Hicketty, hicketty, hoecum!
Blicketty, blicketty, blocum!
Ziss-boom! Ziss-boom!
Come back, Slowcum!
(*Sounds of great storm offstage. In slides* SLOWCUM, *hat smashed in, clothes torn, dragging torn kite.*)

WITCHES AND WIZARDS: (*gathering around* SLOWCUM) Are you all right? What happened?

GRAND WIZARD: (*hands on hips, glowering at* SLOWCUM) All right, Slowcum, what happened?

SLOWCUM: (*meekly*) I took your suggestion, sir. I flew on a kite.

GRAND WIZARD: My suggestion? "Go fly a kite?" That's just an expression.

SLOWCUM: Yes, sir, I know; but it's a good suggestion, too. Flying on a kite was glorious, wonderful, until . . . .

GRAND WIZARD: Until what? I bet you got off course. Will you never learn to ride on course?

SLOWCUM: No, sir. I mean, yes, sir. This time I was on course, and so was a satellite. I bumped into a satellite.

GRAND WIZARD: *(alarmed)* A satellite! That's dangerous.

WITCHES AND WIZARDS: Yes, yes, yes.

GRAND WIZARD: What shall we do?

SLOWCUM: I know. As the mortals say, "If you can't fight 'em, join 'em."

GRAND WIZARD: What? Join the mortals?

SLOWCUM: No, join the satellites. Let's ride the satellites.

WITCHES AND WIZARDS: Yes! Yes! Ride the satellites.

GRAND WIZARD: *(raising hands)* Quiet! Let me think. Witches and wizards riding satellites. That's not customary.

OLDROT: No, sir. But it sounds like fun.

SLOWCUM: And I've thought of a new chant.
Away with brooms!
Away with kites!
Witches ride
The satellites! Zoom!

GRAND WIZARD: That's good. We'll do it. Ready?

WITCHES AND WIZARDS: Away with brooms!
Away with kites!
Witches ride
The satellites! Zoom!
(Witches and Wizards exit saying chant, "Away with brooms!" etc. in a snake chain.)

- Who are the characters in *Operation Satellite*?
- What is the scene?
- Where are the characters and the scene listed?
- Why is each character's dialogue easy to find?
- Find some stage directions that tell how a character speaks or moves.

When you read a play, pay attention to the characters, scene, stage directions, and dialogue.

Working It Through

A. Match column A with column B.

Column A

1. characters
2. scene
3. dialogue
4. stage directions

Column B

a. tells where the play is
b. are the people in the play
c. tells how to speak or move
d. is what the characters say to each other

B. Add to the scene for *Operation Satellite* in your own words. Think about the answers to these questions to help you.

1. What would witches and wizards be wearing?
2. Where would witches and wizards meet?
3. What time of day would it be?
4. What might be in the pot?

C. Describe the Grand Wizard and Slowcum. Think about the answers to these questions to help you.

1. Is the Grand Wizard grouchy? funny? angry? strict? friendly? old? young?
2. What do you think the Grand Wizard looks like?
3. Is Slowcum clever? timid? impolite? clumsy? imaginative?
4. What do you think Slowcum looks like?

Trying It Out

Read *Operation Satellite* aloud. With your classmates, choose four children to read the parts of the main characters in the play. Choose others to read the parts of the Witches and Wizards.

Writing Dialogue

The dialogue in a play is what the characters say to each other. Most of the story in a play is told by the dialogue.

Thinking It Through

Notice how the characters' words, or dialogue, get the story started in *The Mystery of the Haunted House*.

The Mystery of the Haunted House

Characters: RACHEL   VINCENT   TERRY   SAMUEL

Scene: *It is nighttime. An old and empty house is in the background. Two girls are standing close to each other, staring at the house. Two boys are swinging on a rusty gate, which makes a squeaking sound.*

RACHEL: *(to* TERRY*)* Do you believe in haunted houses and ghosts and all of that scary stuff?

TERRY: Not one bit!

VINCENT: *(coming over to where the girls are)* Well, I *do*. My cousin Freddie told me what happened to him one night.

SAMUEL: Baloney! He was just afraid and his mind played tricks on him. I don't believe in any ghost nonsense at all.

RACHEL: If that's true, then you won't mind a dare from me. I dare you to spend an hour in that house *(points to the old house)*. As a matter of fact, I double dare you!

- How many characters are in the play? Who are they?
- What is the scene?
- How does the dialogue get the story of the play started?

Two marks of punctuation are used very often in plays—a **colon** (:) and **parentheses** ( ).

- In the play on page 200, what punctuation separates the characters' names from their words?
- What punctuation marks go around the stage directions?

The dialogue is the most important part of the play. It tells the story. The stage directions help tell the story by explaining how the characters should speak or move. A colon often follows the name of the speaker. Parentheses often go around the stage directions.

Working It Through
A. Add colons and parentheses where they are needed.

PATTY   *pointing to the sign* Well, today is the Best Detective Agency's first day of business.

DAVID   I hope we get some work soon.

PATTY   *opening door* What's happened? This place is a mess!

DAVID   It looks as if someone doesn't want us in this business!

B. Give names to the two characters in each example. Write 2 or 3 sentences of dialogue for the examples.
   1. a boy taking his first airplane ride with his uncle
   2. two girls seeing smoke coming out of a house
   3. a boy and a girl caught in a sudden rainstorm
   4. a boy and a girl on the first flight to Venus

Trying It Out
Finish *The Mystery of the Haunted House*, begun on page 200. Tell what happens when the characters get inside the house. You can use only the characters listed, or add some new characters. Use correct punctuation. Make the dialogue tell most of the story.

Lesson 3   Improving Your Writing

Using correct play form will improve your writing.

Thinking It Through

Read the beginning of *An Empty Planet*. The proofreading marks tell you what changes have to be made.

Proofreader's Marks

≡	Make a capital letter.
⊙	Add a period.
ℓ	Take out.
∧	Put in one or more words.

An Empty Planet

Characters: SARAH   JOHN   MARIA

   Scene: *Dusty, red planet.* ∧*There is no sign of life*⊙ *Spaceship is in the background. (Three young people in spacesuits are looking around.)*

SARAH: *(softly)* I don't think anybody lives here ⊙

JOHN : ≡ no people and no plant life, either. Wow! ∧ We are totally alone.

MARIA: (*looking around*) We don't know that for sure ⊙ ℓ for certain. Come on. Let's do some exploring.

● What changes does the writer plan to make?

To improve your writing when you write a play, mark the changes you want to make. Then write a new copy of your play.

Working It Through

A. Rewrite *An Empty Planet*. Put in all the changes that were marked.

202

B. Find the 5 errors in the play. There are 2 capital letters,
1 period, 1 colon, and 1 word you should add.

The Class Quiz

Characters: ANNOUNCER

JOSH

STEVEN

Scene: *an educational quiz show. The two players have a tied*
score. The final question will determine the winner.

ANNOUNCER: I'm in the solar system   I'm the sixth largest planet.
I   the second closest to the sun. What is my name?

JOSH: mercury.

ANNOUNCER: Incorrect. If you can answer it Steven, you will be the
winner.

STEVEN   *(excitedly)* Venus.

ANNOUNCER: Congratulations to our winner, Steven!

Trying It Out

Use the proofreading marks on page 202 to improve the
play you wrote for Lesson 2. Then rewrite your play or
you could finish *An Empty Planet* and improve it by using
the proofreader's marks.

Planning a Play Performance

When you want to perform a play, plan where and when to perform it and who will act in it. You might also plan scenery, props, and sound effects.

Thinking It Through

Before you put on a play, you need to plan your performance. Answer these questions in a class discussion:
- Which play will be performed?
- When and where will the play be given?
- Who will be the performers?

When you have answered these questions, you can plan what you need to make your play more true to life. Keep these points in mind as you plan:

1. You can use **scenery,** such as painted sheets or paper or boxes, to make the stage look like a certain place. If your play takes place during a rainstorm, you might want to paint dark clouds for the scenery.

2. **Props** are objects used by the characters or put on the stage to make the play look real. If part of a play takes place in a rainstorm, the characters might need umbrellas and boots.

3. **Sound effects** are the sounds that make your play seem real, such as shaking marbles in a box to make a sound like thunder.

When you want to perform a play, begin by planning where and when the play will be performed and who will act in it. You might also plan the scenery, props, and sound effects.

Divide your class into 4 groups. Choose a team captain to
be in charge of each group. Answer the questions listed for
your group.

Acting Group
1. Who will be each character in
   the play or plays?
2. When will they practice their
   parts?
3. Where will they practice?
4. Who will make copies of the
   play for each performer?

Props Group
1. What props do you need?
2. Where can you get them?
3. Who will get each prop?
4. Are there any other props that
   would be nice to have and easy
   to get?

Scenery Group
1. What scenery is necessary?
2. How will it be made?
3. Who will make it?
4. Is there any other scenery that
   would be nice to have and easy
   to make?
5. Who will make that?

Sound Effects Group
1. Are there any sound effects that
   would add to the play?
2. How can the noises be made?
3. Who will be responsible for
   making each sound effect at the
   right time?

Trying It Out
A. Bring the groups together. The
team captain of each group should
report what the group decided. Make
sure all of the plans go together.

B. Carry out the plans you
decided on.

Writing an Invitation

An invitation should include information about the place, date, and time of the event.

Thinking It Through

You might want to invite another class to see your play. Read this invitation, and answer the questions in the checklist.

date ——

greeting ——

body ——

closing ——

signature ——

January 19, 19 _ _

Dear Ms. Murray and class,

We would like to invite you to see our play, "The Mystery of the Haunted House." Could you join us in our classroom on Friday, January 21, at 10:30?

We are excited about our play. We hope you can come.

Sincerely,

Mr. Thomas and class

- Date: What goes in the upper right-hand corner of an invitation? What three parts does a date include? What punctuation separates the day from the year?
- Greeting: Which words are capitalized? What punctuation comes after the greeting?
- Body: Does the invitation include the place, date, and time of the event? Where is a colon used?
- Closing: What kind of letter does the closing begin with? What punctuation comes after the closing?
- Signature: Which word or words in the signature are capitalized? Why?

Working It Through

A. Read the invitation Karen sent her cousin, Julie. Use the checklist on page 206 to find what is wrong with Karen's invitation.

> October
>
> Dear Julie,
>   I am having a birthday party sometime soon. Everyone is coming, I hope! Will you be able to come? Let me know if you can.
>
>   Love,
>   Karen

B. Rewrite the invitation. Make the corrections.

C. Write an invitation asking your family to come to your class open house. Use this information.

    date of the invitation: January 21, 19___
    place of the open house: your school
    date of the open house: February 16, 19___
    time of the open house: 6:30 p.m.

Use the checklist on page 206 to help you write the invitation.

Trying It Out

Write an invitation to another class in your school. Invite the teacher and class members to see a performance of your play. Use the checklist in Thinking It Through to proofread your invitation.

Writing Direct Quotations

A direct quotation is the exact words spoken by a person. Punctuation is used to separate a quotation from the rest of the sentence.

Thinking It Through

The exact words a person says are called **direct quotations.** Quotation marks (" ") show where the exact words begin and end. Other punctuation separates a quotation from the rest of the sentence. Read these rules.

When the speaker's name comes before the quotation, use a comma. When the speaker's name follows the quotation, use
—a comma for a statement
—a question mark for a question
—an exclamation mark for an exclamation.

<u>Al said,</u> "I liked the play."

"I took pictures," <u>added Ed.</u>
"How many pictures?" <u>asked Ann.</u>

"I have twenty!" <u>Ed remarked.</u>

Read what Chiyo and her friends said about their play.
Chiyo said, "I think the scenery looked good."
"How do you think the thunder sounded?" asked Karl.
"I think it sounded like a dog barking!" replied Carla.
"I liked the thunder," declared Tom.

- In which sentence is the speaker's name before the quotation? What punctuation is used? Where is it put?
- In which sentences do the speakers' names follow the quotations? What punctuation is used? Where is it put?

A direct quotation is written with quotation marks. A comma, a question mark, or an exclamation mark can be used to separate the quotation from the rest of the sentence. Punctuation at the end of a direct quotation comes before the last quotation mark.

A. Copy the sentences. Underline the direct quotations. Circle the quotation marks.

   1. The magician said, "I can saw a woman in half."
   2. "Is it difficult?" asked Sam.
   3. "No, I learned it as a child," said the magician.
   4. Sam inquired, "Are there any more children at your home?"
   5. "I have several half-sisters," stated the magician.

B. Rewrite the sentences. Add the missing punctuation.

   1. I love geography,   said Carlos.
   2. "I like history better " said Cleo.
   3. Ted said "Art is my favorite subject.
   4. Do you like English   asked Laura.

C. Make each sentence a direct quotation. Add a speaker and the correct punctuation.

   1. Did you like the movie?   **3.** I liked the music.
   2. I thought it was dull.   **4.** I never want to see another movie!

Trying It Out

The animals in the picture are talking about the new road being built through their marsh. Write the conversation they are having. Use each group of words below as part of a sentence.

   growled the giant green frog
   cried the tiny tadpole
   said the good-natured squirrel
   stated the grouchy brown toad

Use quotation marks and correct punctuation in each sentence.

Review • Writing Dialogue

A. Read this part of a play. Notice how the dialogue gets the story started.

The Biggest Strawberry in the World

characters: KIM GREGORY
ANNETTE CARLOS

scene: *A yard with a garden and fence. Two girls are walking by the garden. Two boys are hiding behind the fence.*

KIM: *(picking up some dirt)* This dirt feels like any other dirty dirt. How can you grow huge strawberries?

ANNETTE: *(holding a bottle)* The secret is in here! Think what vitamins can do for strawberries!

KIM: *(jumping)* So all we have to do is plant vitamin pills?

ANNETTE: No! *(whispering in Kim's ear)* Here's what we do.

GREGORY: *(looking at Carlos)* What are they doing?

CARLOS: *(peaking over fence)* Something strange! Do you think we could find out?

1. How many characters are in the play? Who are they?
2. What is the scene?
3. How does the dialogue get the story started?
4. What punctuation separates the characters' names from their words?
5. What punctuation marks go around the stage directions?

B. Add at least one example of dialogue for each character. Include some stage directions. Be sure to put colons and parentheses where they are needed.

C. Answer these questions.
1. Did your dialogue tell a little more about the story?
2. Did you use colons and parentheses correctly?

Evaluation • Writing Dialogue

A. Improve the following play. Add stage directions where they are needed. Finish Carol's sentence. Put colons after the characters' names and parentheses around the stage directions.

The Float

characters: SUSAN   RANDY

MIKE   CAROL

scene: *It is a Saturday afternoon. The children are in a basement trying to decide on a float to make. Newspapers, paste, paint, and chicken wire are on a table.*

SUSAN   *(shrugging her shoulders)* We can't just make an ordinary float. We'll never win the contest.

MIKE   Here's the wire. We better get started on something. The parade is next week.

RANDY: A float is a float! *sitting down* I can't think of any new ideas.

CAROL: I can! We'll make a big brown-and-white float with a huge straw. We'll _____

_____.

B. Think about what could happen next in the above play. Write at least two examples of dialogue for each character. Add stage directions.

You will be evaluated on your dialogue, your stage directions, and on the following:

   colons after the characters' names

   parentheses around the stage directions

Spotlight • Language Changes

Languages are always changing. A language keeps growing with new words as long as people speak it.

The English language has changed since William Shakespeare's time. Shakespeare was a famous writer of plays, who lived in England about three hundred years ago. Below are some lines from a play he wrote. Read them and see how well you can understand them.

LUCIUS: Sir, 'tis your brother Cassius at the door, who doth desire to see you.

BRUTUS: Is he alone?

LUCIUS: No, sir. There are moe with him.

BRUTUS: Do you know them?

LUCIUS: No, sir. Their hats are pluck'd about their ears, and half their faces buried in their cloaks, that by no means I may discover them by any mark of favour.

The same lines in modern English might read this way:

LUCIUS: Sir, your brother Cassius is at the door, and he wants to see you.

BRUTUS: Is he alone?

LUCIUS: No, sir. There are other people with him.

BRUTUS: Do you know them?

LUCIUS: No, sir. Their hats are pulled down, and they've hidden their faces in their coat collars. I can't tell who they are.

Spotlight • Stage Talk

Knowing the parts of a stage can help you read and act out plays. How many stage words do you know? How many can you learn from the picture?

Suppose you are in the audience. You may wonder why *Stage Left* is on your right side, and *Stage Right* is on your left side. Also, *Downstage* is closer to you than *Upstage*. It is because the parts of the stage are named from the players' way of looking at the stage.

Pretend you are a director sitting in the audience. The empress is standing at Stage Left. You direct her to go to her throne. What part of the stage would she go to?

213

Pronouns in the Subject

Pronouns take the place of nouns. The pronouns *I*, *you*, *he*, *she*, *it*, *we*, and *they* are used in the subject part of the sentence.

Thinking It Through

A **pronoun** is a word used in place of a noun. Notice the underlined nouns and pronouns in the paragraphs below.

Al put on a wig. The wig was red. Al looked funny. Sue found a wand. Sue waved it.

Al said, "Sue should buy the wand."

Al and Sue found more wigs.

Sue said, "Al and Sue like the wigs. Sue and Al will get the wand and the wigs."

Al put on a wig. It was red. He looked funny. Sue found a wand. She waved it.

Al said, "You should buy the wand."

They found more wigs.

Sue said, "Al and I like the wigs. We will get the wand and the wigs."

- What are the underlined nouns in the first paragraph?
- What are the underlined pronouns in the second paragraph?

The pronouns *I, you, he, she, it, we,* and *they* are used in place of nouns in the subject part of sentences. When you name other people along with yourself in the subject, be sure to write about them first: *Sue and I.*

Pronouns in the Subject
I
you
he
she
it
we
they

Working It Through

A. Read the sentences. Use a pronoun in place of the underlined word or words. Use the chart to help you.

1. Rachel came to the party. Rachel dressed as a pirate.

2. David came as a clown. David wore big shoes.

3. Brad and I came as carrots. <u>Brad and I</u> won the prize.

4. Mickey and Lela brought games. <u>Mickey and Lela</u> shared the games.

5. The party was fun. <u>The party</u> was over too soon.

B. Choose the correct pronoun in parentheses for each underlined subject. Write the sentences.

  1. Dana said, "Bill and <u>Dana</u> are having a treasure hunt."   (I, it)

  2. She told Mark, "<u>Mark</u> should come."   (You, I)

  3. <u>Bill and I</u> invited ten people.   (They, We)

  4. <u>The treasure hunt</u> will be exciting.   (It, She)

C. Complete each sentence by choosing the correct subject.

  1. (My parents and I, I and my parents) went to Mexico.

  2. (I and Dad, Dad and I) wore sombreros to protect us from the hot sun.

  3. (I and Mom, Mom and I) took pictures of an ancient volcano near Mexico City.

  4. (Dad and I, I and Dad) visited a marketplace.

Trying It Out

Read all the directions before starting the activity.

  1. Look at the Pronoun Pyramid at the right.

  2. Starting with the number 1, find a sentence below that has the same pronoun in the subject.

> Joe, Judy, and <u>I</u> were swallowed by a giraffe.
> They were both angry.
> It laughed us right out of its stomach.
> She was surprised.
> You should never get too close to a hungry giraffe!
> He was frightened.
> We tickled the giraffe's stomach with a feather.

Pronoun Pyramid

1. I

2. He   3. She

4. They   5. We

6. It   7. You

  3. Write the sentence.

  4. If you write the sentences in order, you will have a story.

215

Pronouns After Action Verbs

The pronouns *me, you, him, her, it, us,* and *them* follow action verbs.

Thinking It Through

The pronouns *me, you, him, her, it, us,* and *them* follow action verbs. Notice the underlined pronouns in these sentences.

> Uncle Dan baked two loaves of bread. He baked them today. Joan and I helped him. He told us what to do. He let me take the bread out of the oven. After one loaf cooled, Joan sliced it. I watched her. Uncle Dan said, "Soon I will teach you how to bake pies."

- What kind of verb comes before each pronoun? What are they?
- What pronouns follow the action verbs?

Use the pronouns *me, you, him, her, it, us,* and *them* after action verbs.

Working It Through

A. Replace the underlined word or words in each sentence with the correct pronoun. Use the chart to help you.

1. Sam got some books about horses from Grandfather, and he read <u>the books</u> for hours.
2. Sam saw <u>Grandfather</u> yesterday.
3. Sam said, "Thank <u>Grandfather</u>!"
4. Grandfather also gave a book to Mom, and she read <u>the book</u>.
5. Grandfather said, "Get in the car. I want to surprise <u>Mom and Sam</u>."
6. He took <u>Mom and me</u> to a horse show.
7. Afterwards, he said, "Call <u>Grandfather</u> tomorrow."

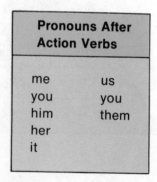

Pronouns After Action Verbs	
me	us
you	you
him	them
her	
it	

B. Complete each sentence by choosing the correct pronoun that follows an action verb. Write the sentences. Underline the action verbs.

1. Harriet called (I, me) yesterday.
2. I helped (her, she) make some kites.
3. Dad saw (they, them) after we had finished.
4. We told (him, he) how we learned to make kites in school.
5. Dad praised (we, us) for our fine work.

C. Use both of the words in parentheses to complete each sentence. Be sure you use the correct pronoun in the subject and after the action verb.

1. ____ is my friend, and I like ____. (he, him)
2. ____ came over, and I helped ____ make cookies. (her, she)
3. ____ hid from us, but we found ____. (them, they)
4. ____ raced to the pool, but Juan beat ____. (we, us)
5. ____ went to the store for Mr. Tate, and he thanked ____. (me, I)

Trying It Out
Write sentences about what is happening in the picture. Use the pronouns below in your sentences. Underline each pronoun. For example: The girl is chasing <u>him</u>.

me	him	it	them
you	her	us	

Take Another Look Did you remember to use the pronouns *me, you, him, her, it, us,* and *them* after the action verbs in your sentences?

Pronouns Ending in Self and Selves

Pronouns ending in -*self* refer to one person. Pronouns ending in -*selves* refer to more than one person.

Thinking It Through

Look at the pronouns in the chart.

Singular Pronouns Ending in -*self*	Plural Pronouns Ending in -*selves*
I saw *myself.* *You* saw *yourself.* *He* saw *himself.* *She* saw *herself.* *It* saw *itself.*	*We* saw *ourselves.* *You* saw *yourselves.* *They* saw *themselves.*

- Which pronouns end in -*self?* Are they singular or plural?
- Which pronouns end in -*selves?* Are they singular or plural?
- *Myself* refers to the subject pronoun *I.* How are the other pronouns matched?

A pronoun that ends in -*self* refers to one person and is singular. A pronoun that ends in -*selves* refers to more than one person and is plural.

Remember to use *himself* instead of *hisself, ourselves* instead of *ourself,* and *themselves* instead of *themself.*

Working It Through

A. Choose the correct pronoun ending in -*self* for each sentence. Use the underlined subject to help you.

1. <u>I</u> want to learn to roller skate by ____. (myself, itself)
2. Don't you remember when <u>you</u> learned by ____? (yourself, myself)

3. She taught ____ in a week.   (herself, myself)

4. He taught ____ yesterday.   (itself, himself)

5. Once my skate rolled across the rink by ____.
(herself, itself)

6. I laughed at ____ when I saw my skate.   (himself, myself)

B. Complete each sentence with a pronoun ending in *-selves*. Write the sentences.

1. They can wash their clothes by ____.

2. We clean our rooms ____.

3. You do chores for ____ also.

4. We remind ____ to help at home.

C. Find the incorrect forms of the pronouns ending in *-self* or *-selves*. Write the sentences.

1. He has not felt like hisself lately.

2. We want to rake the leaves by ourself.

3. They want to make dinner by themself.

4. He likes to do everything hisself.

5. We built the sand castle ourself.

6. They can take care of themself.

Trying It Out

Write about your favorite make-believe characters. Tell what makes each one special. Use at least 5 pronouns ending in *-self* or *-selves*. For example:

Superseal can leap over icebergs by itself.

Sentences That Command or Request

Some sentences make commands or requests. Their subjects are understood. The end punctuation may be a period or an exclamation mark.

Thinking It Through

Have you ever been asked or ordered to do these things?

Wake up!

Brush your teeth.

Feed your alligator!

Please get on the bus.

Do pages 1–1,000!

Finish your work.

Hop on your magic carpet.

Hurry home!

You is the subject of the sentence *Wake up! (You wake up!)* The word *you* is not written, but the listener understands that he or she is the one being spoken to.
- What is the understood subject of the other sentences?
- What two kinds of punctuation do you find at the end of these sentences?

Sentences like these are called **commands** or **requests.** A command or request has an understood subject—*you.* The end punctuation may be a period or exclamation mark, depending on how the sentence is said. If the sentence is said with strong feeling, use an exclamation mark.

Working It Through

A. Write a command or request sentence for each situation below.
  1. Tell your aunt to open her birthday present.
  2. Tell your classmate to give you a pencil.

3. Tell your younger brother to leave your basketball alone.
4. Tell your dog to get the newspaper.
5. Tell your younger sister to make her bed.
6. Tell your friend to play a game with you.
7. Tell your brother to open the door.
8. Tell your friend to walk to the park with you.

B. Tell which sentence in each pair is a command or request.

1. Did you comb your hair? Comb your hair!
2. Mow the lawn. Have you mowed the lawn?
3. The phone is ringing. Answer the phone!
4. I like broccoli. Please eat some broccoli.

C. Find the command or request sentences below.

1. Will you go to the hobby show with me?
2. I like pickles.
3. Climb down the ladder.
4. Did you run all the way?
5. Wait for me!
6. Please let the cat out.
7. The plane flew out of sight.
8. Put your shoes on!

Trying It Out
Read all the directions before starting the activity.

1. Pretend you are a famous cook.
2. Tell how to make a special sandwich.
3. Write at least 6 command or request sentences that tell how to make the sandwich.

Nouns of Address

> When you speak to a person and use the person's name, the name is called a noun of address. A noun of address is separated from the rest of the sentence by a comma.

Thinking It Through

Read the little play about Nettie's visit to the doctor.

To Play the Piano

Characters: DOCTOR   NETTIE

Scene: *Doctor's office.* (DOCTOR *is seated.* NETTIE *is standing with a big bandage around one hand.*)

DOCTOR: There you are, <u>Nettie</u>. Keep the bandage on your hand. Don't worry, the cut will heal.

NETTIE: <u>Doctor</u>, I've been wondering.

DOCTOR: About what, Nettie?

NETTIE: When my hand gets well, will I be able to play the piano?

DOCTOR: Of course, you can play the piano, Nettie.

NETTIE: That's good news! I couldn't play the piano before I cut my hand!

- In the first line of the dialogue, what person's name does the doctor say because he is speaking to her?
- How is Nettie's name separated from the rest of the sentence?
- How does Nettie address the doctor?
- How is *doctor* separated from the rest of the sentence?
- Can you find other examples of nouns of address in the dialogue? Where are they?

When you speak to a person and use the person's name, the name is called a **noun of address.** A noun of address is separated from the rest of the sentence by a comma.

Working It Through

A. Use either *Judy* or *Joe* as the noun of address in each sentence. Write the sentences.

1. ____, where is the globe?
2. The globe is on the table, ____.
3. ____, I can't find the Hawaiian Islands.
4. Look in the Atlantic Ocean, ____.
5. Here they are! ____, the Hawaiian Islands are in the Pacific Ocean.

B. Find 3 sentences in which the nouns of address are not written correctly. Rewrite the sentences.

1. Please be quiet Tom.
2. Kim, bring me the glasses.
3. Where is the milk Henry?
4. Caroline pour the milk for me.
5. Susan, we need another fork.

C. Write the sentences. Underline the nouns of address and the commas used with them.

1. I'll see you later, Sally.
2. Whatever you say, Jeff.
3. Rover, get down!
4. I can't hear you, Mr. Thomas.
5. Mother, will you help me?

Trying It Out

Pretend you are putting on a play in your backyard. Write the sentences you could say to your friends. Use at least 6 nouns of address in your sentences, such as *Janice, tie the rope to the tree.*

Take Another Look Did you set off each noun of address with a comma?

Contractions

Some contractions are made from pronouns and verbs.

Thinking It Through

A pronoun and verb can be put together to form a contraction. The chart below shows how some of the contractions are made.

Pronoun + verb *will*	Pronoun + verb *is*	Pronoun + verb *are*
I + will = I'll	she + is = she's	you + are = you're
we + will = we'll	he + is = he's	they + are = they're
they + will = they'll		we + are = we're

- What letters does the apostrophe stand for when you make a contraction with a pronoun and *will?*
- What letter does the apostrophe stand for when you make a contraction with a pronoun and *is?*
- What letter does the apostrophe stand for when you make a contraction with a pronoun and *are?*

When you write a contraction made from a pronoun and a verb, you will always need to use an apostrophe to show where a letter or letters were left out.

Working It Through

A. Match each contraction on the left with the words that make up the contraction. Write both forms.

1. she's		I will
2. they're		he is
3. we'll		we are
4. he's		she is
5. I'll		they will
6. we're		they are
7. you're		you are
8. they'll		we will

B. Write the contraction that the underlined words in each sentence would make.

1. <u>You are</u> getting ready for the bike trip, aren't you?
2. We need to clean the bikes because <u>they are</u> dusty.
3. <u>We are</u> also going to pack some food.
4. Remember to keep the backpacks light so <u>they will</u> be easy to carry.
5. <u>I will</u> draw a map of our route.
6. <u>We will</u> leave about 9:00 in the morning.
7. Ask your brother to be ready, so <u>he is</u> on time.
8. Aunt Peg will be happy to see us because <u>she is</u> always glad when we visit her.

C. Choose the correct contraction for each sentence. Write the sentences.

1. (We'll, She's) turn our bunk beds into a fort.
2. (We'll, We're) good at building bunk bed forts.
3. (I'll, They're) easy to make.
4. (I'll, He's) get some blankets from the closet.
5. My sister can hang them from the top bunk because (we're, she's) taller than I am.
6. The blankets will be walls and (you're, they'll) hang all around the lower bunk.
7. Our dad is coming home, and (they're, he's) bringing a flashlight.
8. There are many ways to make forts, if (we'll, you're) interested.

Trying It Out

Read the contractions listed below. Use each one in a song title. You can use the name of a song you've heard or one you make up, such as "*We're* Two Lonely Salamanders Stranded on a Lily Pad."

I'll	they'll	he's	they're
we'll	she's	you're	we're

Review • Pronouns and Punctuation

A. Copy the sentences. Underline each pronoun. You should find 13 pronouns.

1. She told me about Texas.
2. Does Sam want him to come here?
3. He helped her make it for us.
4. Rodolfo and I told them a story.
5. We will bring some milk for you.
6. They measured the flour and gave it to the cook.

B. Copy each sentence. Underline the action verb. Complete the sentence with a pronoun in place of the words in parentheses.

1. Alfredo always wears ____. (a hat)
2. Ester dressed ____. (a baby girl)
3. Tatsuo watched ____. (two lions)
4. The dog barked at ____. (you and me)
5. The speaker praised ____. (a man)

C. Decide if each statement is a question or a command or request. Add correct ending marks to each.

1. Is the store open
2. Don't run
3. Hurry back
4. Please be careful
5. Don't talk to strangers
6. Did you put the food away

D. Copy the sentences. Put in commas where needed.

1. Can I see you   Sam?
2. Tuffy   get off the sofa!
3. How do you use this tool   Dad?
4. Nikki   you really run fast!

For extra practice turn to pages 336–338 and 343.

Take Another Look   Copy the sentence. Complete it with a contraction of the two words in parentheses.

They ____ think it will rain today.   (do not)

Did you use *don't*?

For more practice turn to pages 328–329.

Evaluation • Pronouns and Punctuation

A. Write the letter of the response that gives the correct
pronoun for each blank.

1. Ed raced ____ to school.
   a. her   **b.** she
2. I gave ____ the gift.
   a. he   **b.** him
3. She told ____ a joke.
   a. us   **b.** we
4. Mom told ____ to study.
   a. I   **b.** me
5. Get my hat and put ____ away.
   a. we   **b.** it
6. We want ____ with us.
   a. they   **b.** you
7. Ella saw ____ at the show.
   a. them   **b.** they

8. ____ love the beach.
   a. I   **b.** Me
9. ____ are good friends.
   a. Them   **b.** They
10. ____ is a fast reader.
    a. She   **b.** Her
11. ____ drank all the milk.
    a. You   **b.** Him
12. ____ went to Alabama.
    a. Him   **b.** He
13. ____ saw a butterfly.
    a. We   **b.** Us
14. ____ is cold today.
    a. Her   **b.** It

B. Write the letter of the response that tells what kind of
sentence each statement is.

1. Where are you?
   a. command or request   **b.** question
2. Hurry up!
   a. command or request   **b.** statement
3. I want to play the piano.
   a. command or request   **b.** statement

4. Please come inside.
   a. command or request   **b.** statement
5. Don't run.
   a. command or request   **b.** question
6. Dorsey is so happy!
   a. command or request   **b.** exclamation

C. Write the letter of each word that should be followed
by a comma.

1. Betty will you call me?
     a   b   c   d   e
2. Let's go to the store Mom.
     a b c d   e   f

3. How do you bake a cake Sue?
     a   b c   d   e   f   g
4. Sandra you wrote a good story.
     a   b   c d   e   f

Spotlight • Activities to Choose

1. Change a fairy tale. Write a new ending for a fairy tale you learned when you were younger. You could have the story of the three bears take place in your city. Write the new ending in the form of a play. List the characters, tell the scene, give stage directions, and write the dialogue. Make sure the dialogue you write tells the story.

2. Make a play poster. Draw a poster to advertise the fairy tale you wrote or the play you completed in Lesson 2 or 3. Make sure the poster gives the date, time, and place where your play will be performed. Display your poster where other people in your school will notice it.

3. Play circle of commands. Form a group with three of your classmates. Start the game by giving a command like this one: "Sit down, Francine." Your command must include a noun of address. The person you addressed follows your command, repeats it out loud, and adds another command. For example: "Sit down and put your hand on your head, Bill."

Players lose if they don't give a noun of address, don't follow the commands, or forget part of the commands. Continue the circle until only one player—the winner—remains.

4. Make a chain of pronouns. Draw some people who are all telling a secret. Then write under each picture who told the secret to whom. Use these subject pronouns: *I, you, he, she, it, we,* and *they.* Use these pronouns after action verbs: *me, you, him, her, it, us,* and *them.* Here is the beginning of the chain:

228

Will You Sign Here, John Hancock?
by Jean Fritz

You know John Hancock as the first person to sign the Declaration of Independence. But why was his signature so large? You can learn the answer when you read about John Hancock's life. You'll feel as if you know this famous early American.

Fun Time Plays and Special Effects
by Cameron Yerian and Margaret Yerian

Do you want to write a play? What a great idea! Will you make your own scenery, props, and stage and sound effects? This book is loaded with great ideas and activities to help you put on your own play. There is also a play that you can use in the book.

Best Wishes, Amen: A New Collection of Autograph Verses
by Lillian Morrison

Did you ever wish for a new and clever saying to write in a friend's autograph book? This book has over 300 autograph verses you can use to amuse your friends. Part of the book has a collection of autograph verses in Spanish with English translations.

Unit Eight

Have you ever had trouble using the telephone? Read about an elephant's problems with a telephone.

Eletelephony

Once there was an elephant,
Who tried to use the telephant—
No! no! I mean an elephone
Who tried to use the telephone—
(Dear me! I am not certain quite
That even now I've got it right.)

Howe'er it was, he got his trunk
Entangled in the telephunk;
The more he tried to get it free,
The louder buzzed the telephee—
(I fear I'd better drop the song
Of elephop and telephong!)

Laura E. Richards

In this unit, you'll learn about many things in everyday life, like reading a newspaper index, using the Yellow Pages, and reporting an emergency on the telephone.

Lesson 1   **Using a Newspaper Index**

An index helps you find information in a newspaper quickly.

Thinking It Through

A newspaper gives information about business, sports, and many other subjects. The information is given in the different parts, or sections, of the newspaper.

A newspaper index tells you which section and page have the information you want. The index is usually on the first or second page of the newspaper. The subjects in the index are listed in alphabetical order.

Index	Section	Page
Business	3	2
Classified Ads	4	6-15
Comics	2	15-16
Farm News	3	5-6
Movies	2	13-14
Senior Citizen News ...	1	7-8
Sports	4	1-3
TV and Radio	2	13
Weather	1	9

- Why are *Movies* listed after *Business* in the index?
- In which section will you find the farm news?
- In which section and on which pages will you find sports articles?

Nikki Johnson wanted to buy a puppy. She looked in the newspaper index for the classified ads. The **classified ads** list things people want to buy and sell. They also list jobs for people.

- In which section of the newspaper would Nikki find the classified ads? on which pages?

An index shows where to find different kinds of news in a newspaper. Newspaper indexes list subjects in alphabetical order and give the sections and pages. The index usually comes at the beginning of a newspaper.

Working It Through

A. Use the index on page 232 to answer the questions.

1. Which would come first in a newspaper index, comics or classified ads? Why?
2. In which section and on which page would you find information about the weather?
3. In which section and on which page would you find business information?
4. Which section are the comics in? How many pages of comics are there? What are the page numbers?

B. Answer the questions. Use the index on page 232 to help you.

1. Louise's grandmother graduated from college when she was 75 years old. The newspaper wrote a story about her. Where would you find the story?
2. Ken grew the tallest corn in the county on his farm. Where can you read about it?
3. Barry wanted to buy a used bicycle. Where would he look to find used bicycles for sale?
4. Gail wanted to find a part-time job. Where would she find a list of jobs that are available?

Trying It Out

Look at the index from a newspaper in your own city. Write down the section and page number or numbers where you could find the following information.

1. Classified Ads
2. Weather
3. Comics
4. TV and radio listings
5. Movies
6. Sports

Filling in an Application Form

When you fill in an application form, be sure that your information is correct and complete and that your handwriting is clear.

Thinking It Through

Nikki found a puppy by reading the classified ads. Then she had to fill in a form to get a license for her puppy.

CITY OF TOMÁS, TEXAS   19--
DOG LICENSE APPLICATION

Date _March 10_____, 19--

NAME _Nikki Johnson_

ADDRESS _616 Carmel Drive_____ _Tomás, Texas 79788_
     Number   Street   City   State   Zip
PHONE _729-3996_

BREED _Collie_   AGE _6 mo._   MALE ☒ FEMALE ☐

NAME _Bouncer_   COLOR _white and tan_

RABIES TAG 936	DATE	VACCINATED
CERT. NO.	VACCINATED	BY
1-267836	March 8, 19--	Edward Kelly, DVM

A RABIES CERTIFICATE OR A COPY MUST ACCOMPANY APPLICATION FEE $4.00

WRITTEN SIGNATURE OF OWNER _Nikki Johnson_

- Did Nikki fill in all of the information?
- Is all of the information in the right place?
- Is the writing easy to read?

An application form should be filled in carefully and accurately. The handwriting should be clear and easy to read.

A. Complete the sentences below with the information that Nikki used in her application form.

1. Nikki's last name is ____ .
2. Nikki's street is ____ .
3. Nikki's dog is a ____ .
4. Nikki's dog is named ____ .
5. Bouncer was vaccinated on ____ .
6. Bouncer was vaccinated by ____ .

B. Apply for a license for your bicycle. Make up any information that you do not know to fill in this form.

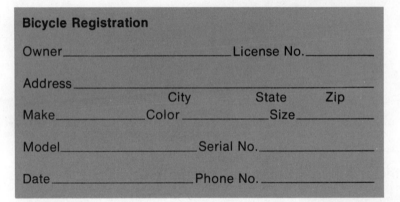

Bicycle Registration

Owner_____License No._____

Address_____
                    City   State   Zip
Make_____Color_____Size_____

Model_____Serial No._____

Date_____Phone No._____

Trying It Out

Carolyn Chen moved to Geneva, New York. Her new address is 423 Elmdale Road. Her phone number is 284-3995. Her mother, Mrs. Anna Chen, went with her to apply for a library card.

   Copy the form at the right. Correct any mistakes Carolyn may have made.

Library Card Application

Name _Carolyn Chen_____
                (print)
Address _423 Elmdale Rd. Geneva_
Home phone _484-3395_____
Parent or Guardian_____
Your signature _Carolyn Chen_____
                        (written)

Take Another Look   Did you put the information in the right places? Did you fill in every blank that you should? Is your writing clear?

Addressing an Envelope

When you address an envelope, be sure that your
information is correct and complete and that your
handwriting is clear.

Thinking It Through

Nikki addressed the envelope below so that she could mail
her application form for a dog license.

return
address

Nikki Johnson
616 Carmel Drive, Apt. 31
Tomás, Texas 79788

Dog License Bureau
930 San Pedro Street
Tomás, Texas 79788

mailing
address

- Which address is the return address? Which is the
  mailing address?
- What information did Nikki include in each address?
- What punctuation did she use?
- What might happen if Nikki didn't write clearly?

When you address an envelope, write the mailing
address in the middle of the envelope and the return
address in the upper left-hand corner. Be sure that the
information in both addresses is correct and easy to read.

Working It Through

A. Use the envelope on this page to help you complete the
sentences.

    1. The bureau Nikki addressed the envelope to is ____.

    2. The street address of the Dog License Bureau is ____.

3. The rest of the mailing address is ____.

4. Nikki's complete return address is ____.

5. Nikki used a period after ____.

6. In both addresses, Nikki used commas to separate ____.

B. Nikki soon received a dog license for her puppy in the mail. Fold a sheet of paper to the size of an envelope. Address the envelope to Nikki Johnson from the Dog License Bureau. Use the addresses on the envelope on page 236.

C. Kirsten sent a letter to his cousin Marian. When he addressed the envelope, he made 6 mistakes. Write the return address and the mailing address correctly. Make up the information that you do not know.

Kristen
865 Greenleaf Avenue
Rhode Island 03509

Marian Rowe
1234 Bumblebee Drive, Apt. 4C
Honey Farm

Trying It Out
Fold a sheet of paper to the size of an envelope. Address the envelope to your family. Put your school address on the envelope. Write a note to your family about what you are learning in school. Put it in the envelope. Give the envelope to your family.

Take Another Look Did you put each address in the right place? Did you remember the Zip Codes? Is all your information correct? Did you write clearly?

Using the Yellow Pages

The Yellow Pages is a telephone directory that lists entries by the type of business or service offered. The entries are in alphabetical order.

1620   Veterinarian–Violins

▶**Veterinarian**

BEST ANIMAL CLINIC
  Cohn, Jake, DVM
  Lowenski, Renee, DVM
  4204 W. Johnson Ave 665-4700
CAT CLINIC
  Sanchez, Manuel, DVM
  Practice Limited to Cats
  1009 E. Wood Rd 995-2345
CORTEZ, MARY, DVM
  981 E. Oak 343-7250
  Night Emergency Phone 343-8500
DOGWOOD ANIMAL HOSPITAL
  By Appointment Only
  Hours 9-5 Mon.-Fri.
  15870 W. Dogwood Ln 283-6740
KELLY, EDWARD, DVM
  Mobile Veterinary Clinic
  House Calls Only
  6338 S. 100th St 332-2323
MAPLE STREET ANIMAL HOSPITAL
  Hours 10-5 Mon.-Sat.
  No Appointment Necessary
  35 W. Maple St 853-0050

Thinking It Through

The **Yellow Pages** is a telephone directory that lists names of businesses and services in alphabetical order. The Yellow Pages can help you find information on such things as bicycle stores, camps, restaurants, and veterinarians.

When Bouncer needed to have shots, Nikki looked in the Yellow Pages to find the name of a veterinarian. The information at the left shows what Nikki found.

First she looked at the guide words to find the right page.

● What guide words helped Nikki?

Then Nikki looked at the entries until she came to **Veterinarian.** The list of veterinarians included the names of doctors, clinics, and hospitals. Nikki decided to call Dr. Kelly.

● What kind of clinic does Dr. Kelly have?
● What is the address of the clinic?
● What is the phone number?

The Yellow Pages has guide words and entries in alphabetical order. Entry names are followed by an address and phone number, and often other special information.

Working It Through

A. Use the information from the Yellow Pages on page 238 to answer these questions. Write complete sentences.

1. Which is listed first under Veterinarian—the Best Animal Clinic or the Cat Clinic? Why?
2. When is the Maple Street Animal Hospital open? What is the address? What is the phone number?
3. What special information is given under the Cat Clinic?
4. What two telephone numbers are listed for Dr. Cortez? When would you use each number?
5. How many veterinarians are at the Best Animal Clinic? Who are they?

B. Let the clues given below direct you to the correct entry name. Write the answers.

1. You want a doctor who treats only cats. What is the name of the doctor who treats only cats?
2. Your puppy is very sick during the night. Who has a night emergency phone number? What is it?
3. If you needed help fast, would you go to the Maple Street Animal Hospital or to the Dogwood Animal Hospital? Why?

Trying It Out

Make a Yellow Pages listing of your own for something you might want to phone, like *Hobby Shops*, *Costumes*, *Sleeping Bags*, or *Musical Instruments*. Make up a list of 5 places, addresses, and phone numbers. Add other information if you like. Arrange the entry names as they would appear in the Yellow Pages.

Learning About Emergency Numbers

It is important to know where to look for emergency numbers and to know which number to call.

Thinking It Through

In an emergency, it is important to find the right number quickly. You can usually find emergency numbers on the inside front cover or first page of a phone book. Look at the emergency numbers in Nikki's phone book.

EMERGENCY NUMBERS

FIRE
(also Ambulance) **911**

POLICE
(also Tornado) **911**

Dial the number **0** for **Operator** in any emergency.

Personal Emergency Numbers

Veterinarian _496-1000_

Doctor   office _664-7553_

home _853-4112_

Hospital and
Poison Information Center _731-2158_

- What is the emergency number for the police and fire departments? For what other emergencies can you use *911?*
- What person can you call in any emergency? How do you dial *Operator?*
- What personal emergency numbers are listed in Nikki's phone book?
- What emergency number did Nikki add?

You should keep your phone book near the phone so that you can quickly find emergency numbers. If you are not sure what number to call, use the number *0* for *Operator.*

A. Use the emergency numbers on page 240 to tell what number and what person or office Nikki should call in each situation.

1. Nikki's dog Bouncer is sick.
2. Nikki sees a dark cloud with a point moving close to the ground. It could be a tornado.
3. Nikki's younger brother has swallowed some bleach that is poisonous.

B. What emergency number and person or office should you call in each of these situations? Explain why you would call each number.

1. You look out the window and see smoke coming from the upstairs window next door.
2. Someone has moved the phone book, and you need to call the police. Who else can you call?
3. You see two children on bicycles run into each other. One of the children is hurt.

C. Tell whether the right person or office was called in each situation. If the wrong person or office was called, tell who should have been called.

1. Mr. Reeves broke his leg. He called the veterinarian.
2. Ms. Hattori's car has been stolen. She called the police.
3. Mrs. Wood's son has eaten some berries that may be poisonous. She wanted to call the Poison Information Center, but she didn't remember the number. She called the operator.

Look in your phone book. Find the emergency numbers and make a list of them. Be sure to include emergency numbers for your doctor and any others you may need. Keep the list near your telephone.

Reporting an Emergency

When you report an emergency, be sure to speak clearly and give the necessary information.

Thinking It Through

Nikki heard Bouncer barking in the backyard. She looked out the window. The garage was on fire! Nikki looked at the list of emergency numbers by the phone. She quickly called the fire department. Read what Nikki said when she reported the emergency.

> "Our garage is on fire! My name is Nikki Johnson. I live at 616 Carmel Drive. My phone number is 729-3996."

- What information did Nikki give when she called the fire department?
- Why was it important for Nikki to tell where she lived?
- What might have happened if Nikki had not spoken clearly or had not given the correct information?

When Nikki reported the emergency, she told what happened. Then she gave her name, address, and telephone number. When you report an emergency, be sure to speak clearly and give all the necessary information. Do not add any information that is not needed.

Working It Through

A. Mrs. Connie Rivera called the Coast Guard when she saw an accident. Read the report and answer the questions.

"I just saw a sailboat turn over in Crystal Bay, south of the lighthouse. There were three people in the boat. My name is Mrs. Connie Rivera. I am calling from 839-5762."

1. Where did the accident happen?
2. What happened?
3. When did it happen?

4. Why was it important to tell how many people were in the boat?

5. Who reported the accident?

6. What is the phone number?

B. Read about each emergency below. Choose only the facts you should report. Write them on a sheet of paper.

1

Smoke is coming from an upstairs window of my house. My name is _____. I am a teacher. I live at 310 W. Grove Avenue. I am calling from a neighbor's phone. She is nice. The number is _____.

2

My sister fell in the yard. Her leg hurts, and she can't stand up. She has brown eyes. My name is _____. My address is 386 Peachtree Street. It is a big house. The yard is big too. My number is _____.

C. Pretend you are going to report each emergency in Exercise B. What person or office should you call? Read aloud what you would say. Remember to speak clearly.

Trying It Out

1. Look at the picture. Pretend you are the person in the drugstore using the phone. You are reporting the accident.

2. On a sheet of paper, write what you would say on the phone.

3. Practice saying your report aloud to a partner.

243

Review • Reporting Information

A. Read the information below. Notice that Terri gave all the necessary facts and that she told the facts in order.

My sister fell down the stairs in our house. My name is Terri Stevens. I live at 5872 Laurel Street. My telephone number is 251–3306.

1. What did Terri say first?
2. After she told what happened, what other information did she give?
3. Should Terri have said that her sister tripped on the carpet? Why or why not?
4. Terri spoke clearly when she reported the accident. Why was this important?

B. Read the information below. Find 2 facts that should not be reported.

My brother fell when he was roller-skating in front of our house. His skates are the fastest in our neighborhood. My name is Stanley Davis. I am a good skater too. I live at 302 Westmore Drive. My telephone number is 462–1180.

C. Read the information below. Write the facts in order.

I live at 1224 Fifth Street. The tiger that escaped from the circus is in my front yard. My telephone number is 749–2255. My name is Linda Alvaro.

D. Answer the questions.
1. Which fact did you write first?
2. Which facts did you add?
3. Why is it important to keep to the subject and tell facts in order when reporting information?

Evaluation • Reporting Information

A. Improve the emergency report. Ask yourself the questions below it to decide where to make changes. Rewrite the report.

> I am calling from a neighbor's house. The telephone number is 692–1583. My neighbor has a white fence around her yard. I just saw someone break a window in my house and go inside. I hit a baseball through Mr. Gray's window last summer. I live at 1852 Forestview Lane, Apartment 1–C. My name is Timothy Reeves.

  1. Are all the facts necessary?
  2. Are the facts in the right order?

B. Write an emergency report. Use the information below. Write the information in complete sentences. Be sure not to write any facts that are not necessary.

what happened:	It was raining so I couldn't play outside. I looked out of the window in the living room for a while. I saw a car skid and hit three cars parked in front of my house. I also saw my friend Bobby running home in the rain.
name:	(your name)
address:	(your address)
phone:	(your phone number)

You will be evaluated on the following:
  putting the facts in order
  including only the necessary facts
  writing correct information
  using complete sentences

Spotlight · Language from Place to Place

frying pan
skillet
spider

corn-on-the-cob
sweet corn
roasting ear

bag
sack
poke

faucet
spigot
tap

peanut
goober

firefly
lightning bug
fire bug

woodchuck
groundhog

People from different parts of the country often use some words that are different from words used in other parts of the country. The picture shows some things that can have different names. Can you think of others?

Spotlight • What Is It Called?

Do you know the names of the things in the pictures? See if you can tell what they are. Check your answers by turning the book upside down.

1. The hole in a shoe or sneaker that you put the shoelace through.

2. The sidepiece on a pair of glasses, the part that fits over the ear.

3. The little knob you turn to wind your watch.

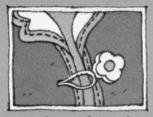

4. A fancy fastening on the front of a coat made of a button and a loop.

5. The roof over a theater entrance.

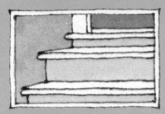

6. The part behind a step that you bump your toes against.

7. The dimple in the bottom of an apple.

8. A South American fish, not over 1 1/2 feet long, that will attack and eat humans and other large animals.

Answers: 1. eyelet, 2. temple, 3. crown, 4. frog, 5. marquee, 6. riser, 7. basin, 8. piranha

247

The Sentence-Building Game

Adding adjectives and adverbs to a sentence can make the sentence more interesting.

Thinking It Through

Read the steps below.

1. Begin with a subject and a word that tells what the subject did.

1. The children laughed.

Now you have a sentence to build upon.

2. In the subject part of the sentence, add an adjective that tells how many.

2. The four children laughed.

3. In the subject part of the sentence, add an adjective that tells what kind.

3. The four happy children laughed.

4. In the predicate part of the sentence, add an adverb that tells how.

4. The four happy children laughed hilariously.

5. In the predicate part of the sentence, add more words that tell when, where, or how.

5. The four happy children laughed hilariously during *King Kong Meets the Monsters.*

You can make your sentences more interesting by adding adjectives and adverbs to them.

A. Think of some adjectives for the subject parts of each sentence below. Write the sentences.

1. The monsters growled.
2. The trees shook.
3. The coconuts fell.
4. The monsters left.

B. Think of words that tell when, where, or how for the predicate parts of the sentences you wrote in Exercise A. Write the sentences.

C. Think of some adjectives and adverbs to add to these sentences. Choose at least 4 of the sentences. Write the sentences.

1. The teacher smiled.
2. The boots leaked.
3. An ostrich hid.
4. The doors slammed.
5. A telephone rang.
6. The pipe burst.
7. The players won.
8. A kangaroo jumped.

Trying It Out

Add adjectives and adverbs to each sentence to tell what is happening in the picture. Write the sentences.

1. The parachute opened.
2. The capsule landed.
3. The astronauts bounced.
4. The water splashed.
5. The ship arrived.

Sentence Building

Adding details to a sentence can make the sentence more interesting.

Read the sentence below the pictures.

The horse ran.

- What does each horse look like?
- How is each horse running?
- Where is each horse running?

When Mark answered the questions, he wrote these sentences.

> The wild red horse ran swiftly through the desert.
> The fat brown horse ran slowly to the barn.
> The magical white horse ran beautifully through the forest.

- Why are Mark's sentences more interesting than the sentence beneath the pictures?
- What details did he add to each sentence?

Adding details to your sentences can make your sentences more interesting.

A. Add details to each sentence below. The words in parentheses are clues to help you. Use the questions in the chart to help you add details that fit the clues.

1. The rain fell (in a desert).
   The rain fell (in a jungle).
2. The bear sniffed (smoke).
   The bear sniffed (berries).
3. The boy gulped (orange juice).
   The boy gulped (salt water).
4. The kitten licked (sour milk).
   The kitten licked (its fur).
5. The letter carrier walked (through deep mud).
   The letter carrier walked (on the sidewalk).

Questions
What kind?
Where?
How?
When?
Why?

B. Add details to each sentence below. Use the questions in the chart to help you. Write the sentences.

1. The river flooded.
2. The beaver dam collapsed.
3. The beavers ran.
4. One beaver was hurt.
5. Some children came.
6. They found the beaver.
7. They helped the beaver.
8. The beaver found its family.

Look at the pictures. Write 4 sentences, one about each picture. Make sure you include details, so that your sentences will be clear and vivid. You can use the questions in the chart to help you.

Lesson 9 Combining Sentences

The words *and*, *but*, and *or* have different meanings. You can use these words to combine sentences.

Thinking It Through

Read what three children said about going to a rodeo.

Brenda: I would love to go to the rodeo, and I think I would enjoy it.

Allen: I would love to go to the rodeo, but I was there last week.

Jeremy: I would love to go to the rodeo, or I would love to go to the movies.

The words *and*, *but*, and *or* can be used to combine sentences. Each of these words has a special meaning that gives you a clue about what the second part of the new sentence will say.

The word *and* tells you that there is another idea coming in the sentence.

● What was Brenda's other idea?

The word *but* tells you that there is a problem with the first idea in the sentence, or that there is a big difference between the first and second ideas.

● What was Allen's problem about going to the rodeo?

The word *or* tells you that there is a choice in the sentence.

● What was Jeremy's choice?
● What punctuation is used before *and*, *but*, and *or* in the combined sentences?

And, *but*, and *or* have different meanings. Make sure you use them correctly when you write.

Working It Through

A. Combine the two sentences. Use *and, but,* or *or,* whichever word fits the meaning best. Put a comma before the word you use.

1. Mark wanted to roller skate. It was raining.
2. He stayed home. He decided to paint.
3. He could paint his pottery jar. He could paint a picture.
4. He decided to paint his jar. He couldn't find it.
5. The jar could be at school. It could be at home.
6. He finally found the jar. He started to paint.

B. Think of an idea that will complete each of these sentences. Write the sentences.

1. A bicycle can move, but _____.
2. A train moves fast, and _____.
3. A car can be parked on the street, or _____.
4. An airplane flies, but _____.
5. I can walk, or _____.
6. A boat floats, and _____.

Trying It Out

Read all the directions before you begin the activity.

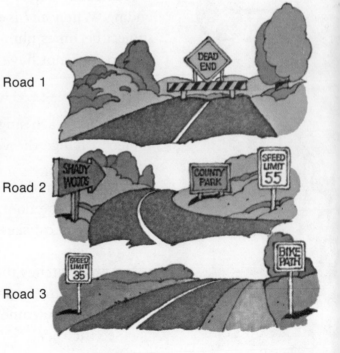

Road 1

Road 2

Road 3

1. Write 2 sentences about each road.
2. Combine each pair of sentences into one sentence.
3. Use *but* to combine the pair of sentences about Road 1, *and* to combine the sentences about Road 2, and *or* to combine the sentences about Road 3.

Subject-Verb Agreement

The subject and the verb of a sentence must agree.

Thinking It Through

Read the sentences below.

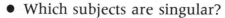

Singular	Plural
The blue marble rolls.	The blue marble and
The red marble rolls.	the red marble roll.

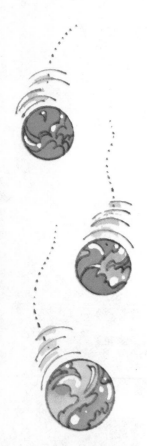

- Which subjects are singular?
- What verb goes with the singular subjects?
- What word was used to put the two singular subjects together to make a plural subject?
- What is the plural subject?
- What verb goes with the plural subject?
- How do the singular and plural verbs differ?

When the subject is a singular noun, the verb has an *-s* ending. When *and* is used to combine singular subjects, the subject becomes plural. The verb that goes with a plural subject does not have an *-s* ending.

Working It Through

A. Combine each singular subject to make a plural subject. Change the verb to make it agree with the plural subject.

1. A green marble rolls on the floor. A yellow marble rolls on the floor.
2. A plump cat sees the marbles. A little kitten sees the marbles.
3. Anna watches the cats play with the marbles. Al watches the cats play with the marbles.
4. Their mom comes to see the cats. Their dad comes to see the cats.

B. Choose the correct form of the verb in parentheses. Write the sentences.

1. Hot weather and rain _____ the Amazon rain forest steamy.   (make, makes)
2. An Indian girl _____ her family grow manioc for food.   (help, helps)
3. The toucan and the tarantula _____ in the rain forest.   (live, lives)
4. A brightly colored macaw _____ over the rain forest.   (fly, flies)

C. Find the plural subjects. Write the sentences. Draw one line under each subject. Draw two lines under the verb that agrees with the subject.

1. Sue and Sam (look, looks) out the window.
2. The rain (keep, keeps) them inside.
3. Their mother and father (cook, cooks) breakfast.
4. The morning and the afternoon (go, goes) by quickly.

Trying It Out

1. Find a child in the picture who is like the person named in each sentence below.

   Danny likes orange sweaters.
   Paula puts on funny masks.
   Jeff always wears hats.
   Anita loves long hair.
2. Add the child's name to the sentence.
3. Write the new sentences.

Take Another Look   Does each verb agree with the plural subject?

255

Using Verbs

The verbs *do, go, come, run, take,* and *fall* do not end in *-ed* to show past tense.

Read what the girl and boy are saying about their problem. Notice the underlined verbs.

> I <u>came</u> home from school. I <u>went</u> into the kitchen. I <u>did</u> the dishes. A plate <u>fell</u> on the floor. I <u>ran</u> outside. I <u>took</u> a long walk.

> I <u>come</u> home. I <u>do</u> my homework. I <u>go</u> into the kitchen. I <u>fall</u> on the broken plate. Mom <u>runs</u> to help. I <u>take</u> the blame for the broken plate.

- Who is talking about the problem in the present tense?
- Which verbs are in the present tense?
- Who is talking about the problem in the past tense?
- Which verbs are in the past tense?

The verbs *come, do, go, fall, runs,* and *take* show action that is happening now. They are in the present tense.

The verbs *came, went, did, fell, ran,* and *took* show action that happened in the past. They are in the past tense. These verbs do not end in *-ed*.

A. Tell whether each sentence shows past or present action.

1. My dog Barney does tricks.
2. Yesterday he did a new trick.
3. Today I take pictures of Barney.
4. Yesterday I took pictures of him too.

B. Complete each sentence with verbs from the Verb Box. Write the sentences to show action that is happening in the present.

1. Sid ____ the 50-yard dash well.
2. He ____ exercises before the race.
3. His sister Reba ____ to see him race.
4. She ____ pictures of Sid.
5. Sid's watch ____ off his arm, but he wins the race.
6. He ____ to the gym to take a shower.

Verb Box	
Present	**Past**
does	did
goes	went
comes	came
runs	ran
takes	took
falls	fell

C. Chose the past tense of the verbs in parentheses to complete each sentence. Write the sentences.

1. Ted (runs, ran) the 50-yard dash last week.
2. Sid and Reba (come, came) to see Ted run.
3. Once Ted almost (fell, falls) down.
4. He (does, did) his best and won.
5. Reba and Sid (took, take) Ted out to celebrate.
6. They (go, went) to a restaurant to eat pizza.

Trying It Out

1. Look at the pictures below.
2. Write a paragraph that tells how the girl helps people in her neighborhood. Use the present tense of the verbs *do*, *run*, and *take*.
3. Write a second paragraph that also tells how the girl helps people. Use the past tense of the verbs *do*, *run*, and *take*.

Using Other Verbs

The verbs *know, grow, see, fly,* and *draw* do not end in *-ed* to show past tense.

Thinking It Through

Read the two police reports by Officer C. Straight. Notice the underlined verbs.

> **Report 1**
> I <u>see</u> a spaceship. It <u>flies</u> over my head. I <u>know</u> it is strange. It <u>grows</u> bigger before my eyes. I <u>draw</u> a picture of it.

> **Report 2**
> What I really <u>saw</u> was a firefly. It <u>flew</u> by my head. It <u>grew</u> bigger as it got closer. The picture I <u>drew</u> was wrong. I <u>knew</u> I should have gone to the eye doctor.

- Which report shows action that is happening now?
- Which verbs are in the present tense?
- Which report shows action that happened in the past?
- Which verbs are in the past tense?

The verbs *see, flies, know, grows,* and *draw* show action that is happening now. They are in the present tense.

The verbs *saw, flew, grew, drew,* and *knew* show action that happened in the past. They are in the past tense. These verbs do not end in *-ed.*

Working It Through

A. Tell whether each sentence shows past or present action.

1. Mr. Reed grows watermelons.
2. Last year, he grew the biggest one in the county.
3. Today Marco and I see one of the giant watermelons with our own eyes.
4. Yesterday Lisa saw one of the watermelons.

258

B. Complete each sentence with the past or present tense of the verb in parentheses. Use the Verb Box to help you.

1. Today Ms. Lambert _____ a picture to show us what her plane looks like.   (draw)
2. This morning, she _____ her plane to St. Louis.   (fly)
3. She _____ how to get from Chicago to St. Louis. (know)
4. Last week, we _____ Ms. Lambert take off in her plane.   (see)
5. She went to the city where she _____ up.   (grow)

Verb Box	
Present	**Past**
know	knew
grow	grew
see	saw
flies	flew
draw	drew

C. Choose the past or present tense of the verbs in parentheses for each sentence below.

1. I (see, saw) strange flowers as I walk through the yard.
2. I wish I (know, knew) how they got there.
3. They (grow, grew) last night after I went to bed.
4. When I touched one of the flowers, a silver petal (fly, flew) away.
5. Other petals fall off as I (draw, drew) pictures of the flowers.

Trying It Out

1. Look at the picture.
2. Write a paragraph that tells about the boy's three hobbies. Use the present tense of the verbs *fly, grow,* and *draw.*
3. Write a second paragraph that also tells about the boy's three hobbies. Use the past tense of the verbs *fly, grow,* and *draw.*

Review • Subject-Verb Agreement

A. Choose the verb that agrees with the subject of each sentence. Write the sentences.

1. Reiko and Mario often (stay, stays) for lunch.
2. Our pet robin (hop, hops) very close to us.
3. Mom and I (like, likes) to shop for food.
4. She and I (study, studies) the prices carefully.
5. We (look, looks) for bargains.
6. Food (cost, costs) a lot these days.
7. Emiko (pick, picks) apples to earn money.
8. Toshio (cook, cooks) supper on the grill.
9. Those trees (bloom, blooms) in the spring.
10. That squirrel (jump, jumps) from tree to tree.

B. Complete each sentence with the correct form of the verb in parentheses.

1. Mike (does, did) his work yesterday.
2. Kenji studies and (knows, knew) his lessons.
3. His horse (run, ran) away last summer.
4. The girl (sees, saw) and talks to her teacher now.
5. Paula (goes, went) to the dentist now.
6. Leonora (goes, went) skiing last week.
7. Last Monday Ira (sees, saw) the eclipse.
8. My dad (runs, ran) or swims for exercise.
9. Our dog (knows, knew) when it is dinnertime.
10. Elena (does, did) her homework yesterday.

For extra practice turn to pages 340–341.

Take Another Look   Copy the sentence. Put each pronoun in parentheses in the correct blank.

_____ gave _____a frog.   (he, him)

Did you write *He* in the first blank and *him* in the second blank?

For more practice turn to pages 326–327 in the Handbook.

Evaluation • Subject-Verb Agreement

A. Write the letter of the response that completes each sentence correctly.

1. Mom and Sue **a.** drives **b.** drive the car.

2. He **a.** keeps **b.** keep the key in the box.

3. The dogs **a.** likes **b.** like to run.

4. My banana **a.** tastes **b.** taste delicious.

5. The air **a.** feel **b.** feels cold.

6. Sammy **a.** is **b.** are my cousin.

7. My friends **a.** is **b.** are nice.

8. The wind **a.** feel **b.** feels cold.

9. Kim **a.** is **b.** are learning to drive.

10. Joy and Ed **a.** washes **b.** wash the car.

11. Joe's aunt **a.** was **b.** were in Canada.

12. The girls **a.** sing **b.** sings well.

B. Write the letter of the present tense verb that completes each sentence.

1. Al ____ good work.
   a. does   **b.** did

2. She ____ to work every day.
   a. went   **b.** goes

3. Our dog ____ running to us.
   a. came   **b.** comes

4. It ____ a long time to grow.
   a. takes   **b.** took

5. The old car ____ like new.
   a. runs   **b.** ran

6. I don't ____ well anymore.
   a. see   **b.** saw

7. Lou ____ my secret.
   a. knows   **b.** knew

C. Write the letter of the past tense verb that completes each sentence.

1. He ____ to see me yesterday.
   a. come   **b.** came

2. Jo ____ her time reading.
   a. took   **b.** takes

3. Ali ____ his homework early.
   a. did   **b.** does

4. She ____ slowly over the bumps
   a. goes   **b.** went

5. The old clock ____ down often.
   a. runs   **b.** ran

6. I studied so I ____ the answer.
   a. know   **b.** knew

7. Meg ____ the sunset yesterday.
   a. see   **b.** saw

Spotlight • Activities to Choose

1. Collect news. Invite some friends to write weather reports, comic strips, sports news, movie news, and school news. Collect the news and put the papers in a folder. Ask other classmates to add news reports. Number the pages and make sections if you wish. Then make an index. Write a name for your newspaper on the top of the first page.

2. Exchange addresses and emergency numbers. Ask a friend for his or her home address. Make an envelope. Address the envelope to your friend. Write your home address as the return address. Write a note to your friend. Tell your friend what number or numbers to call in case you have an accident. You might include your parents' work numbers or numbers of neighbors. Exchange envelopes.

3. Describe a picture. Draw a picture of an imaginary place, or make a finger painting of something unusual, such as an undiscovered planet or a deep tunnel. Use the sentence-building game on pages 248–249 to write an interesting sentence about your picture. Write the sentences beneath your picture. Display your picture and sentence on the bulletin board. Invite your classmates to write additional sentences about your picture.

The silvery light glowed in the deep tunnel through the dark.

4. Climb the verb ladder. Choose a classmate to lead the game. The leader draws two or more ladders on the board. Each ladder should have 11 steps. The leader selects a player for each ladder. Then the leader calls out these present tense verbs: *do, go, come, run, take, fall, know, grow, see, fly,* and *draw*. The players must write the correct past-tense form of the verb on a step. Whoever fills in the most steps correctly wins and becomes leader for the next round.

Who Goes There, Lincoln?
by Dale Fife

When Lincoln Farnum and his friends hold their club initiation in the old firehouse, they run into ghosts and trap doors. But they also make an important discovery that ties the old firehouse to the Civil War. Read about Lincoln's discovery in this mystery book.

Help! Emergencies That Could Happen to You, and How to Handle Them
by Mary Lou Vandenburg

Do you know what to do if your clothes catch fire? Or what to do if you get bitten by an animal or insect? This book tells about emergencies that could happen to you and tells how to handle them. It can be a very important book for you to read.

Fun Time Codes & Mystery Messages
by Cameron Yerian and Margaret Yerian

Would you like to write a friend a secret message in code? This book will show you how to make invisible ink and even how to speak in code. Colorful pictures and step-by-step instructions explain each code clearly.

Unit Nine

Do you ever think about how you are changing and growing every day? Some of the same ideas you have had may be in this poem.

Message
from a Caterpillar

Don't shake this
bough.
Don't try
to wake me
now.

In this cocoon
I've work to
do.
Inside this silk
I'm changing
things.

I'm worm-like now
but in this
dark
I'm growing
wings.

Lilian Moore

In this unit, you will learn to write about the events and adventures in your own life.

Lesson 1   A Diary

A diary is a daily record of what happens to the person who writes it.

Thinking It Through

A **diary** is a day-by-day record. Some diaries tell only facts about what the writer saw or did. Other diaries include the writer's thoughts and feelings.

Melanie's class was reading about a diary written in 1805 by a boy named Noah Blake. Noah's diary was bound in leather, and the pages were made at the paper mill in town. Noah made some butternut ink and a quill pen. His spelling was old-fashioned too.

On the next few pages, you can find out what Melanie's class read in Noah's diary.

> March 25, 1805 – This diary was given to me by Father Izaak Blake and my Mother Rachel upon the fifteenth year of my life.
>
> March 28, 1805 – Snow stopp'd during the night but it is very cold. My window glass is frosty and my ink froze.
>
> April 27, 1805 – The Adams arrived with six townspeople at sunrise. We made a fine bridge. We knocked down the old bridge, which made me feel a little sad.
>
> May 23, 1805 – Father and Mr. Beach started on the mill.
>
> July 4, 1805 – Never heard so many bells and cannon shots. Several wagonloads were on their way as we walked to the village. Mr. Adams was reading the Declaration of Independence when we arrived. Father bought a horse and a wagon!

NOAH BLAKE BRIDGE
Please walk your horse!
Foot passengers --------- 1 cent
Horned cattle ---------- 3 cents
4 wheel carriage -------- 10 cents
Sleds or sleighs ------- 6 cents
1805

July 18, 1805 - We collected our first toll over the new bridge! A waggon crossed over, carrying a merchant and his wife.

August 2, 1805 - Some Indians came this evening with gifts. They had dinner with us.

November 6, 1805 - Father and I have the mill roof all but shingled. It is fun working at night, but the weather is most cold.

December 11, 1805 - Our first business, at the mill! An order for sawing pine floor boards, for Mr. Thoma.

December 14, 1805 - We took off the day. General Washington died this day six years ago. We could hear a cannon salute all the way from the village.

- What facts did Noah write about on March 28, 1805?
- What facts and feelings did he write about on April 27, 1805?
- Tell about some other facts and feelings that Noah wrote about.
- How did each entry begin?

Diaries are day-by-day records of what happens to the people who write them. Diaries often include the writers' thoughts and feelings.

Working It Through

A. Imagine that Wilbur Wright, who helped invent the airplane, recorded these facts in his diary.

December 17, 1903 — Today Orville and I made the first airplane flights in history near Kitty Hawk, North Carolina. Orville made the first flight. The plane flew 120 feet and stayed in the air 12 seconds. We made three other flights today. My flight was the longest — 852 feet in 59 seconds.

1. List 3 facts recorded in Wilbur's diary.

2. Write 3 facts that tell what happened to you today.

B. Imagine that Orville Wright, Wilbur's brother, wrote this in his diary.

December 17, 1903 — Today was one of the most important days in history. Wilbur and I have flown in an airplane! Now I know how a bird must feel. Flying is wonderful. Our hard work has been rewarded.

1. How is Orville's account different from Wilbur's?

2. What is one feeling Orville described?

3. Write 3 feelings about the facts you wrote in Exercise A.

Trying It Out

You may want to keep a diary of what happens to you at home and at school. Remember to write a date before each entry. Try to include both facts and feelings in your diary. You can keep your diary secret or share it with a friend.

Lesson 2   Listing Facts and Feelings

You can write facts and feelings about yourself.

Thinking It Through

Melanie and her classmates decided to write about their lives as Noah Blake did. They talked to their families about different things that happened when they were little. They thought about new kinds of things that were happening now or that could happen in the future. Here is the list Melanie made.

When I Was Little
I was a messy eater when I was a baby.
When I first walked, I was only eight months old.
I drew my first picture when I was a year old.

Now
My ninth birthday was very exciting.
I felt sad when my friend Jan moved away.
My first day in the fourth grade was very unusual.

In the Future
Mom is going to help me build a treehouse this summer.
Next year, I am going to Alaska to see my brother.
I want to be on the basketball team in junior high.

● Melanie told about a variety of facts and feelings in her list. What are some of them?

The children in Melanie's class chose one experience when they were little to write about. Melanie wanted to choose the most interesting experience from her list. She decided to write about what happened when she drew her first picture. She added these facts and feelings.

My First Picture

I drew my first picture when I was a year old.
My brother Rob left a big yellow box of crayons on the edge of the table.
I toddled over to the table.
Grabbed the crayons.
Drew some red crooked lines all over the kitchen floor.
I felt very clever.
When I looked up, I saw my mom staring down at the floor.
My mom's mouth.
I was unhappy when she washed the floor.

- What are some facts and feelings Melanie added to tell about her first picture?
- Is every note a complete sentence? Which notes are incomplete sentences?
- What subjects and predicates can you think of to complete Melanie's incomplete sentences?

When you write about your life, it is helpful to begin with lists of your facts and feelings.

Working It Through

A. Melanie wrote her notes as sentences in a paragraph. Read the paragraph. Notice the 3 incomplete sentences that are underlined. Think of a subject or predicate for each one. Write the paragraph correctly.

I drew my first picture when I was a year old. <u>My brother Rob.</u> I toddled over to the table. I grabbed the crayons. <u>Drew some crooked red lines on the kitchen floor.</u> I felt very clever. Then I looked up, and saw my mom staring down at the floor. <u>My mom's mouth.</u> I was unhappy when she washed the floor.

B. Alex wrote a paragraph about an experience he had when he was little. Read the paragraph. Find the 4 incomplete sentences. Think of a subject or predicate for each one. Write the paragraph correctly.

When I was two years old, my dad took me to the store. Put me in a shopping cart. My dad stopped in the fruit section. Reached over and grabbed an orange. Then one orange after another. Soon all the oranges were on the floor. My dad. He didn't take me to the store for a while.

Trying It Out

1. Make a list of facts and feelings about yourself. Be sure to include things that happened when you were little, things that are happening now, and things that could happen in the future. Keep this list for the next 3 lessons.

2. Look at your list. Choose one experience that happened when you were little to write about. Try to choose the experience you think is the most interesting.

3. Write details about your experience. Then write a paragraph. Be sure you write complete sentences.

Lesson 3   Working with Topic Sentences

Sometimes a paragraph has a topic sentence that states the main idea of that paragraph.

Thinking It Through

Melanie's teacher asked the class to write about some experiences that happened recently. Melanie looked at her list and decided to write about her first day in the fourth grade. She added these facts and feelings.

My First Day in the Fourth Grade

My first day in the fourth grade was very unusual.
I woke up late, and I had to rush to get ready for school.
As I ran to catch the bus, I fell and broke my arm!
My grandfather taught me how to make ice cream.
I felt sad when I thought I would miss the first day of school.
I was able to go to school that afternoon.
Jan and I slept in my backyard once.
I was thrilled when everyone in my class signed my cast.

- What are some of the facts and feelings Melanie added to tell about her first day in the fourth grade?
- Which sentences do not tell about her first day? Do they belong in her list? Why or why not?
- When Melanie writes her paragraph, what do you think her topic sentence should be? Why?

When you write a paragraph about yourself, remember to write a topic sentence. Make sure each sentence in the paragraph tells something about the topic sentence.

Working It Through

A. Melanie wrote her sentences in a paragraph. Take out the 2 sentences that do not tell about the topic sentence. Write the paragraph. Underline the topic sentence.

My first day in the fourth grade was very unusual. I woke up late, and I had to rush to get ready for school. As I ran to catch the bus, I fell and broke my arm! My grandfather broke his arm once. I felt sad when I thought I would miss the first day of school. I was able to go to school that afternoon. My school is new. I was thrilled when everyone in the class signed my cast!

B. Melanie's friend wrote a paragraph that needs to be improved.

A funny thing happened to me when I went to the movies with my friends. I went to get some popcorn. When I came back to my seat, my friends were gone! I got lost at the beach once. I saw my friends when the movie was over. They had left their seats to get some water. I really felt silly after I found them.

1. What proofreading mark needs to be used?
2. What sentence should be taken out?
3. Write the paragraph correctly.
4. Underline the topic sentence.

Proofreader's Marks

= Make a capital letter.

⊙ Add a period.

ℓ Take out.

∧ Put in one or more words.

Trying It Out

Choose a recent experience from the list you made in Lesson 2. Add facts and feelings about your experience. Then write a paragraph. Be sure that your paragraph has a topic sentence and that all the sentences in your paragraph tell about the topic sentence. Remember to keep your list from Lesson 2 for the next lesson.

Lesson 4 **Working with Sentence Beginnings**

Using a variety of sentence beginnings will make your sentences more interesting.

Thinking It Through

Melanie wanted to write about another experience she had recently. She looked at her list. Melanie remembered how exciting her ninth birthday had been. She wrote these facts and feelings about her birthday.

> <u>My Ninth Birthday</u>
>
> I had an exciting ninth birthday.
> In the afternoon, I helped Dad put on a magic show.
> I couldn't find Mom after the show.
> I felt terrible.
> I finally looked in the backyard.
> I saw Mom holding a pizza.
> On top of the pizza were nine candles.
> I was really surprised!
> I thought Mom had done some magic too.

- What are some facts and feelings Melanie included about her birthday?
- Which sentence begins with words that tell when?
- Which sentence begins with words that tell where?
- What do all the other sentences begin with?
- How could Melanie change the order of the third sentence so the sentence begins differently?
- What words could she add to the sixth sentence so the sentence begins differently?

274

When you write about yourself, don't start each sentence with *I*. Use different sentence beginnings to make your sentences more interesting.

Working It Through

A. Rewrite Melanie's paragraph. Change the third sentence so that it doesn't begin with *I*. Begin the fourth sentence with words that tell when. Add any other sentence beginnings you can think of.

> I had an exciting ninth birthday. In the afternoon, I helped Dad put on a magic show. I couldn't find Mom after the show. I felt terrible. I finally looked in the backyard. I saw Mom holding a pizza. On top of the pizza were nine candles. I was really surprised! I thought Mom had done some magic too!

B. Read Ken's paragraph. Add the sentence beginnings at the left to some of the sentences in the paragraph. Write the paragraph.

Sentence Beginnings

From now on

On the top of my head

Yesterday

I slipped on the sidewalk. Mom rushed me to the hospital. I have two stitches. I will try to be more careful.

Trying It Out

Choose a recent experience from the list you wrote in Lesson 2. Write facts and feelings about your experience. Then write a paragraph. Begin some sentences with words that tell when and some sentences with words that tell where. Keep your list from Lesson 2 for the next lesson.

Take Another Look   Read the paragraph you just wrote. Did you begin most of your sentences with *I?* If so, rewrite some of your sentences so that they begin differently.

Working with Words and Sentences

Using exact words will help you make your writing clear and interesting.

Thinking It Through

Melanie wanted to write about an experience she might háve in the future. She looked at her list. She decided to write about her trip to Alaska next year.

My Trip to Alaska

Next year, I am going to Alaska to *see* my brother.
When Mom said I could go, I went to tell all my friends!
I will go in an airplane.
I am so happy!
My brother is a worker in Nome.
He said he would let me ride in a dog sled.
I want to learn to wear snowshoes.
I will probably walk *badly* at first.
I saw *nice* pictures of Alaska in a good book.

- What verb could Melanie use instead of <u>see</u> to make her sentence clearer and more interesting?
- What adverb could she use instead of <u>badly</u> to describe how she might walk?
- What adjective could she use instead of <u>nice</u> to describe the pictures?
- What other exact words could Melanie use to make her sentences better?

When you write about yourself, choose exact words to make your sentences clear and interesting.

Working It Through

A. Rewrite Melanie's paragraph. Change the underlined words to make the sentences clearer and more interesting.

Next year, I am going to Alaska to <u>see</u> my brother. When Mom said I could go, I <u>went</u> to tell all my friends! I will <u>go</u> in an airplane. I am so happy! My brother is a <u>worker</u> in Nome. He said he would let me ride in a dog sled. I want to learn to wear snowshoes. I will probably walk <u>badly</u> at first. I saw some <u>nice</u> pictures of Alaska in a <u>good</u> book.

B. Rewrite Russell's paragraph. Choose one of the words in parentheses to make each sentence clearer and more interesting.

I (will plant, will make) a flower garden in the spring. I already have a (good, sunny) place picked out for my garden. My flowers will have (brilliant, pretty) blossoms. I (will take, will dig) out all the weeds and watch (constantly, closely) for bugs. I will (carefully, quickly) pick some (nice, fresh) flowers for my room each day.

Trying It Out

Look at the list you wrote in Lesson 2. Choose an experience that you might have in the future. Write a paragraph about it. Try to use exact words to make your sentences as clear and interesting as possible.

Take Another Look   Did you use exact verbs, adverbs, and adjectives in your sentences? Did you indent the first line of your paragraph?

Improving Your Writing

Using exact words and good sentences in your paragraphs will improve your writing.

Thinking It Through

Use the proofreader's marks to help you when you make changes in your story.

Read this part of Sam's story. Notice the changes he marked.

Proofreader's Marks

≡ Make a capital letter.

⊙ Add a period.

ℓ Take out.

∧ Put in one or more words.

> Many different things are
> happening to me now. One day last
> week, I got a shirt when I woke up
> late. Everybody ~~laughed~~ *howled* when I got
> to school because the shirt said
> SUE'S SHIRT! it was my sister's!
> When I was a baby, I almost chewed
> up my blanket. I played a terrible
> joke on Sue this morning. I scared
> her horribly. I acted badly.

- What is the topic sentence?
- Are Sam's facts and feelings in the order that they happened?
- Which sentence did Sam take out? Why?
- What other changes did he want to make?

Working It Through

A. Answer these questions about Sam's story.

1. What exact word did Sam use to describe how everybody laughed at his shirt? to describe the joke? to describe how he scared Sue?

2. Think of some other exact words that Sam could use instead of *different, got,* and *badly.* Write them on a sheet of paper.

3. Which words besides *I* did Sam use to begin his sentences?

4. Think of another sentence beginning for the fifth sentence that Sam might have used. Write it on a sheet of paper.

B. Rewrite Sam's story. Make the changes that are marked. Also add some of the exact words and the sentence beginnings that you thought of in Exercise A.

C. Improve the paragraph. Make the incomplete sentence complete. Find the sentence that doesn't belong. Think of another word to use instead of <u>like.</u> Change some of the sentences so that they don't all begin with *I.*

> I <u>like</u> many sports now. I learned to swim last year. Learned how to ice skate this winter. I feel so free when I skate. I want to be a good soccer player too. I like to go to the movies too.

Trying It Out

1. Look at the four paragraphs you have written in Lessons 2–5. Decide what changes you need to make. Use the proofreader's marks on page 278 to help you. Rewrite the paragraphs, making the changes you marked.

2. Congratulations! You now have four good paragraphs. You have written many different things about yourself as Noah Blake did. You may wish to put your paragraphs in a folder with your name.

Review • Working with Sentences

A. Look at the sentences in the paragraph George wrote about his roller-skating class.

On Tuesdays after school, I go to my roller skating class. At first, the skates kept falling off my shoes. The other kids flew past me. My legs trembled. I clung to the railing with my sweaty hands. At every class, I worked hard. Now I move gracefully and get up swiftly when I fall.

1. George's sentences do not all begin the same way. Which sentences begin with words that tell when? with words that tell where?
2. George used exact words to make his sentences clear and interesting. What exact verb did he use in the third sentence? in the fourth sentence? What exact adjective did he use in the fifth sentence? What exact adverbs did he use in the last sentence?

B. Remember a time you were scared. Think about what you saw or heard and how you felt. Then write 5 sentences about that time. Put your sentences in a paragraph.

C. Answer the questions.
1. Which sentence do you like best? Why?
2. Did you use words that tell when or where to vary your sentence beginnings?
3. Did you use exact verbs, adverbs, and adjectives to make your sentences clear and interesting?
4. Did you write complete sentences?
5. Did you indent the first line of your paragraph?

280

Evaluation • Working with Sentences

A. Improve the sentences in the paragraph below.
Follow steps 1–5. Rewrite the paragraph.

> My grandma and I looked in her attic.
> Everything was covered with sheets. We found
> some pictures in an old trunk. In one picture,
> Grandma was smiling at me when I was only
> a week old.

1. Think of some word or words that tell when to add to the beginning of the first sentence.
2. Think of an exact verb to use instead of *looked in* for the first sentence.
3. Think of some words that tell where to add to the beginning of the second sentence.
4. Think of an exact adjective to use instead of *old* for the third sentence.
5. Think of an exact adverb to tell how Grandma was smiling in the last sentence.

B. Write some sentences about a place that is special to you. Think about the exact words and sentence beginnings you can use. Put your sentences into a paragraph.

You will be evaluated on your use of exact words, different sentence beginnings, and on the following:
    using complete sentences
    indenting the first line of your paragraph

Spotlight • Old and New Ways of Saying "Yes" and "No"

The first colonists used the words *yea* and *nay* to mean *yes* and *no*. Since then Americans have added other ways to say *yes* and *no*. How many do you know from the lists below? Notice the dates when they were first used.

Yes
uh-huh, 1830s
O.K., 1840
yes indeedy, 1856
sure, sure thing, 1896
You said it! 1919
absolutely! 1922
yeah, 1920s
yowzer, 1930s
You can say that again! 1941
Right on! 1967

No
uh-uh, 1830s
N.G. (no good), 1839
nix, 1855
nope, 1890s
Are you kidding? 1890s
nothing doing, 1902
no can do, 1923
no soap, 1924
I should say not!, 1934
No way! 1960s

Spotlight • The Names of Dogs

Dogs have been friends with people for thousands of years. In all parts of the world, dogs have helped people as hunters, protectors, and friends.

1.

3.

4.

2.

5.

1. **Golden Retriever**
2. **Australian Terrier**
3. **English Sheepdog**
4. **German Shepherd**
5. **Longhaired Dachshund**

Many names for kinds of dogs include the names of countries. Often the dogs come from those countries. For instance, there are Australian Terriers and English Setters. How many more kinds of dogs do you know that have place names?

Other names describe the dog or its occupation. Some of these are Golden Retriever and Longhaired Dachshund. Can you name more? Some names combine place names and description. like German Shepherd and English Sheepdog.

An Adventure Story

An adventure story is a story about an unusual, exciting, or dangerous experience.

Thinking It Through

An adventure story tells about an unusual, dangerous, or exciting experience. It usually begins with a description of where the story takes place, the most important character or characters, and a problem the characters have. Then the story tells what happens to the characters and how they solve the problem.

The Swiss Family Robinson is an adventure story that takes place over 150 years ago. It is about a family from Switzerland. The family includes a mother, father, and three children—Fritz, Ernst, and young Francis. On the way to New Guinea, the Robinsons' ship is wrecked in a storm. They use a raft to reach an island. In this part of the story, Fritz, Ernst, and their father use the raft to return to the shipwreck to save their farm animals trapped on the wreck.

The ship was lodged fast where it had struck a huge jagged rock. Pounding waves crashed against the hull. When they reached the wreck, Fritz at once started making life preservers out of kegs for the animals. Suddenly Ernst gave a shout, "There's a ship!"

Ernst was perched halfway up a shattered mast. He was waving toward the horizon and calling wildly, "Ship ahoy! Ahoy there!"

The father had found a telescope, and he raised it to his eye—but a moment later his face grew very worried.

He spoke rapidly. "It's the pirate ship that chased us into the storm. Ernst, come down from the mast. Better keep down, Fritz; try not to let them see you . . ."

- Where does this part of the story take place?
- Who are the characters?
- What do you think their problem might be?

Now all three were huddled on the ship. The telescope up to his eye again, the father said, "They're bringing a cannon into position . . . they're preparing to fire."

Fritz glanced about. Their "ship" had a cannon too!

"Do you know how to fire it?" asked Ernst.

The father rushed off, calling back over his shoulder. "I'll get a keg of powder. Ernst, see if you can find any kind of rags we can use for wadding."

The father had just returned with a powder keg when the pirates fired their first shot. As the ball whistled overhead, Fritz said, "That was just to warn us."

The father's face was white. "We'll have only one shot," he said. "Let's wait until we can't possibly miss."

"How are these for wadding?" asked Ernst, rushing back with an armload of flags and banners.

"Good!" said Fritz. "Rip them into ribbons!"

Ernst and the father dropped to their knees. The father was about to tear a yellow banner with a large black ball in the center of it—when suddenly he stopped. A moment later, he got to his feet and moved off, taking the banner with him.

By now, Fritz was ramming a load of powder into the muzzle. Ernst moved in with some ripped bits of flags, and they both poked the wadding down the muzzle.

Fritz swallowed hard. "Let's see how lucky we are," he said.

- What problem do Fritz, Ernst, and their father have to solve?
- How do the boys try to solve the problem?

Fritz bent to take a sighting. But then, squinting along the muzzle, he saw the pirate ship wheeling about in the wind, moving *away* from them.

Fritz rubbed his eyes with disbelief. "They're leaving!"

Then, turning to the father who had just returned, Fritz asked, "Do you know what they're up to?"

Instead of replying with words, the father turned his eyes up toward the top of the shattered mast. Staring up, his sons saw the yellow banner with the black-ball center fluttering there. Fritz asked, "What's that?"

"Quarantine flag," the father said. "Warning that there's the black death aboard."

The two boys shook their heads in awe at their father's clever plan. "But how'd you know *that*?" asked Ernst.

With a twinkle in his eye, the father answered, "I do a bit of reading, too, you know."

- Who solves the problem? How does he do it?
- How did the boys feel about the solution?

Working It Through

Discuss answers to the following questions with your classmates.

1. If the Swiss Family Robinson had an adventure in the space age, where might it take place?
2. Who would the characters be? What other people or things might be in the adventure?
3. What problem could the characters have? Who might be chasing them instead of pirates?
4. How could the characters try to solve the problem?
5. How could the characters solve the problem in the end? How would the characters feel about the solution?

Trying It Out

Think about an adventure you have had or have read about. Was it exciting? Did it scare you? Tell your classmates where it took place, who the characters were, and what happened. You can tell how the adventure ended or ask your classmates if they can guess the ending.

Where Does It Happen?

The setting of a story is where the action takes place.

Thinking It Through

A setting is where the action of a story takes place. Often stories begin with a description of the setting.

The paragraph below is the beginning of "On the Edge," an adventure story you will read in the next several lessons. Notice the setting. You will learn about the character in the next lesson.

> From the training camp, the deep valley stretched out in the June sunshine. Five hundred feet below, the tops of the evergreens sloped sharply to the Little Salmon River that wound like a silver thread through the purple shadows. It looked as if Marta could reach out and pick up that thread.

- What is the setting?
- What details help you picture the setting?

An adventure story often begins with a description of the setting so you know where the action of the story takes place. Sometimes the setting gives other information you need at the beginning of a story, such as the kind of day, the time of day, or the season.

Working It Through

A. Read the following paragraphs. Then answer the questions.

1

> It was a cold, rainy day when we took a walk along the river. The weeds and bushes were a soft, bright green. Mud squished under our feet. The only sounds we heard were the rain, the squishing, and a few fish jumping.

The gym in our school has a shiny wood floor, bright lights, and beams in the ceiling where volleyballs get caught. There's a very soft breeze in the gym, and it's always cooler there than in the rest of the school. Being in the gym almost feels like being outside.

1. What was the setting in the first paragraph? in the second paragraph?
2. What kind of day was it in the first paragraph? What kind of floor did the gym have?
3. What other details were used to describe each setting?

B. Below are three story settings. Think of details about each one to make a clear and interesting description.
1. a busy street during rush hour
2. a carnival on a hot day in the summer
3. a playground where you play kickball

Trying It Out
1. In this lesson and the next three lessons, you will write an adventure story of your own. You can write the story you told in Lesson 7 or a new one. Before you begin to write, think about the setting for your story, the characters, the problem in the story, the ways the characters try to solve the problem, and the final solution.
2. Begin your adventure story by writing the setting. Make a list of details about the setting. Write your list of details in sentences. Then put your sentences into a paragraph. Be sure to keep your work for the next lesson.

Who Is It About?

The characters in a story are who the story is about. Often the characters' problem is introduced with the characters.

Thinking It Through

The characters in a story are who the story is about. Sometimes you learn about the problem the characters need to solve when the characters are introduced.

These paragraphs introduce the character in "On the Edge." Notice who she is and what her problem might be.

"Distances are tricky in the mountains, very tricky," she could almost hear the voice of Mr. Johnson, the climbing instructor. "That's why nobody, but *Nobody*, goes into the mountains alone."

But Mr. Johnson didn't seem to understand that sometimes a person needed to be alone. So on this last morning of the training camp, Marta had crept from the sleep-filled cabin in the dawn stillness, and climbed Old Baldy. Now, she sat on the peak gazing into the distance. She felt good, but she was tired. Drowsy . . . suddenly she found herself slipping down the steep slope on which she sat.

The bang and scrape of granite, fingers clawing at rounded stone, arms and legs flailing, then the drop—four more feet to a ledge where, shuddering, she clung to a naked rock wall.

- Who is the character in the story?
- What problem do you think Marta might have to solve?

Working It Through

A. Read the paragraphs below. Then answer the questions.

1

Mr. Piazza had run the gas station as long as I remember. He had a big smile and dirty hands. In the summer, he looked skinny. In the winter, he looked fat because he wore three layers of clothes. He cleaned the windows on cars until they sparkled, and he always helped us put air in our bike tires. All this changed when a new gas station opened across the road.

2

Grandpa has many habits. He always wears dark pants, white shirts, and skinny ties. He always sits in the green chair in his living room. He drives his car slower than anybody else on the road. His best habit is meeting my sister and me after school on Wednesday afternoons to take us for a small treat. But one Wednesday he didn't come.

1. Who is the character described in the first paragraph? in the second paragraph?
2. What details help you know what Mr. Piazza is like?
3. What details help you know what Grandpa is like?
4. What problem is introduced at the end of the first paragraph? at the end of the second paragraph?

B. Think about your favorite friend or relative. Make a list of details to describe that person. Write the list in sentences. Turn your sentences into a paragraph.

Trying It Out

Add characters to the adventure story you started in Lessons 7 and 8. First name the characters. Then list details that describe them. Turn your details into sentences and your sentences into a paragraph. After you have added your characters, suggest the problem they will have in the story. Keep your work for the next lesson.

What Happens?

What the characters do to solve the problem in a story is the action of a story, or what happens.

Thinking It Through

How the characters in a story try to solve a problem is what happens in a story. Notice what happens as Marta tries to solve her problem.

> Marta shouted: HELP! HELP! HELP! Her call soared over the empty valley, which threw back three faint cries, mocking her weakness.
>
> Mr. Johnson's voice echoed in Marta's mind. "That means *nobody* goes into the mountains alone." Marta understood now. If she had had a partner up there with a rope—but nobody was there.
>
> She studied the cliff. Near the top, a crack zigzagged along. If I could get back up to that crack, she thought, I could make it. She sighed. If she had only left her rope buckled to her belt. But what good would a rope do? She couldn't just toss the end up into the air and then climb up. It would have to be tied to something at the top.
>
> If I tied a big enough knot in the end, I could toss it up there and jam the knot so that it wouldn't pull through. That might work.

- What problem does Marta need to solve?
- What attempts does she make and think of making to solve the problem?

What the characters do to solve the problem is the action of a story, or what happens. Usually the characters try several solutions before they find the one that solves the problem at the end of the story.

Working It Through

A. On a school field trip to the museum, Doug got separated from his classmates. Read the list of possible solutions to Doug's problem on the left. Then answer the questions on the right.

He retraced his steps, but his classmates had moved on.

He guessed where they might be and went there, but he still couldn't find them.

1. What solutions did Doug think of to solve his problem? Did they work? Why not?
2. What other solutions can you think of for Doug's problem?

He asked a guard to help him, but the guard hadn't seen them.

B. Read about the problem Sally had. Then write a list of possible solutions. Tell why each solution doesn't solve the problem.

Every Saturday morning, Sally collected old newspapers from the neighbors. She piled them high on her wagon and pulled her load to the recycling center. One Saturday, her wagon suddenly collapsed under the heavy stack of newspapers. Sally had to get the papers to the center by noon when it closed. But there were too many papers to carry in her arms.

Trying It Out

1. Think about the problem the characters in your story have. Then list the different ways they can solve the problem. Tell why each solution doesn't solve the problem. As you think of attempted solutions, you may think of one that works. Keep this in mind to use when you write the end of your story in the next lesson.
2. Turn your list of attempted solutions into a paragraph or paragraphs about what happens in your story. Keep your work for the next lesson.

How Does It End?

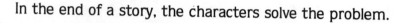

In the end of a story, the characters solve the problem.

Thinking It Through

In the end of a story, the characters solve the problem they have been trying to solve.

Notice how Marta finally solves the problem in "On the Edge."

> Marta took off her jacket, and cut it into long even strips, tying them carefully together, testing each knot. The big knot was going to be a problem. She hunted about the ledge for a loose stone or a dead branch, but there was nothing except her shoes. Why not? Picking up her right shoe, she flexed the heavy leather. Perfect!
>
> Marta took the end of the rope in her right hand, gathered the rest in her left, and swung the shoe. On the third try, the line disappeared and the shoe stuck in the crack. Harder and harder she tugged, until she pulled herself off her perch. Then she climbed for her life—up and up—clawed her way over the edge to safety.
>
> She lay gasping, partly with relief, partly with fear and partly with shame, but with a new sense of how beautiful it was to be alive.

● How does Marta solve her problem?

The end of a story comes when the characters think of a solution that finally solves the problem.

Working It Through

A. Roger's cat, Purr, got stuck high in a tree. She had jumped from one limb to another, but then she got scared.

Purr was afraid to jump to another branch or climb down. Read the list of solutions Roger tried.

1. Roger tried to coax Purr to climb down by showing her a bowl of food, but Purr couldn't be coaxed.
2. He thought of climbing the tree himself, but he knew that would be dangerous.
3. He looked for a ladder he could use, but he couldn't find one tall enough.
4. He called his uncle at the paint company to get a tall ladder. His uncle came and rescued Purr.

Now answer the questions.
1. Which solutions are attempts to solve the problem? Why didn't they work?
2. Which solution is the solution that works?
3. What other solutions can you think of for the problem?

B. Read about the problem Kim and her friends had. Then make a list of solutions that they can try and one solution that finally works.

Mr. Mixer never liked to have Kim and her friends play softball on the empty lot next to his house. He feared a ball would crash through one of his windows one day, and one day, his fear came true. If Kim and her friends wanted to continue using the lot, they had to find a way to protect Mr. Mixer's windows.

Trying It Out
Think of a solution that works for the problem in your adventure story, or use the final solution you thought of in Lesson 10. Then write a paragraph about how that solution solves the problem. Keep your work for the next lesson.

Improving Your Writing

Improve your writing by making sure that each part of your story is complete. Using exact details will help too.

Thinking It Through

David was going to be in a huge parade. He wanted to win the prize for the best costume. In this part of the story, David is just waking up on the day of the parade. Notice the changes made in the story.

Proofreader's Marks

≡ Make a capital letter.

⊙ Add a period.

ℓ Take out.

∧ Put in one or more words.

> Rosie, David's dog, was staring at him when he woke up. Rosie looked shy, as if she had done something wrong. When david looked at his ∧cowboy costume, he understood. Rosie had chewed the hat and vest.
>
> David didn't (not) have time to lose. He tried to sew his costume, but he couldn't find any thread.

- What is David's problem?
- How many solutions did David think of? What other solutions can you think of?
- Why was the word *cowboy* put in?
- What other changes are marked in this part of the story?

Working It Through

A. Write a setting for the story about David. Think of some good details to describe David's room.

Answer the following questions to help you write your setting.

1. How big is the room?
2. What color is the room? Is it bright or dull?
3. What objects do you see in his room? Is there a goldfish bowl? Are his clothes put away?
4. Are there pictures on the wall? What do the pictures show?

B. Now rewrite the part of the story on page 296. Make the changes that are marked. Write at least 2 more solutions that don't work and a solution that does.

C. Write a title for the story about David. Make sure you capitalize the first word, the last word, and all the important words.

Trying It Out

1. Improve your adventure story. Answer these questions to help you.
   a. Is the setting clear and interesting?
   b. Do the characters have a problem to solve?
   c. Do your characters try at least two solutions that don't work?
   d. Does the solution at the end of your story solve the problem?
   e. Have you used good details to make your sentences clear and interesting?

2. Give your story a title. Make sure you capitalize the first word, the last word, and all the important words. Add your name under the title. You have worked hard!

3. Put your story in a folder. Put the folder on a table or in your school library so other pupils can read it.

Review • Writing Story Beginnings

A. Rachel wanted to write a story about when she got stuck in the mud by a swamp. This is what happened. She had been told never to go near the swamp, but she was taking a shortcut and she got lost. She called for help when she realized she was stuck, but no one heard her. She kicked and squirmed, but moving made it worse. She finally freed herself by using a strong tree branch.

1. If you were writing a story about what happened to Rachel, what setting would you describe?
2. Who would be the main character?
3. What would Rachel's problem be?
4. What attempts would she make to solve the problem?
5. What would happen in the end of the story?

B. Write the beginning of Rachel's story.

1. In the first paragraph, describe the setting. What is the swamp like? Why is it a dangerous place?
2. In the second paragraph, describe the main character. What is Rachel like?
3. In the third paragraph, describe the problem. What events caused her problem? Why can't Rachel walk out of the mud? How deep is she in the mud?

C. Answer the questions.

1. Did you add information in the first paragraph to make the setting clear and interesting?
2. Did you add information in the second paragraph to tell what Rachel is like?
3. Did you explain the problem and the causes of the problem clearly?
4. Which paragraph was the hardest for you to write? Why?
5. Which paragraph do you like best? Why?

Evaluation • Writing Story Beginnings

A. Read the beginning of the story about Dan. Use the questions below to help you improve it. Rewrite the beginning of the story.

> Dan's father took him to the grand opening of the shopping mall. They saw fountains and ate free popcorn. They went in a toy store. When Dan turned around to show his father a battery-operated dumpster, his father wasn't there.

1. What information can you add about the setting so that it is as clear as possible?
2. What information can you add about Dan to tell what he is like?
3. What information can you add about Dan's problem in the story? How did Dan feel when he realized he was separated from his dad?

B. Write the beginning of an adventure story about a time that you or someone you know was lost or scared.

You will be evaluated on making the setting, character, and problem clear and interesting, and on the following:

    capital letters at the beginning of sentences
    complete sentences
    end punctuation
    paragraph indention

Spotlight • Activities to Choose

1. Make a diary. Choose two colorful pieces of construction paper to use as covers. Put some sheets of your notebook paper inside. Ask your teacher to help you staple the 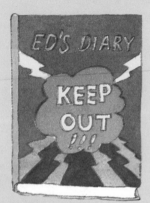 pages to the folder. You may wish to draw a picture or write your name on the cover. Write in your diary whenever you wish.

2. Find out more about yourself. Were your ancestors from Norway, England, Africa, Japan, or some place else? Ask your family what country your ancestors came from and what they were like. You can also find interesting information about other countries in books. See if you can find the answers to these questions.

Where is the country?

Who are some famous people from that country? What did they do?

What language did they speak?

Do you know any of the words?

What foods are they famous for?

You could write a report, draw a map of the country, teach your friends some of the words you know, or make one of the foods to share with your classmates.

3. Paint a mural. Get large sheets of paper and tape them together. Put the paper on a wall in your classroom. Have several classmates paint their own versions of scenes from *The Swiss Family Robinson*. The pictures could show the island, the wrecked ship, and the pirate ship. Keep the pictures on the wall for your classmates to enjoy. You could also use the pictures as background scenery and retell the adventures of *The Swiss Family Robinson* to another class.

4. Solve the problem. Divide into groups. The leader of each group begins a story by giving a setting and some characters. Then he or she tells about the problem in the story and how the characters try to solve it. The group members must each write a solution. After all the solutions are discussed, the group chooses the best solution. The person who had the best solution becomes the new leader.

Spotlight · Books to Read

From Anna
by Jean Little

Nine-year-old Anna never did anything right. She felt misunderstood by the rest of her family. When her family moved to Canada, it was discovered that Anna was handicapped. The book will help you understand how she felt and how her world changed for the better.

Cricket's Jokes, Riddles and Other Stuff
compiled by Marcia Leonard

If you need a good laugh, you've come to the right place. This book of sillies includes limericks, ghostly giggles, tongue twisters, jokes, the "riddlediculous," and much more to laugh about. It's a wonderful book to share with your friends.

The Dancing Kettle and Other Japanese Folk Tales
retold by Yoshiko Uchida

The fourteen Japanese folk tales in this book will take you to temples, small villages, fish markets, delicate gardens, and the wooded hills of Japan. You can find out about princes, princesses, and even an eight-headed dragon.

Unit Ten

You will probably understand this poem, even though you won't know the meanings of most of the words.

Mean song

Snickles and podes,
Ribble and grodes:
That's what I wish you.

A nox in the groot,
A root in the stoot
And a gock in the forbeshaw, too.

Keep out of sight
For fear that I might
Glom you a gravely snave.

Don't show your face
Around any place
Or you'll get one flack snack in the bave.

Eve Merriam

You understood the poem because you understand how language works. With Unit Ten you'll review some important knowledge you have about language.

Subjects and Predicates

Look at the sentence and think about its parts.

| complete | simple | simple | complete |
| subject | subject | predicate | predicate |

The funny <u>clowns</u> | <u>rode</u> bicycles.

If you need help, see pages 44–47 or page 319.

A. There are 5 incomplete sentences below. Tell whether the missing part is a subject or a predicate. Then complete each sentence.

The class ____. The field trip ____.
____ climbed the steps to the top. ____ looked through the telescope. The bus ____.

B. Copy the sentences. Put one line under the complete subject. Put a second line under the simple subject.

1. The plane took off smoothly.
2. The pilot flew over the crowd.
3. A woman climbed out on a wing.
4. The small plane banked steeply.
5. The daring acrobat stood on her head.
6. The cheering crowd roared in its enjoyment.
7. The brave stuntwoman turned a cartwheel on the wing.
8. The noisy plane buzzed down to land.

C. Copy the sentences. Put one line under the complete predicate. Put a second line under the simple predicate.
  1. Some people went on a cruise.
  2. A woman fished all day.
  3. A man took a sun bath on deck.
  4. One person watched the birds.
  5. The captain saw some dolphins.
  6. The dolphins leaped out of the water.
  7. The passengers watched the dolphins a long time.
  8. Soon the dolphins swam away.
  9. The people loved the dolphins.

Review 2 **Nouns**

Look at the sentences and notice the underlined nouns.

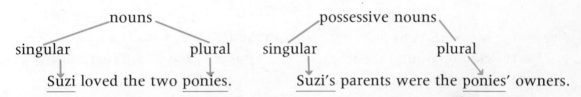

Suzi loved the two <u>ponies</u>.   <u>Suzi's</u> parents were the <u>ponies'</u> owners.

If you need help, see pages 80–87 or pages 322–323.

A. Copy the sentences. Write the noun that belongs in each sentence.

1. Two (child, children) went for a walk in the park.
2. Ray picked a (daisies, daisy).
3. Some (goose, geese) were swimming in a lake nearby.
4. Joyce watched a (bees, bee) sitting on a flower.
5. Ray bought a balloon from a (man, men).
6. Joyce and Ray sat on a (blankets, blanket) to rest.
7. They each ate two (sandwich, sandwiches).
8. They each drank a (cups, cup) of milk.
9. Both of Joyce's (foot, feet) hurt after the walk.

B. Make the underlined nouns show possession. Add 's to the singular nouns and to the plural nouns that do not end in s. Add an ' to the plural nouns that end in s. Write the sentences.

1. The <u>women</u> camping trip lasted three days.
2. The <u>wolves</u> howls kept us up all night.
3. The <u>boy</u> invention did not work.
4. The <u>men</u> hats were on the top shelf.
5. The <u>dogs</u> tails wagged.
6. The <u>foxes</u> noses were long and pointed.
7. The <u>mice</u> fur was covered with soot.
8. The <u>girl</u> job was to keep score.
9. The <u>puppies</u> food is in the pantry.

Review 3 Verbs

Look at the sentences and notice the verbs.

action verbs

Present: Mr. Sims <u>runs</u> fast.
Past: He <u>ran</u> around the track.
Future: He <u>will run</u> again tomorrow.

linking verbs

Present: Mr. Sims <u>is</u> a coach.
Past: He <u>was</u> my coach last year.

If you need help, see pages 110–115 or pages 323-325.

A. Choose the correct tense of the verb in each sentence. Write the sentences.

1. Sandra (takes, took) me to her ball game yesterday.
2. She (wear, wore) her uniform and took her bat.
3. She (runs, ran) and hits well.
4. Now I (am, was) interested in baseball.
5. I (will go, went) to all her games next year.

B. Copy the sentences. Underline the action verb. Write whether the verb is *present, past,* or *future tense.*

1. Ed makes a picture.
2. He brings it home.
3. His sister Sue drew a picture.
4. She put it in the frame.
5. Ed and Sue will wrap the picture.
6. They will give it to their father.
7. Gina learned about camels.
8. She saw some pictures in a book.
9. She likes the book about camels.
10. Gina goes to the library.
11. She will get more books.
12. Then she will write a report.

C. Copy the sentences. Underline the linking verb. Write whether the verb is *present* or *past tense.*

1. My mom is a writer.
2. I am a writer too.
3. Books are fun to write.
4. My work is interesting.
5. I was a good student in English.
6. My teachers were helpful.
7. We are on the train.
8. I am so excited!
9. Mom is asleep.
10. Dad and Pat are asleep too.
11. I was glad when we got home.
12. We were tired after the trip.

Review 4 **Adjectives**

Look at the sentences and notice the adjectives.

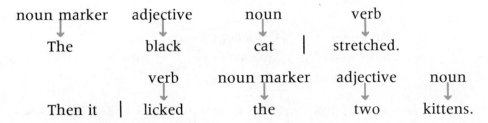

noun marker	adjective	noun	verb
↓	↓	↓	↓
The	black	cat	| stretched.

	verb	noun marker	adjective	noun
	↓	↓	↓	↓
Then it	| licked	the	two	kittens.

If you need help, see pages 144–149 or page 326.

A. Complete each sentence with an adjective at the right
or use one of your own. Write the sentences.

1. I have a _____ eggs.
2. I mix them in a __ bowl.
3. I am baking a _____ cake for Grandpa.
4. The _____ icing tastes delicious.
5. It is Grandpa's _____ birthday.

ninetieth
delicious
sticky
glass
dozen

B. Copy the sentences. Draw a line between
the complete subject and predicate. Label each
word in the subject. Use the letters **NM** for
noun marker, **A** for *adjective*, and **N** for *noun*.

1. A banana peel caused the accident.
2. The injured girl fell on the street.
3. A big bump was on her head.
4. A worried boy called for help.
5. A kind nurse helped the girl.

C. Copy the sentences. Draw a line between the complete
subject and predicate. Label each word in the predicate.
Use the letters **NM, A, N,** and **V** for *verb*.

1. Syreeta wore an expensive dress.
2. She was the star performer.
3. Syreeta sang a popular song.
4. The audience clapped a long time.
5. Syreeta enjoyed the thunderous applause.

Review 5 **Adverbs**

Read the sentences and notice what the adverbs tell you about the verbs.

where ──→ The baby sleeps <u>here</u>.
when ──→ She is awake <u>now</u>.
how ──→ Talk <u>softly</u> to her.

If you need help, see the lesson on pages 178–179, or see page 326.

A. Write the sentences. Add an adverb that answers the question after each sentence.

1. Crickets chirp ____ all night.   (How?)
2. The crickets live ____ the house.   (Where?)
3. We hear crickets ____.   (When?)
4. I sleep ____ when I hear the crickets.   (How?)

B. Choose an adverb that answers the question following each sentence. Write the sentences.

1. My brother and I made bread ____.   back
   (When?)   later
2. We took the ingredients ____ of the   out
   cupboard.   (Where?)   yesterday
3. We measured the ingredients ____.   carefully
   (How?)
4. We put the dough ____ in the bowl to
   rise.   (Where?)
5. ____ we baked the bread.   (When?)

C. Write the sentences. Underline the adverb in each sentence that answers the question following the sentence.

1. The team ran onto the field quickly.   (How?)
2. The game should start now.   (When?)
3. We are sitting outside to watch the game.   (Where?)
4. I hope it doesn't rain soon.   (When?)

Review 6 Pronouns

Pronouns in the Subject

Look at the chart. Notice how the pronouns in the chart are used in the paragraph.

Pronouns in the Subject	
I	we
you	you
he	they
she	
it	

Sue, Tom, and <u>I</u> went fishing. <u>She</u> caught a huge catfish. <u>You</u> should have seen that fish. <u>It</u> had whiskers! Tom caught three fish. <u>He</u> threw the fish back in the water. <u>They</u> were too small. <u>We</u> all had a nice afternoon.

If you need help, see pages 214–215 or page 327.

A. Use a pronoun in place of the underlined word or words. Write the sentences.
1. Dr. Finn told Alex, "<u>Alex</u> should eat more apples. Apples are delicious and <u>apples</u> are good for you."
2. Greg likes apples and <u>Greg</u> eats one every day.
3. Ellen made an apple pie and <u>Ellen</u> gave us some.
4. I had a slice and <u>the slice</u> was delicious.
5. Sam and Ann love baked apples and <u>Sam and Ann</u> made some last night.
6. My dad and I bought some apple cider and <u>my dad and I</u> drank two cups.
7. Bertha said "<u>Bertha</u> will pick apples next October."

Pronouns After Action Verbs

Look at the chart. Notice how the pronouns in the chart are used in the paragraph.

Pronouns After Action Verbs	
me	us
you	you
him	them
her	
it	

Uncle Grant asked Annette and <u>me</u> to come see <u>him</u> and Aunt Alice. They took <u>us</u> to the car show. We bought <u>them</u> a bumper sticker. We put <u>it</u> on the car. The sticker said, "Thank <u>you</u> for driving carefully!"

If you need help, see pages 216–217 or page 327.

B. Use a pronoun in place of the underlined word or words. Write the sentences.

1. Mom told <u>Tom and me</u> to take Al to the doctor.
2. We asked <u>Mom</u> to come too.
3. We put a blanket around Al, but he shook <u>the blanket</u> off.
4. Al got two shots and he didn't like <u>two shots.</u>
5. "Al will be better now, Tom. Thank <u>Tom</u>," said Mom.
6. Al was unhappy about the trip and he didn't like <u>the trip.</u>
7. Al barked happily when we took <u>Al</u> home.

Review 7 Punctuation and Capitalization

Sentence Punctuation

Read the sentences and notice the end punctuation.

Statement:	I am going to the water show.
Question:	Would you like to go?
Exclamation:	The high diving will be exciting!
Command or Request:	Please come with me.

If you need help, see pages 42–43 or pages 318–319.

A. Write the sentences. Add the correct end punctuation to each sentence.

1. I am making hamburgers
2. Would you like one
3. Oh no, I almost burned them
4. Please pass the catsup

Capitalization and Special Titles

Read the sentence and notice the underlined nouns.

Dr. Marsha Dawes went to Asia last Monday.

Dr. Marsha Dawes, *Asia*, and *Monday* are proper nouns. They begin with capital letters.

Dr. is a special title. It is an abbreviation that begins with a capital letter and ends with a period.

If you need help, see pages 78–79 and 152–153, or page 321 and 331–332.

B. Write the sentences. Capitalize the proper nouns and special titles.

1. I went to see supt. rourke at washington school.
2. On saturdays, mrs. bonelli works at the hospital.
3. lt. mary wilson sailed across the pacific ocean.
4. I went fishing with ms. jones in deer river.

Commas

Read the sentences and notice where the commas are.

> Doug, are you in the attic?
> Yes, I am trying to find a suitcase.
> It is so hot, stuffy, and dusty up here.
> I am going to Boulder, Colorado.
> I am leaving on July 17, 1979.

If you need help, see pages 34–35, 150–151, 188–189, 222–223, and 236–237, or pages 333–334.

C. Write each sentence. Put commas where they belong in the sentences.

1. Would you like to go to the museum Glenn?
2. Yes let's ask Cory and Pat to go too.
3. Rachel hurry or the bus will leave us.
4. No we have plenty of time.
5. I hope the museum is not as dark crowded and stuffy as last week.
6. Cory look at that dinosaur skeleton!
7. Dinosaurs lived millions of years ago Pat.
8. Many of them were gigantic scaly and ferocious.

D. Write each sentence. Put commas where they belong in the sentences.

1. The parade is on August 21 1980.
2. We rode the train to Sandusky Ohio.
3. I live in Pittsburgh Pennsylvania.
4. John and I were both born on May 10 1969.
5. It rained all week in Tampa Florida.
6. I will visit my sister on April 12 1981.
7. Uncle John lives in Plainview Nebraska.
8. He will be here on November 13 1980.

Read the paragraph. The topic sentence and three of the
descriptive details are underlined.

> I had fun visiting my grandmother last summer. The
> window in my room overlooked the garden. I could smell
> the damp earth and the sweet honeysuckle. We ate
> vegetables from the garden. She taught me how to fix
> corn on the cob. I tore off the soft green husks and pulled
> away the silky threads. Then we cooked the corn and ate it.

If you need help, see pages 68–69 and 100–101.

A. Rewrite the paragraph below. Underline the topic
sentence and 3 of the details in the paragraph.

> I like sitting in a car as it goes through the automatic
> car wash. It's scary, but fun. First, water pounds down
> on the car, like a hard rainstorm. Then the big brushes
> swish and thump all over the car. After the rinse, a
> terrific wind blows the car dry.

B. Think about a grocery store you
have been to. What did you see?
colorful signs? rows of shelves? What
did you hear? babies crying? cash
registers working? What did you
smell? baked goods? peaches? What
things did you touch that felt soft?
slippery? rough?

Write a paragraph about the
grocery store. Write a topic sentence
for the paragraph. Include at least 3
good details.

Evaluation

A. Write the letter of the response that tells what the underlined part of each sentence is.

1. The red dog ran outside.
  a. complete subject
  b. simple subject

2. The wild vine grew up the tree.
  a. complete subject
  b. simple subject

3. The girls picked apples.
  a. complete subject
  b. simple subject

4. Our uncle came to dinner.
  a. complete subject
  b. simple subject

5. Sue and I washed dishes.
  a. complete predicate
  b. simple predicate

6. The nurse helped the boy.
  a. complete predicate
  b. simple predicate

7. Alicia rode the bus to work.
  a. complete predicate
  b. simple predicate

8. The old cat slept all day.
  a. complete predicate
  b. simple predicate

B. Write the letter of the response that tells what kind of noun the underlined word in each sentence is.

1. Two men went fishing.
  a. singular noun
  b. plural noun

2. My bicycle is red.
  a. singular noun
  b. plural noun

3. Cheese sandwiches are good.
  a. singular noun
  b. plural noun

4. Both of my feet hurt.
  a. singular noun
  b. plural noun

5. The candles burnt out.
  a. singular noun
  b. plural noun

6. The women's club meets now.
  a. singular possessive noun
  b. plural possessive noun

7. June's parents are here.
  a. singular possessive noun
  b. plural possessive noun

8. The boy's hat is lost.
  a. singular possessive noun
  b. plural possessive noun

9. The wolves' howls are scary.
  a. singular possessive noun
  b. plural possessive noun

10. Al's shoes need to be shined.
  a. singular possessive noun
  b. plural possessive noun

C. Write the letter of the response that tells what tense the underlined verb in each sentence is.

1. Bob <u>stirs</u> the soup.
   a. present   **b.** past
2. Ms. Carr <u>will visit</u> soon.
   a. present   **b.** future
3. The girl <u>bought</u> a gift.
   a. past   **b.** present
4. My mother <u>is</u> an artist.
   a. past   **b.** present
5. She <u>knew</u> me last year.
   a. past   **b.** present
6. They <u>were</u> happy yesterday.
   a. past   **b.** present
7. Jody <u>was</u> in every race.
   a. past   **b.** present
8. You <u>are</u> a good skater.
   a. present   **b.** past
9. I <u>raked</u> the leaves.
   a. future   **b.** past
10. Tom <u>runs</u> home every day.
    a. past   **b.** present

D. Write the letter of the response that tells what the underlined part of each sentence is.

1. The <u>black</u> horse ran fast.
   a. adverb   **b.** adjective
2. I saw a <u>pink</u> shell.
   a. adverb   **b.** adjective
3. A <u>big</u> rock fell on the road.
   a. adverb   **b.** adjective
4. I'll see you <u>soon</u>.
   a. adverb   **b.** adjective
5. I like to play <u>outside</u>.
   a. adverb   **b.** adjective
6. We laughed <u>loudly</u> at the show.
   a. adverb   **b.** adjective
7. <u>He</u> is my brother.
   a. pronoun   **b.** adverb
8. Allen told <u>me</u> a secret.
   a. pronoun   **b.** adverb
9. Al gave a gift to <u>her</u>.
   a. pronoun   **b.** adverb
10. Tom reads, and <u>I</u> write.
    a. pronoun   **b.** adverb

E. Write the letter of the response that gives the correct form of each underlined word or words.

1. I met <u>dr.</u> Burr at <u>oak hospital</u>.
   a. Dr.   **c.** Oak hospital
   b. Dr   **d.** Oak Hospital
2. I saw <u>aunt lila</u> in <u>new england</u>.
   a. aunt Lila   **c.** new England
   b. Aunt Lila   **d.** New England
3. My dad is <u>lt.</u> Jones from <u>Fox lake</u>.
   a. Lt.   **c.** Fox Lake
   b. Lt   **d.** fox lake
4. I saw <u>mrs.</u> Hand on <u>state street</u>.
   a. Mrs.   **c.** State street
   b. mrs   **d.** State Street

F. Write the letter of each word or number that should be followed by a comma.

1. No I can't go.
   a b c   d

2. It is cold dark, and damp.
   a b c   d   e   f

3. Burt lives in Houston Texas.
   a   b   c   d   e

4. Mom was born April 1 1956.
   a   b   c   d e   f

5. Bob are you ready?
   a   b   c   d

6. I was born on May 27 1943.
   a b   c   d   e   f   g

7. Janice can I see you?
   a   b c d   e

8. Where are you Tom?
   a   b   c   d

9. Yes you can come.
   a   b   c   d

10. I am thin tall and happy.
   a b   c   d   e   f

G. Think about something you have made in art class or at home.

Did you make a picture? a kite? a model? a gift? a photo album?

Did you make it with bright paint? thin tissue paper? wood or plastic?

Does it make any noise? How big is it? What shape is it?

Write a paragraph about what you made. Include a topic sentence and at least three good details to describe it.

You will be evaluated on your topic sentence, good details, and the following:

    capital letters at the beginning of each sentence
    complete sentences
    correct ending marks for the sentences

Handbook

Sentences

A sentence may be a statement, a question, an exclamation, or a command or request.

A sentence always begins with a capital letter and has end punctuation.

> It's pet day at school.

Kinds of Sentences

A statement tells something and ends with a period.

> A hamster is a good pet.

A question asks something and ends with a question mark.

> Is this your pet hamster?

An exclamation shows strong feeling or surprise and ends with an exclamation mark.

> The cage door is open!

A command or request orders or asks for something. It has an understood subject—*you.* The end punctuation may be a period or an exclamation mark.

> Run fast!   Please sit down.

Practice

Write the sentences. Begin each sentence with a capital letter and use correct end punctuation to show what kind of sentence it is.

1. an ant farm is interesting
2. i like to watch the ants through the glass case
3. have you ever seen ants moving bits of soil
4. please be careful when you handle my ant farm

5. once my cousin broke the glass
6. i was really angry
7. he felt terrible about it
8. my aunt helped us clean up
9. i take good care of my ant farm now

Parts of Sentences

A sentence has two parts—a subject and a predicate.
The complete subject is all the words in the subject.
The complete predicate is all the words in the predicate.

The furry kitten│jumped over the sleeping dog.

The simple subject tells who or what the sentence is about.
The simple predicate is the verb that usually tells what the subject does.

The angry dog│chased the kitten.

Practice

Copy the sentences below. Draw a line between the complete subject and complete predicate. Then draw one line under the simple subject and two lines under the simple predicate.
1. The Brown family owns an ice-cream parlor.
2. They use real cream in their homemade ice cream.
3. Many people order chocolate ice cream.
4. The ice-cream parlor sells over thirty flavors.
5. I tasted a different kind every day last week.
6. I like peppermint the best.
7. Mom and Dad always eat ice cream with chocolate sauce on the top.

Combining Sentences

Two sentences can be combined by placing *and, but,* or *or* between them. A comma is used before *and, but,* or *or* when sentences are combined.

> Gigi got up early, and she fixed her kite.
> She wanted to go to the park, but it was raining.
> She couldn't play outside, or she would get wet.

Practice

Use the word in parentheses to combine the two sentences. Place commas where they belong.

1. We are going on a trip. We are leaving today.   (and)
2. We got the car all packed. There was no place for me to sit.   (but)
3. We should stop at a service station soon. The car will run out of gas.   (or)

Sentences with adjectives that describe the same noun can often be combined. A comma comes between each adjective in a series.

> The dog was big.
> The dog was brown.   The dog was big,
> The dog was clumsy.   brown, and clumsy.

Practice

Combine each group of sentences. Separate the adjectives in a series with commas. Remember to add the word *and.*

1. The house was old. The house was dark. The house was dusty.
2. Bob's ring was gold. Bob's ring was new. Bob's ring was shiny.

Nouns

A noun is a word that names a person, place, or thing.
A noun marker signals that a noun will soon appear.
A, an, and *the* are noun markers.

A squirrel saw an acorn in the tree.

Practice

Copy the sentences. Put one line under the noun markers
a, an, and *the* and two lines under the nouns that follow
them.

1. The mask has an eye
   and a nose.

2. The bird sees a stick
   and an acorn by a twig.

Common and
Proper Nouns

A proper noun names a particular person, place, or thing
and begins with a capital letter. All other nouns are
common nouns.

Common	Proper	Common	Proper
person	Ed Martin	continent	Asia
place	Utah	region	Midwest
pet	Bouncer	ocean	Indian Ocean
holiday	Labor Day	lake	Fox Lake
country	Mexico	river	Ohio River

Practice

Find the common and proper nouns in the sentences.
Write the common nouns in one column and the proper
nouns in another column.

1. We had a cookout in our yard on Labor Day
2. We invited Uncle Harry and his dog Champ.
3. He lives in the South near the Mississippi River.
4. He told us about his trip to Europe last summer.

Singular and
Plural Nouns

A singular noun names one person, place, or thing. A plural noun names more than one person, place, or thing.

Plural nouns are formed by:

adding -*s* to most singular nouns

book   books

adding -*es* to nouns ending in *ch, sh, s, ss,* or *x*

sandwich	sandwiches	guess	guesses
brush	brushes	box	boxes
walrus	walruses		

changing *y* to *i* and adding -*es* to nouns ending in *y* preceded by a consonant

cherry   cherries

adding -*s* to nouns ending with a vowel and *y*

highway   highways

Some nouns are made plural by changing some of the letters within the words or by adding letters.

| foot | feet |
| child | children |

Practice

Notice the underlined nouns. Make each one a plural noun.
1. Two <u>man</u> sold some <u>box</u> of fruit.
2. Some <u>girl</u> bought <u>bunch</u> of grapes.
3. Mr. Barkley bought <u>berry</u> to make <u>pie</u>.
4. Three <u>child</u> carried some fruit on their <u>tray</u>.
5. <u>Toothbrush</u> and <u>glass</u> were also on sale.

A possessive noun shows ownership.

Mary's sweater is green.

An apostrophe and the letter *s* (*'s*) are added to a singular noun to form the possessive.

the doctor's office   Jake's boat

Only an apostrophe (*'*) is added to a plural noun that ends in *s* to form the possessive.

the boys' pencils   the puppies' paws

An apostrophe and *s* (*'s*) are added to a plural noun that does not end in *s* to form the possessive.

the children's toys   the mice's tails

Add *'* or *'s* to the underlined nouns to show possession.
1. The cat nose was covered with milk.
2. The teachers meetings are tomorrow.
3. A squirrel is in the children tree house.
4. The women teams scored the most points.
5. My cousins rooms are upstairs.
6. The boy bike is in front of the house.

Verbs

Verbs are words that show action in a sentence or that link the subject to a word or words in the predicate.

The boat drifted out into the lake. (Action Verb)
It is past the lighthouse. (Linking Verb)

Tenses of
Action Verbs

The tense of a verb tells whether the action of the sentence takes place in the present, past, or future.

Present	Past	Future
walks	walked	will walk

Practice

Write the verb in each sentence. Then write *present, past,* or *future* to tell the tense of the verb.
1. We see Mr. Grant.
2. He plays with us.
3. Mr. Grant moved away.
4. We will miss him.

Some verbs do not end in *-ed* to show past action.

Present	Past	Present	Past
bring	brought	hear	heard
buy	bought	know	knew
catch	caught	run	ran
come	came	see	saw
do	did	sell	sold
draw	drew	take	took
fall	fell	teach	taught
fly	flew	tear	tore
go	went	tell	told
grow	grew	wear	wore

Practice

Write the sentences. Change the verbs in each sentence to show action that happened in the past.
1. Dad (tells) us a story.
2. Earl (comes) home early.
3. I (bring) them home.
4. We (grow) vegetables.
5. Tim (sees) you yesterday.
6. Angie (wears) boots.

A linking verb can show present or past tense.

Present	Past
I am	I was
You are	You were
He is	He was
She is	She was
It is	It was
We are	We were
You are	You were
They are	They were

Practice

Copy the sentences. Put a line under the linking verbs.
Write whether each verb is present or past tense.
1. My shoes are in boxes.
2. My coat is in the closet.
3. Books were on the shelf.
4. Paper was in the basket.
5. I am proud of my room.
6. I am happy with myself.

**Subject-Verb
Agreement**

The subject and the verb in a sentence must agree. If the
noun in the subject is singular, the verb must be singular.
If the noun in the subject is plural, the verb must be
plural.

A snake slithers.   Snakes slither.

Practice

Choose the verb that agrees with the subject in each
sentence. Write the sentences.
1. Julie (lives, live) on
   an island.
2. Birds (sings, sing) there.
3. A fawn (plays, play) by
   its mother.
4. The sun (sets, set) softly.

Adjectives

Adjectives are words that describe nouns by telling what kind or how many.

The <u>scary</u> monster ate a <u>dozen</u> trees.

Practice

Tell what adjective describes the underlined noun.
1. The cassowary is an unusual <u>bird</u>.
2. It is a fast <u>runner</u>.
3. It can jump six <u>feet</u> in the air.
4. The cassowary lives in only a few <u>places</u>.

Adverbs

Adverbs are words that tell more about verbs by telling when, where, or how. Adverbs often end in -ly, as in *eagerly*.

Nancy bought some dog food <u>yesterday</u>.　(When?)
She fed her dog <u>downstairs</u>.　(Where?)
The dog ate the food <u>eagerly</u>.　(How?)

Practice

Write the sentences. Underline the adverb in each sentence that answers the question following the sentence.
1. Greg will go to a volleyball game tomorrow.　(When?)
2. The teams will play outside.　(Where?)
3. Greg will cheer loudly for his team.　(How?)

Pronouns

Pronouns take the place of nouns.

<u>Joe</u> washed the <u>dishes</u>. Then <u>he</u> dried <u>them</u>.
<u>Marsha</u> got an <u>apple</u>. <u>She</u> ate <u>it</u>.

Pronouns in the Subject	Some pronouns are used in the subject parts of sentences. When you name other people along with yourself in the subject, write about them first.

<table>
<tr><td colspan="2">Pronouns in the Subject</td></tr>
<tr><td>I</td><td>we</td></tr>
<tr><td>you</td><td>you</td></tr>
<tr><td>he</td><td>they</td></tr>
<tr><td>she</td><td></td></tr>
<tr><td>it</td><td></td></tr>
</table>

I went to a garage sale.
He bought an old bike.
We both got some old toys.
Alex and I went home.

Pronouns After Action Verbs	Some pronouns follow action verbs.

<table>
<tr><td colspan="2">Pronouns After Action Verbs</td></tr>
<tr><td>me</td><td>us</td></tr>
<tr><td>you</td><td>you</td></tr>
<tr><td>him</td><td>them</td></tr>
<tr><td>her</td><td></td></tr>
<tr><td>it</td><td></td></tr>
</table>

Jan called me.
I met her after school.
Jan's Aunt Alice took us to the skating rink.

Practice

Complete each sentence by choosing the correct pronoun in parentheses.
1. Bobby and (I, me) went to a radio station.
2. (Us, We) met an engineer.
3. Bobby asked (she, her) about her job.
4. The disc jockey showed (him, he) the equipment.
5. Now (he, him) wants to be an engineer.
6. (I, Me) would like to read about it too.
7. Our librarian will help (us, we) find good books.

Pronouns
Ending in *Self*
and *Selves*

Pronouns that end in *self* refer to one person and are singular. Pronouns that end in *selves* refer to more than one person and are plural.

Singular Pronouns Ending in Self	Plural Pronouns Ending in Selves
I saw myself. You saw yourself. He saw himself. She saw herself. It saw itself.	We saw ourselves. You saw yourselves. They saw themselves.

Practice

Complete each sentence with a pronoun ending in *self* or *selves*. Write the sentences.
1. Can you make up a joke by _____?
2. We made up three jokes by _____.
3. Roy and Sue made up a joke by _____.
4. I chuckled to _____.
5. Bob chuckled to _____.

Contractions

Two words can often be put together to make a contraction, or shorter word. Many contractions are formed by combining a verb and the word *not*. An apostrophe shows where a letter or letters were left out.

is not	isn't	has not	hasn't
are not	aren't	have not	haven't
was not	wasn't	had not	hadn't
were not	weren't	can not	can't
does not	doesn't	will not	won't
do not	don't		

Some contractions are made from pronouns and verbs.

Pronoun + verb	Pronoun + verb	Pronoun + verb
I + will = I'll	she + is = she's	You + are = you're
we + will = we'll	he + is = he's	they + are = they're
they + will = they'll		we + are = we're

Practice

Write the contractions for these words.

1. she is   4. was not   7. are not   10. does not
2. have not   5. you are   8. they are   11. can not
3. will not   6. they will   9. I will   12. we are

Problem Words

any, no

To make a sentence mean "no," use only one word that means "no."

Incorrect—Two "No Words"	Correct—Only One "No Word"
There aren't no letters.	There aren't any letters. There are no letters.
There wasn't no post card.	There wasn't any post card. There was no post card.
Ed hasn't no mail for me.	Ed hasn't any mail for me. Ed has no mail for me.

Practice

Choose the correct word in parentheses. Write the sentences.
1. Elena hasn't (any, no) salt.
2. There aren't (any, no) onions.
3. There wasn't (any, no) garlic either.
4. There were (any, no) fresh tomatoes.
5. There is (any, no) way she can make spaghetti.

329

good, well

The word *good* is used to describe nouns. The word *well* can be used to describe verbs.

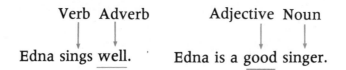

Verb Adverb   Adjective Noun

Edna sings well.   Edna is a good singer.

Practice

Complete each sentence with *good* or *well*.

1. George is a ____ baker.
2. He bakes cakes ____.
3. He has many ____ recipes.
4. He cooks ____.

Homophones

Some words called homophones sound alike, but they have different meanings and spellings.

to	We went up to the attic.
two	We found two old pictures of Dad.
too	It was too hot up there.
there	My aunt and uncle live there.
their	Their house is the oldest one in town.
they're	They're going to paint the house today.
here	The vase fell here.
hear	I didn't hear the noise.
four	I bought four pears.
for	One of them is for my sister.

Practice

Complete each sentence with the correct word in parentheses.

1. I hiked (to, two) miles.
2. (They're, Their) happy.
3. This is (for, four) you.
4. Put the ball (hear, here).

330

Abbreviations

An abbreviation is a shortened form of a word. Abbreviations of days, months, and special titles begin with a capital letter and end with a period.

Days		Special Titles	
Sunday	Sun.	Mister	Mr.
Monday	Mon.	title of a married	
Tuesday	Tues.	woman	Mrs.
Wednesday	Wed.	title of a married	
Thursday	Thurs.	or unmarried woman	Ms.
Friday	Fri.	Doctor	Dr.
Saturday	Sat.	Superintendent	Supt.
		Lieutenant	Lt.
		Governor	Gov.
		President	Pres.

Months

January	Jan.	May	none	September	Sept.
February	Feb.	June	none	October	Oct.
March	Mar.	July	none	November	Nov.
April	Apr.	August	Aug.	December	Dec.

Practice

Write the abbreviations for the days, months, and special titles.

1. Sunday, April 1
2. Friday, May 18
3. Lieutenant Jan Morgan
4. Mister Robert Belton
5. Wednesday, June 6
6. September
7. President Adam Alvarez
8. Sue Jones (not married)
9. Thursday, December 12
10. Doctor Walter Smith
11. Superintendent Mary Polk
12. Tuesday, February 9
13. Ellen West (married)
14. Governor Janet Gibbs
15. Saturday, August 8
16. January

Apostrophes   An apostrophe shows where a letter or letters were left out of a contraction. See *Contractions*, pages 328–329.
An apostrophe is used with nouns to show possession. See *Possessive Nouns*, page 323.

Capital Letters   Capital letters are used for the following:

the word *I*	I am tired.
proper nouns	(See *Common and Proper Nouns*, page 321.)
the first word in a sentence	The baby has teeth.
the days of the week	Monday
the months of the year	January
abbreviations and special titles	Mon. Jan. Dr.
the greeting of a letter	Dear Jack,
the closing of a letter	Your friend,
initials	Joe Mason's initials are J. M.
the first word, the last word, and all important words in titles	A House Full of Mice

Practice   Correct the sentences below by capitalizing 25 words.

1. i live in kansas city near the missouri river.
2. dr. lisa allen visited us on memorial day.
3. she returned tuesday from a trip across the atlantic ocean.
4. dr. allen said she might take me next may or june to south america and australia.
5. she brought me a book called *the weary traveler*.

Colons

A colon is placed between the hour and minutes when the time is written in numbers.

> 12:30

A colon often follows a speaker's name in a play.

> GEORGE: It may rain all day.

Practice

Add 5 colons where they are needed.

DAVID   It's 3 30.
JANE   Can we make it to the game in time?
DAVID   Yes, we can catch the bus at 4 00.

Commas

Commas are used in the following ways:

> between the name of a city and state in an address
>
> > Providence, Rhode Island
>
> between the day and the year in a date
>
> > July 4, 1776
>
> after the greeting in a letter to a friend
>
> > Dear Ann,
>
> after the closing in a letter
>
> > Yours truly,
>
> to separate a quotation from the rest of the sentence
>
> > Doug said, "I will be home soon."

to set off a noun of address

Ed, answer the phone. Open the door, John.

after an introductory *yes* or *no*

Yes, you're right. No, you're wrong.

after adjectives in a series of three or more

The car was old, gray, and noisy.

before *and, but,* or *or* when two sentences are combined

Pat would like to go, but she won't be here.

Practice

Add commas where they are needed in these sentences.
1. I am going to Philadelphia Pennsylvania.
2. Steve do you think I will like it there?
3. Steve said "Yes you will like the beautiful old and historic buildings."
4. I will go by bus or I will take the train.
5. Elena went to San Francisco California.
6. Yes she liked the steep winding and narrow streets.
7. No she didn't ride in a cable car.
8. Elena said "I hope to return to San Francisco soon."
9. Steve went there on August 10 1980.

End Punctuation

A sentence always has end punctuation. See *Kinds of Sentences*, pages 318–320.

| **Proofreader's Marks** | The following marks are used by writers when they improve their writing. |

$\equiv$ Make a capital letter. $\mathcal{e}$ Take out.

$\odot$ Add a period. $\wedge$ Put in one or more words.

Practice

Rewrite the paragraph. Make the changes that are marked.

Quotation Marks

Quotation marks are put at the beginning and at the end of a direct quotation.

Carlos said, "Let's go."
"I'll meet you," said Mary.

Practice

Rewrite the sentences. Add the missing punctuation.
1. Jo asked, Where is the cat?   3. Dad said, I know.
2. It isn't here, said Lois.   4. Where? asked Mom.

Titles of Books

The title of a book is underlined when it is part of a sentence.

My favorite book is <u>The Wind in the Willows</u>.

Practice

Copy the sentences. Underline each book title.
1. Fred read The Red Cat.   2. That book is Fishing Fun.

Extra Practice

Sentences

End Punctuation

Write the sentences. Put a period, question mark, or
exclamation mark at the end of each sentence.

1. I had a silly dream
2. What was it about
3. A frisky squirrel jumped in my room
4. It found my bowl of peanuts
5. It crunched and crunched
6. Then it licked me on the nose
7. I woke up fast
8. What did I see
9. I saw my little brother closing my door
10. I saw an empty bowl of peanuts

Simple and Complete Subjects

Copy the sentences. Underline the complete subject in each
sentence. Put a second line under the simple subject.

1. A big city is an interesting place.
2. Many people live and work in big cities.
3. Some cities have museums.
4. Large cities are crowded.
5. Tall buildings line busy streets.
6. Some people live in these tall buildings.

Simple and Complete Predicates

Copy the sentences. Underline the complete predicate in
each sentence. Put a second line under the simple
predicate.

1. The cowboy sat on the horse.
2. The horse moved restlessly.
3. A girl opened the gate.
4. The horse jumped into the rodeo ring.
5. The horse bucked wildly.
6. The horse galloped around and around the ring.
7. The cowboy held tight to the rope.
8. The crowd cheered excitedly.
9. The horse threw the cowboy.
10. The cowboy got up quickly.
11. He walked out of the ring.
12. Then the horse trotted out of the ring.

Command and Request Sentences

Copy the sentences. Begin each with a capital letter and use ending marks.

1. don't eat so fast
2. please put on your coat
3. don't miss the bus
4. do your work carefully
5. please pick up litter
6. please tell me

Nouns

Plurals

Fill in each blank with the plural form of the underlined noun.

1. one pound of cheese—two ____ of cheese
2. one bee—five ____
3. one sandwich—one dozen ____
4. one radish—one bag of ____
5. one box—four ____
6. one jelly glass—two jelly ____
7. one bakery—six ____
8. one foot—two ____
9. one key—five silver ____
10. one child—three ____

Proper Nouns

Write a proper noun to answer each question.

1. What is the name of your school?
2. In what state do you live?
3. On what continent do you live?
4. What city would you most like to visit?
5. What is your favorite holiday?

Possessives

Choose the correct possessive for each noun. Write the sentences.

1. The (city, cities') problems are serious.
2. The (streets', streets's) names are misspelled.
3. (Tom's, Toms') mother is nice.
4. My (grandchildren's, grandchildrens') clothes will come tomorrow.

337

5. The (dresses's, dresses') belts are lost.
6. The (tigers', tigers's) cages need cleaning.
7. One (wagon's, wagons') wheel is broken.

8. The (trucks', trucks's) rumblings awoke me.
9. The (sheeps', sheep's) wool is soft.
10. The (officers', officers's) badges were shiny.

Nouns of Address

Punctuation with Nouns of Address
Copy the sentences. Add commas where they are needed.
1. Please stand up Sue.
2. Judy can you go with me?
3. I can't hear you Paul.
4. Cynthia will you help me?
5. Where is my hat Mother?
6. Tom can you come over?

Verbs

Tenses of Action Verbs
The action verb in each sentence is underlined. Write the sentences. Then write whether the verb is in the past, present, or future tense.
1. Spaghetti <u>tastes</u> delicious.
2. Tim <u>eats</u> it with a fork.
3. Mom <u>made</u> some spaghetti sauce yesterday.
4. It <u>tasted</u> hot and spicy.
5. Mom <u>will teach</u> me to make some tomorrow.
6. I <u>will buy</u> the groceries.

Tenses of Linking Verbs
The linking verb in each sentence is underlined. Write the sentences. Then write whether the verb is in the past or present tense.
1. I <u>am</u> hungry today.
2. Terry <u>is</u> hungry too.
3. I <u>was</u> in the kitchen again.
4. We <u>were</u> here ten minutes ago.

Tenses of Other Verbs

buy, catch, bring, teach
Choose the verb in each sentence that shows present
action. Write the sentences.

1. Tom (buys, bought) some gerbils
   and a cage.
2. He (taught, teaches) them to stand
   up.
3. He (brings, brought) them some
   lettuce.
4. Tom (caught, catches) one gerbil
   under a chair.

Choose the verb in each sentence that shows past action.
Write the sentences.

1. Mr. Barton (caught, catches) fish
   every summer.
2. He (brings, brought) them home.
3. Once he (caught, catches) a bass
   and a trout.
4. He (taught, teaches) his daughter
   to fish.
5. Mr. Barton (buys, bought) her a
   fishing pole.
6. She (brings, brought) it with her.

hear, tell, tear, sell, wear
Choose the verb in each sentence that shows present
action. Write the sentences.

1. Jan (heard, hears) about a
   tug-of-war.
2. She (told, tells) Anita.
3. They (wore, wear) new jackets.
4. Anita (tore, tears) her jacket at the
   game.
5. Jan (sold, sells) some candy apples
   at the game.

Choose the verb in each sentence that shows past action.
Write the sentences.

1. Mrs. James (hears, heard) about
   the school play.
2. She (told, tells) her brother.
3. He (sells, sold) tickets.
4. He (tears, tore) them carefully.
5. Mrs. James (wore, wears) her new
   shoes to the play.
6. She (tears, tore) her heel on the
   seat.
7. We (told, tell) her how to fix it.

do, go, come, run, take, fall
Choose the verb in each sentence that shows present
action. Write the sentences.

1. We (went, go) to the beach with Father.
2. Please (come, came) with us to the beach today.
3. Mom (takes, took) some food.
4. My sister (does, did) cartwheels in the sand.
5. I (ran, run) in the waves.
6. My sister (falls, fell) in the sand at the beach.

Choose the verb in each sentence that shows past action.
Write the sentences.

1. Carolyn (went, goes) to the art museum.
2. She (came, comes) here last week too.
3. Carolyn (takes, took) some paper and pencils.
4. She (went, goes) early.
5. She (does, did) a sketch from a painting.
6. Once her pictures (fall, fell) to the floor.
7. Carolyn (ran, runs) home to show her sister.
8. Her sister (does, did) a sketch too.

know, grow, see, fly, draw
Choose the verb in each sentence that shows present
action. Write the sentences.

1. Ann (knew, knows) about airplanes.
2. She (draws, drew) pictures.
3. Ann (saw, sees) a plane take off.
4. She (grew, grows) more interested in being a pilot.
5. Ann (flies, flew) in her uncle's airplane.

Choose the verb in each sentence that shows past action.
Write the sentences.

1. The sick bird (flies, flew) to the ground.
2. It (knew, knows) something was wrong.
3. Johnny (see, saw) the bird.
4. He (draws, drew) water for it.
5. Johnny helped the bird until it (grows, grew) stronger.

Subject-Verb Agreement

Copy the sentences. Complete each one with the correct verb.

1. Joe and Al (buys, buy) a book.
2. Joe (reads, read) about metrics.
3. Joe and his brother like to (measures, measure) rooms.
4. Kim (use, uses) metrics when she cooks.
5. Dan and Al (want, wants) to know more about metrics.

Combine the singular subjects to make a plural subject.
Change the verb to make it agree with the plural subject.
Write the new sentences.

1. Rover likes bones. Red likes bones.
2. Rover gets bones from Wally. Red gets bones from Wally.
3. Rover carries the bones. Red carries the bones.
4. Rover digs in the yard. Red digs in the yard.
5. Rover buries the bones. Red buries the bones.
6. Rover runs away. Red runs away.

Adjectives

Identifying Adjectives

A noun is underlined in each sentence. Write the adjective that describes the noun.

1. In 1954 twenty-two gerbils were brought to the U.S.
2. At first few gerbils became pets.
3. Then people discovered that gerbils make perfect pets.
4. They are quiet animals.
5. They can learn simple tricks.
6. They are friendly pets.
7. Alexander got two gerbils yesterday.
8. He got a wire cage and food for them.
9. Alexander wants to teach them many tricks.
10. I want one gerbil.
11. They are cute animals.
12. They have funny faces.

Placement of Adjectives

Divide a sheet of paper into three columns. At the top of
column 1 write *noun marker*. At the top of column 2 write
adjective. At the top of column 3 write *noun*. Write each
underlined word in the correct column.

1. An orange balloon floated
   across the clear sky.
2. The curious farmers watched it.
3. The big balloon came down.

4. A few onlookers came near the
   balloon.
5. Attached to the bottom was an
   open basket.

Punctuation of Adjectives in a Series

Copy each sentence. Use commas where they are needed.

1. Tommy is short slim and silly.
2. Ed is tired crabby and hungry.

3. Tania sometimes feels happy sad
   and confused all at once.

Adverbs

Identifying Adverbs

Write each sentence. Add adverbs that tell more about the
underlined verbs. Use the questions after the sentences.

1. I awoke. (When?)
2. I found the morning
   paper. (Where?)
3. I took it. (Where?)
4. I opened it. (How?)

5. I found the names of the
   winners. (When?)
6. My name was not listed.
   (Where?)
7. I felt. (How?)

Good and Well

Complete each sentence with *good* or *well*.

1. The Apaches were ____ hunters.
2. They lived ____ on the land.
3. But they were forced to leave
   their ____ hunting lands.

4. They did not do ____ on
   reservations.
5. Many times they were not treated
   ____.

Pronouns

Pronouns in the Subject
Write the sentences. Underline the pronouns.
1. Mom, Dad, and I have moved many times.
2. She likes to move.
3. He would rather stay in one city.
4. I like to move and make new friends.
5. They said our next neighborhood will be quieter.

Pronouns that Follow Action Verbs
Complete each sentence with the correct pronoun.
1. Mary is my friend and I like (she, her).
2. She helps (I, me) make models.
3. Our friends like (them, they).
4. Our principal wants (we, us) to display our models at school.
5. We told (he, him) we will bring some to school.

Contractions

Match the pairs of words with their contractions.
1. is not   wasn't
2. are not   doesn't
3. was not   weren't
4. were not   aren't
5. does not   isn't

6. do not   won't
7. has not   don't
8. have not   haven't
9. had not   hasn't
10. will not   hadn't

Problem Words

Copy the sentences. Complete each one with the correct word.
1. Can you (hear, here) the birds?
2. Put your boots (hear, here).
3. (They're, There) moving here.
4. That is (their, they're) house.
5. Sue wants a hat (to, two, too).
6. Chico has (for, four) guppies.

Yes and *No*

Below are Captain Lemo's answers to questions about his
planet Clipton. Rewrite his answers. Put commas where
they are needed.

1. Yes I'm happy to visit Earth.
2. No I like my planet better.

3. Yes it was a smooth flight.
4. No I won't scare you.

Capitalization and Punctuation

Post Card

Copy the post card. Add capital letters and commas where
they belong.

july 10 19__

dear Mom
  Camp is great. Please send more
towels. I go swimming every day.
      love
      Timmy

mrs. janice ashton
410 tripp
lincoln illinois 60010

Invitations and Envelopes

Copy the invitation and the envelope. Add capital letters
and commas where they belong.

may 29 19__

dear Bobbie
  Please come to my end-of-school
party. It will be on Friday, June 10,
at 7:30. I live at 50 Triangle Court.
      sincerely
      sylvia walsh

sylvia walsh
50 triangle court
loden texas 76020

bobbie brown
43 square road
loden texas 76020

Index